Economic Issues, Problems and Perspectives

Financial Institutions and Services

snova
New York

Economic Issues, Problems and Perspectives

Digital Challenges: What Is the Response of the Economy?
Igor Ilin, D.Sc (Editor)
Mariana Petrova, D.Sc (Editor)
2023. ISBN: 979-8-89113-168-2 (eBook)

Case Studies in Economic Survival: Experiences from Sri Lanka
Sumudu Senani Perera, PhD (Editor)
Prathap Kaluthanthri, PhD (Editor)
Janaka Fernando, PhD (Editor)
Ruwini Dharmawardene, PhD (Editor)
2023. ISBN: 979-8-88697-786-8 (Softcover)
2023. ISBN: 979-8-89113-139-2 (eBook)

More information about this series can be found at
https://novapublishers.com/product-category/series/economic-issues-problems-and-perspectives/

Financial Institutions and Services

Credit Reporting: Reforms, Scoring and Policies
Anthony J. Haley (Editor)
2022. ISBN: 979-8-88697-414-0 (Hardcover)
2022. ISBN: 979-8-88697-465-2 (eBook)

SME Finance: Constraints and an Information Asymmetric Perspective
Chokey Wangmo, PhD, Sardar Islam (Editors)
2021. ISBN: 978-1-68507-063-2 (Hardcover)
2021. ISBN: 978-1-68507-141-7 (eBook)

More information about this series can be found at
https://novapublishers.com/product-category/series/financial-institutions-and-services/

Philip Palmer
Editor

A Closer Look at the Child Tax Credit

snova
New York

Library of Congress Cataloging-in-Publication Data

ISBN: 979-8-89113-601-4

Published by Nova Science Publishers, Inc. † New York

Contents

Preface

This book provides an overview of the child tax credit and the newly enacted changes to this program. To analyze the impact of these changes on families' financial well-being, the book provides estimates of the share of families that receive the child credit both before and after the ARPA expansion, followed by estimates of the ARPA expansion's impact on average family income

Chapter 1

The Child Tax Credit: The Impact of the American Rescue Plan Act (ARPA; P.L. 117-2) Expansion on Income and Poverty*

Margot L. Crandall-Hollick
Jameson A. Carter
and Conor F. Boyle

Summary

Congress significantly expanded the child taxcredit for one year as part of the American Rescue Plan Act (ARPA; P.L. 117-2). Specifically, for 2021, the law raised the eligibility age of children to include 17-year-olds; increased the maximum per-child credit from$2,000 to $3,600 for young children (0 to 5 years old) and to $3,000 for older children (6 to 17 years old); and made the credit fully refundable, meaning lower-income taxpayers, including those with no earnings, are eligible to receive the full credit amount. Under ARPA, the increased per-child amounts (an additional $1,600 per young child and $1,000 for older children) phase down to the pre-ARPA levels ($2,000 per child) for most unmarried parents once their income is over $112,500 and for most married parents when their income is over $150,000 (these thresholds are sometimes referred to as the "ARPA thresholds"). Low-income families received little to no benefit fromthe child credit prior to ARPA and are expected to see large increases in income fromthe ARPA

---

* This is an edited, reformatted and augmented version of Congressional Research Service Publication No. R46839, dated July 13, 2021.

In: A Closer Look at the Child Tax Credit
Editor: Philip Palmer
ISBN: 979-8-89113-601-4

expansion. Some moderate- and higher-income families may also receive additional income fromthese changes. ARPA requires that the Treasury issue half of the expected 2021 child tax credit in periodic payments to families beginning July 2021. (The Internal Revenue Service [IRS] has stated it will begin issuing these payments on a monthly basis beginning July 15, 2021.)

In light of the scheduled expiration of the ARPA changes to the child credit, and potential debate as to whether and to what extent Congress should extend the ARPA changes, CRS estimated the impact of the ARPA-expanded child credit on family financial well-being. Given the substantial impact the ARPA expansion is expected to have on poor families in particular, CRS also analyzed the ARPA-expanded child credit's impact on the prevalence of child poverty (i.e., the child poverty rate), as well as on the depth of poverty among families with children (i.e., the poverty gap). In this analysis, the ARPA changes to the child credit—and only the ARPA changes to the child credit—were modeled as if they had occurred in a pre-pandemic economy. These estimates may help policymakers answer the question, "what impact could the ARPA-expanded child tax credit have on families' financial well-being and poverty if it were enacted as a standalone provision in a nonrecessionary economy?"

Estimated Share of Families Receiving the Child Credit After the ARPA Expansion

In a nonrecessionary economy, **84% of families with children** were estimated to receive the child tax credit **prior to ARPA**. After the ARPA expansion of the child credit, 96% of families with children are estimated to receive the credit in a nonrecessionary economy. The largest increase in receipt is estimated to occur among **poor families with children** (i.e., those with family income *less than* 100% of poverty), from **52%** to 94%.

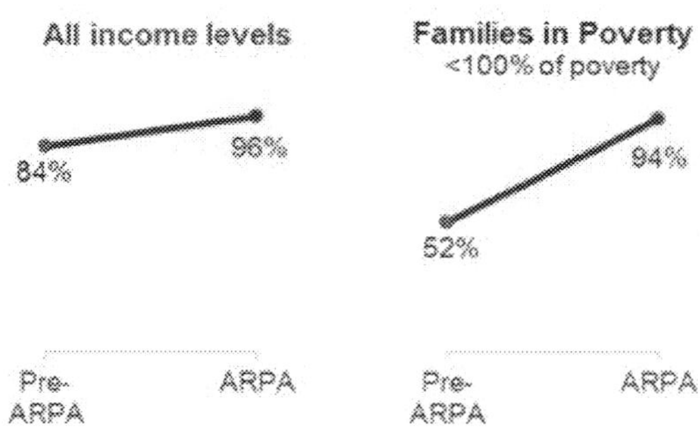

The ARPA-Expanded Child Credit is Estimated to Be a Near-Universal Benefit

CRS estimates suggest that the ARPA expansion transforms the child credit into a near-universal benefit available to all but the highest-income families with children. Specifically, CRS estimates that before the ARPA expansion, 84% of families with children received the child credit, while after the ARPA expansion, an estimated 96% of families with children receive the credit. The greatest increase in credit receipt is estimated to occur among families with children in poverty, as illustrated in the adjacent figure, driven largely by the full refundability of the credit under ARPA.

The ARPA-Expanded Child Credit is Estimated to Increase Family Incomes, Especially the Incomes of Low-Income Families with Children

In addition to increasing the share of families receiving the child credit, CRS's analysis also suggests that the ARPA changes substantially increased the *credit amount* for all but the highest-income families. As illustrated in the figure on the next page (in the leftmost graph), the average family was estimated to receive a $2,597 child credit before the ARPA expansion and a $5,086 child credit after the ARPA expansion, a near doubling of the average credit amount per family. Families in poverty, who tended to receive the smallest benefit fromthe child credit before ARPA, are estimated to receive some of largest gains fromthe ARPA expansion, as illustrated in the same chart (second graph fromthe left). The full refundability of the credit and the larger per-child credit amount are the key factors in this increase. Higher up the income distribution, families are also estimated to receive a larger benefit, although these increases are estimated to be more modest in comparison to the increases received by poor families. Some of the main factors driving this increase further up the income distribution are likely the increased per-child benefit and expansion of the eligibility age to include 17-year-olds.

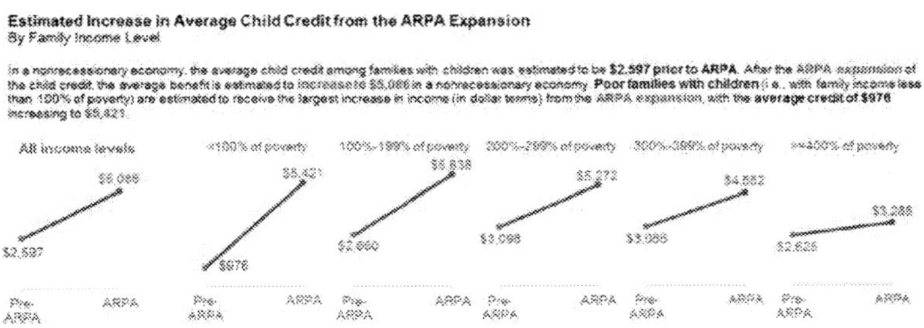

The ARPA-Expanded Child Credit is Estimated to Reduce Child Poverty by Almost Half and Reduce the Degree of Poverty Among Families with Children

The large increases in the credit among the lowest-income families from the ARPA expansion are estimated to significantly boost incomes and reduce the prevalence of child poverty, as illustrated below. The child poverty rate is estimated to fall by almost half (from 13% to 7%, as illustrated in the leftmost graph below) due to the ARPA expansion of the child credit, although racial disparities in child poverty rates would remain.

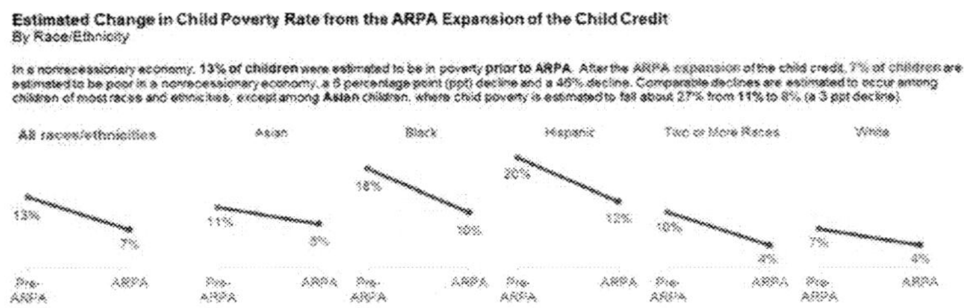

The aggregate poverty gap among families with children—a measure of the degree of poverty—is also estimated to fall by 40% as a result of the ARPA expansion of the child credit, suggesting the ARPA expansion significantly increases income among the poorest families.

Data from the Joint Committee on Taxation (JCT) and the IRS suggest that the ARPA expansion may nearly double the total annual cost of the child taxcredit. The ARPA expansion is also estimated to increase by more than threefold the amount of the credit directed at lower-income families. These estimates suggest that the ARPA expansion of the child credit will likely be, in budgetary terms, the largest cash assistance program for low-income families with children in 2021 (excluding benefits from direct payments). CRS estimates suggest that almost half of additional dollars fromthe ARPA expansion would go to those families with income between 100% and 199% of poverty and about 20% of additional credit dollars wouldgo to families in poverty.

Introduction

Congress expanded the child tax credit for one year—2021—as part of the American Rescue Plan Act (ARPA; P.L. 117-2).[1] The ARPAexpansion of the child credit has often been discussed among its supporters as both a near-universal benefit to help families with the costs of raising children and a program to reduce child poverty.[2] Prior research has indicated that near-universal direct cash assistance to families with children can have significant impact on reducing child poverty and material hardship in the United States.[3] To inform any potential debate about whether and to what extent Congress should extend the ARPA changes to the child credit, this report provides estimates of the potential impact of the ARPA child credit expansion on families' financial well-being prior to the Coronavirus Disease 2019 (COVID-19) pandemic. In other words, the analysis in this report may help policymakers answer the question "what impact could the ARPA-expanded child tax credit have on families' financial well-being and poverty if it were enacted as a standalone provision in a nonrecessionary economy?"

CRS estimates presented in this report suggest the following:

- The ARPA expansion of the child tax credit results in the credit becoming a near- universal benefit generally available to all but the highest-income families with children.

---

[1] The terms "child tax credit" and "child credit" are used interchangeably throughout this report.

[2] For example, see Jason DeParle, "The Tax Break for Children, Except the Ones Who Need It Most," *New York Times*, December 16, 2019; Dylan Matthews, "Mitt Romney and Michael Bennet just unveiled a basic income plan for kids," *Vox*, December 16, 2019; and The White House, *FACT SHEET: Biden-Harris Administration Announces Child Tax Credit Awareness Day and Releases Guidance for Unprecedented American Rescue Plan Investments to Support Parents and Healthy Child Development*, June 11, 2021.

[3] The National Academy of Sciences (NAS) included a "child allowance" as part of a package of policies to reduce child poverty over 10 years. The report included as one of its proposals a monthly benefit of $250 per child ($3,000 per child per year) as a replacement for the current child tax credit and personal exemption. The proposed child allowance would be phased out for families with income between 300% and 400% of poverty. According to estimates from the National Academy of Sciences report, "The more substantial child allowance option ... would generate a 5.3 percentage point reduction in poverty." See Chapter 5: " Ten Policy and Program Approaches to Reducing Child Poverty," in The National Academies of Science, Engineering, and Medicine, *A Roadmap to Reducing Child Poverty* (Washington, DC: The National Academies Press, 2019), p. 152, https://www.nap.edu/catalog/25246/a-roadmap-to-reducing-child- poverty.

- The ARPA changes to the child credit provide the largest benefits to the lowest- income families, significantly reducing both the prevalence of child poverty (i.e., poverty rates) and the depth of poverty among families with children (i.e., the poverty gap).

This report is structured to first provide an overview of the ARPA changes to the child tax credit for 2021. Next, to analyze the impact of these changes on families' financial well-being, the report provides estimates of the share of families that receive the child credit both before and after the ARPA expansion, followed by estimates of the ARPA expansion's impact on average family income. The report then provides estimates of the ARPAexpansion's impact on the prevalence of child poverty (i.e., child poverty rates) and the depth of poverty among families with children (i.e., the poverty gap). To contextualize these impacts, this report also discusses the potential increase in the budgetary cost of the ARPA-expanded child tax credit. *Appendix A* provides an overview of the methodology and data used in this report. *Appendix B* and *Appendix C* provide detailed data cited throughout this report.

Modeling the ARPA expansion of the Child Tax Credit

This report presents estimates of the impact of the ARPA expansion of the child credit using the TRIM3 microsimulation model. This model applies government program rules onto data from the Census Bureau's Current Population Survey Annual Social and Economic Supplement (ASEC), allowing CRS to simulate and estimate how changes in government programs, like the ARPA expansion of the child credit, may impact families. For more information on this model, see CRS Report R46824, *Need-Tested Benefits: Technical Companion to Selected CRS Reports on Need-Tested Benefits Receipt by Families and Individuals* and *Appendix A.*

Caveats with the estimates presented in this report include the following:

Static analysis: Estimates represent *a static analysis* of the ARPA expansion of the child credit and do not incorporate the impact this policy may have on labor force participation, hours worked, or number of children born, for example.

Only the ARPA changes to the child credit are modeled: Estimates reflect the impact of the ARPA expansion of the child credit *exclusively* on family financial well-being. Other changes made by ARPA to other programs (e.g., to nontax programs like Supplemental Nutrition Assistance Program [SNAP] or unemployment insurance or to tax benefits like the earned income tax credit [EITC] or the child and dependent care credit) were not modeled.

Nonrecessionary economy: Estimates reflect the impact of the ARPA expansion of the child credit averaged over 2015, 2016, and 2017. This provides a sense of what the impact of the ARPA expansion could be in a *nonrecessionary economy.*

Eligibility vs. Receipt: Estimates assume that all individuals eligible to receive the child credit do receive the child credit (and hence these terms are used interchangeably throughout the report). Specifically, the TRIM3 model used to simulate the ARPA expansion assumes all households file tax returns (and are in compliance with tax law). However, *in reality not all eligible families actually receive the credit, while some ineligible tax filers may receive the benefit.* As such, the estimates in this report may not reflect actual receipt of the child tax credit, including among many poor families who may have never filed a tax return before due to th eir low incomes.

Administrative changes not modeled: Estimates reflect annual changes in eligibility, income, and poverty and do not model the administration of the ARPA expansion (in particular, the provision requiring the Treasury to advance half of the benefit over the last six months of 2021).

Supplemental Poverty Measure: Estimates are constructed using the supplemental poverty measure (SPM), a statistical measure widely used by researchers to estimate the impact of government policies that are not measured in the official poverty measure (OPM), such as tax credits. These estimates are not reflective of how this policy may affect poverty rates as measured by the OPM. For more information on the SPM, see CRS Report R45031, *The Supplemental Poverty Measure: Its Core Concepts, Development, and Use.*

The ARPA Expansion of the Child Tax Credit

ARPA made several temporary changes to the child tax credit in effect for 2021 only. Under current law, the credit is scheduled to revert to the parameters in place before ARPAbeginning in 2022. (Some of these parameters were enacted as part of P.L. 115-97, commonly referred to as the Tax Cuts and Jobs Act or TCJA, and are scheduled to expire at the end of 2025.)[4]

The Child Credit Before ARPA

For 2021, prior to ARPA, the child tax credit allowed eligible taxpayers to reduce their federal income tax liability by up to $2,000 per qualifying child. A qualifying child was generally any dependent child under 17 years old. The credit was reduced in value, or phased out, by $50 for every $1,000 of income over $200,000 for most unmarried taxpayers or $400,000 for married couples who file joint tax returns (i.e., a 5% phaseout rate).

If a taxpayer owed less in income taxes than the maximum value of the child tax credit, the taxpayer could receive all or part of the difference as the refundable portion of the credit. The refundable portion of the child tax credit—the amount greater than income taxes owed—is often referred to as the additional child tax credit (ACTC) and is calculated using what is sometimes referred to as "the earned income formula." Under the earned income formula, the ACTC gradually increased, or phased in, as earned income rose above a starting threshold of $2,500. Hence, low-income taxpayers with income under $2,500 were not eligible for the credit. The maximum amount of the ACTC was $1,400 per qualifying child. CRS estimates that about one in every five taxpayers (19%) with a credit-eligible child had low incomes that resulted in them receiving less than the maximum credit (i.e., less than $2,000 per child).[5] After 2021, the ARPA expansion described in this report is scheduled to expire, and the credit is to revert to these "prior law" parameters until the end of 2025.

---

[4] For more information, see CRS Insight IN11656, The Child Tax Credit: How Would the Biden Administration's Proposed American Families Plan Change the Child Tax Credit?

[5] For more information, see CRS Insight IN11613, The Child Tax Credit: Temporary Expansion for 2021 Under the American Rescue Plan Act of 2021 (ARPA; P.L. 117-2).

The ARPA Child Credit Expansion

The American Rescue Plan Act of 2021 (ARPA; P.L. 117-2) makes several temporary changes (for 2021 only) that expand the child tax credit, primarily for low-income taxpayers. These changes include the following:

- *Expanding eligibility to 17-year-olds:* The law increases the maximum age for an eligible child from 16 to 17 (there are no other changes to eligibility requirements).[6]
- *Making the credit fully refundable:* The law eliminates the ACTC phase-in based on earned income and eliminates the ACTC cap of $1,400 per child. Hence, the child credit is "fully refundable," and the full value is available to otherwise-eligible taxpayers with no earned income.[7]
- *Increasing the credit for low- and moderate-income taxpayers, with larger increases for younger children:* The law increases the maximum amount of the credit from $2,000 per child to $3,600 per child for a young child (0-5 years old) and $3,000 per child for an older child (6-17 years old). Generally, this increase in the maximum child credit—of $1,600 per young child and $1,000 per olderchild—gradually phases out by $50 for every $1,000 of income over specified thresholds until the credit amount equals the current-law maximum of $2,000 per child (i.e., a 5% phaseout rate).[8] These thresholds (sometimes referred to as the "ARPA thresholds") are
  - $75,000 for single filers;
  - $112,500 for head of household filers, and

---

[6] The age of the child for a given year's child credit is based on their age on December 31 of that year. In other words, for the 2021 child credit, a child who is 17 years old on December 31, 2021, is considered 17 years old for the purposes of the credit.

[7] Full refundability is available to taxpayers whose principal place of abode for more than half of 2021 is the United States or who is a bona fide resident of Puerto Rico for all of 2021. In the case of joint return, only one spouse must meet this "principal place of abode" test to qualify. Given the limitations of the TRIM3 model, this provision is not modeled and so does not affect the estimates presented in this report.

[8] Income for the child credit phaseout is defined as modified adjusted gross income (MAGI) and is equal to adjusted gross income (AGI) increased by foreign-earned income of U.S. citizens abroad, including income earned in Guam, American Samoa, the Northern Mariana Islands, and Puerto Rico. This definition was unchanged by ARPA. Hence, for most taxpayers—those without foreign- or territorial-source income—their child credit phases out by AGI.

- $150,000 for married joint filers.

The actual income level at which the credit phases down to $2,000 per child depends on the number and age of qualifying children. For many families, the credit plateaus at its pre-ARPA level of $2,000 per child over a range of income, before phasing out when income exceeds the current-law thresholds of $200,000 or $400,000 for married joint filers. These second thresholds are sometimes referred to as the "TCJAthresholds" because they were included in the law commonly referred to as the Tax Cuts and Jobs Act (TCJA; P.L. 115-97). For larger families, the credit may never plateau at the $2,000 per child level over a range of income, but simply continue to gradually phase out.[9] A stylized example of the child credit benefit amount by income, before and after ARPA, for an unmarried taxpayer with one young child is provided in Figure 1.

As illustrated in Figure 1, an unmarried taxpayer with one young child and income under $144,500 will receive a larger credit from the ARPA expansion, and will receive the full benefit (i.e., the additional $1,600 per young child) when income is under $112,500. Since a majority of taxpayers have low and moderate incomes—95% of head of household filers and 57% of married joint filers had income under $100,000 in 2018 according to data from the Internal Revenue Service (IRS)—a large share of families with children across the income distribution are expected to benefit from the ARPA expansion of the child credit.[10]

---

[9] The law states that up until a taxpayer's income reaches $75,000 if single, $112,500 if head of household, and $150,000 if married filing jointly, they will receive the maximum child tax credit am ount. This amount is equal to $3,600 multiplied by the number of qualifying children under six years old, plus $3,000 multiplied by the number of qualifying children 6 to 17 years old. After this "first threshold," (i.e., the "ARPA threshold") the credit amount begins to phase down by $50 for each $1,000 over the threshold. The amount by which the credit phases down is limited to the lesser of (a) the "applicable credit increase amount" (the difference between the ARPA credit and the prior -law credit in 2021) or (b) 5% of the "applicable phaseout range" (the difference between the $200,000 and $400,000 phaseouts enacted under P.L. 115-97 and the $75,000, $112,500, and $150,000 phaseouts in ARPA). Notably, 5% of the applicable phaseout range equals $6,250 if single, $4,375 if head of household, and $12,500 if a married joint filer. After the total credit has been phased down by the lesser of (a) or (b), it then remains at its pr e-ARPA level until it is phased out again under the pre-ARPA threshold of $200,000 or $400,000 if married filing jointly (also referred to as the "TCJA threshold").

[10] Internal Revenue Service, *Individual Complete Report (Publication 1304), Table 1.2 (2018)*, https://www.irs.gov/statistics/soi-tax-stats-individual-statistical-tables-by-filing-status.

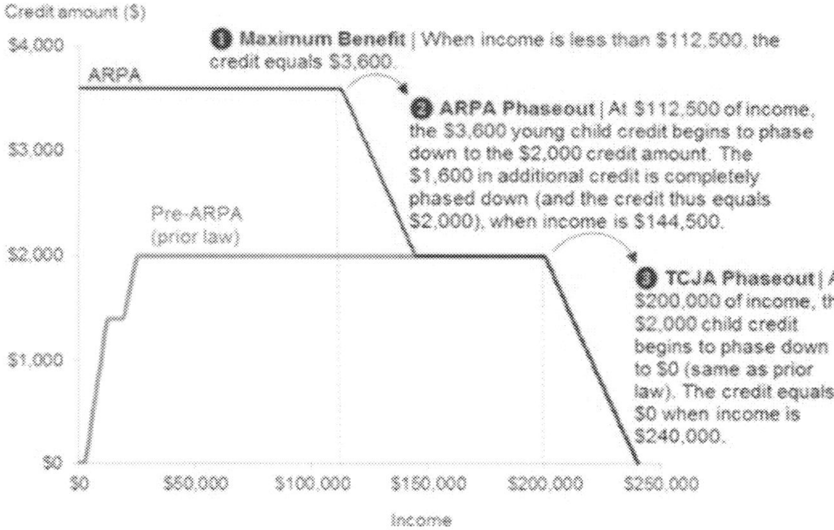

Source: CRS calculations based on Internal Revenue Code §24 and P.L. 117-2.

Notes: A stylized example assuming the taxpayer has one qualifying child and all income is earned income, with no other sources of income and no above-the-line deductions claimed. Unmarried taxpayers with child credit- qualifying children are assumed in this example to file as head of household. For more examples, see CRS Insight IN11613, The Child Tax Credit: Temporary Expansion for 2021 Under the American Rescue Plan Act of 2021 (ARPA; P.L. 117-2).

Figure 1. Child Credit Amount by Income in 2021 Before and After ARPA Unmarried Taxpayer with One Young Child.

Impact of ARPA Child Credit Expansion

CRS estimates that in a nonrecessionary economy, the ARPAexpansion of the child credit will result in nearly all families with children, including the lowest-income families with children, receiving the child credit. While estimates suggest nearly universal benefit receipt as a result of the ARPA expansion, the estimates also indicate that the largest share of new recipients will be the poorest families. CRS's analysis indicates that the largest increases in income are estimated to occur among poor families with children, substantially reducing the prevalence of child poverty (i.e., child poverty rates) and the depth of poverty among families with children (i.e., the poverty gap).

Family as the Unit of Analysis

Although federal income tax provisions like the child tax credit affect taxpayers (sometimes referred to as "tax units"),[11] the impact of the ARPA child tax credit expansion is analyzed in terms of families. This analysis is done at the family level because families can share many resources (like an expanded child credit) and expenses.[12] (Poverty analysis is also generally conducted at the family level.) In some cases, like multigenerational families, a family may be composed of multiple taxpayers. In these cases, any increase in the child credit from the ARPA expansion is aggregated over all taxpayers in the family to determine the ARPA expansion's impact on the family's income. Generally, families discussed in this report are families with children (i.e., they include at least one child under the age of 18).

Family Income Level

Throughout this report, the impact of the child credit is broken down by family income level. In this report, family income level is calculated as the ratio of a family's disposable income to their poverty threshold.[13] This categorization groups families of different sizes, compositions, and income together by similar standards of living. Families are categorized by their family income level before the ARPA expansion to allow comparison of the same families before and after the ARPA expansion.[14] Notably, this definition of income differs from the definition of income used to phase out the credit (which, for most taxpayers, is their AGI).[15]

---

[11] A taxpayer or tax unit is generally composed of all individuals listed on a federal income tax return (IRS Form 1040) and includes an individual, their spouse (if married), and any dependents.

[12] In this report, a family is composed of people living together related by blood or marriage (the family), cohabiting partners, and foster children.

[13] Disposable income is the sum of cash income and cash and noncash need-tested benefits (including refundable tax credits) minus work expenditures, medical expenditures, and taxes owed. This measure of in come is used for grouping families and poverty measurement and differs from adjusted gross income (AGI), used by taxpayers to compute their child credit (and used in the TRIM3 model to compute the credit amount). For more on this topic, see "Family Income Level" in Appendix A.

[14] In other words, while the pre-ARPA child credit is included in income, the increase from the ARPA expansion is not included in income for the purposes of categorizing families by family income level.

[15] For more on this topic, see " Family Income Level" in Appendix A.

Change in the Share of Families Receiving the Child Credit

CRS estimates that as a result of the ARPA expansion of the child credit, the share of families with children that receive the credit will increase from 84% to 96% (as illustrated in Figure 2). The largest increase in child credit receipt is estimated to occur among the lowest-income families. Prior to ARPA, about half (52%) of poor families with children were estimated to receive the child credit. After ARPA, the share of poor families receiving the credit is estimated to increase to 94%, a level comparable to benefit receipt among moderate-income families (as illustrated in Figure 2), albeit slightly lower than the overall percentage (96%).

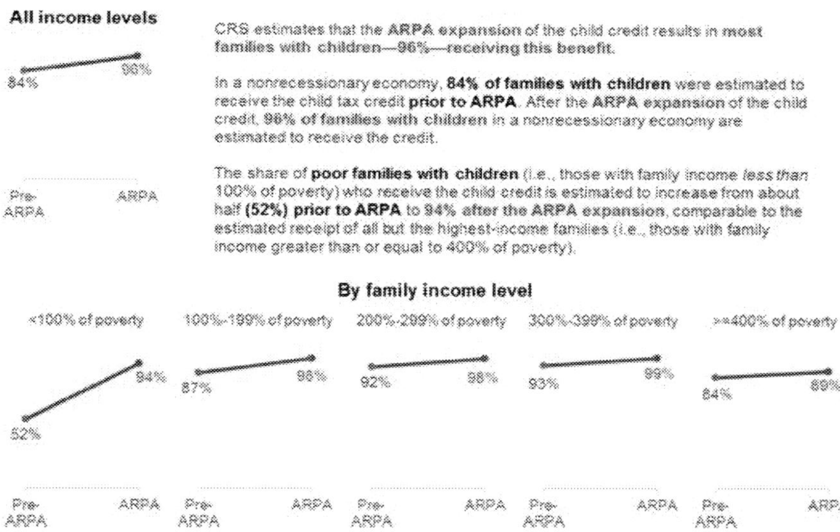

Source: CRS analysis of TRIM3-augmented CPS ASEC files representing data from 2015 to 2017.

Notes: See the notes for Table B-3 and Table C-1. The slopes of the lines in the slope graphs reflect the absolute change before and after ARPA, in percentage point terms.

Figure 2. Estimated Share of Families Receiving the Child Tax Credit Before and After the ARPA Expansion of the Child Credit, by Family Income Level.

The near-universal receipt of the child credit after the ARPA expansion suggested by these estimates is largely influenced by expansion in credit receipt among poor families. And the substantial increase in estimated credit receipt among the poor families is likely driven primarily by the expansion of credit receipt among the poorest families.

Prior to ARPA, very poor families—those with earned income below the $2,500 earnings threshold—were not eligible for the child credit. By making the credit fully refundable, ARPA effectively eliminated the $2,500 threshold. Hence, these estimates suggest that full refundability is a key factor in expanding credit eligibility to the poorest families.[16] Insofar as recipients with incomes under the $2,500 earnings thresholds are part of families with incomes 100%-199% of poverty (e.g., multigenerational families), the elimination of the earnings threshold could contribute to the modest increase in receipt rates among these families. (The increased eligibility age to include 17-year-olds may also expand eligibility for some poor families.)[17]

One reason why poor families may still be less likely to receive this near-universal benefit than moderate-income families (94% compared to 98%-99%, as illustrated in Figure 2) is the ineligibility of certain noncitizen children, specifically noncitizen children without Social Security numbers (SSNs).[18] Under current law, between 2018 and 2025, taxpayers can only receive the credit, including the ARPA-expanded credit, for a child with an SSN. All U.S. citizens, including children, generally receive SSNs. If noncitizen children without SSNs are disproportionately concentrated among

---

[16] As Elaine Maag, of the Tax Policy Center, noted in analyzing the Heroes Act (which was introduced in the 116 th Congress [and did not become law] and was similar to the child credit expansion structured in ARPA), "If Congress makes the credit fully refundable but leaves the maximum credit at $2,000 per child under 17 (as happens after this year under the HEROES Act, as written), it could reduce the annual cost of the CTC expansion to about $ 24 billion. That's because most middle- and high-income families already receive the full $2,000 CTC." Elaine Maag, *Expanding The Child Tax Credit: Full Refundability And Larger Credit*, Tax Policy Center, TaxVox: Individual Taxes, May 26, 2020, https://www.taxpolicycenter.org/taxvox/expanding-child-tax-credit-full-refundability-and-larger-credit.

[17] CRS estimates about 4% of poor families with children have children 17 years old or older.

[18] For more information, see slides 28-31 of this presentation to the National Academies: Dolores Acevedo-Garcia, "Racism and Legality: Undoing the Exclusion of Children in Immigrant Families from the Social Safety Net," April 21, 2021, https://www.nationalacademies.org/en/event/04-21-2021/docs/DBE05DC102C7AEFC1599E30F4052F4AD33B8097928E7. Under statute, only SSNs that are associated with work authorization are acceptable. SSNs issued for nonwork purposes are not considered qualifying SSNs for the purposes of the child credit. For more information on taxes and noncitizens, see CRS Report R43840, *Federal Income Taxes and Noncitizens: Frequently Asked Questions*.

poor families, a lower share of poor families would be expected to receive the child credit (both before and after the ARPA expansion) in comparison to moderate-income families.[19]

A large proportion of moderate-income and some higher-income families with children are estimated to receive the credit, both before and after ARPA.[20] However, the highest-income families (those with income 400% of poverty or more) are least likely to receive the child credit before and after ARPA because of the credit's second or "TCJAphaseout," which was retained by the law. Among moderate- and higher-income families, the expansion of the eligibility age to include 17-year-olds may be a factor in the comparatively modest increases in credit receipt.[21] Another factor that may drive the increase in credit receipt among some higher-income families is that some poor taxpayers who receive the increased child credit from the ARPA expansion may be part of higher-income families. For example, a low -income couple with a young child may live with higher-income relatives. If the couple were ineligible for the child credit before ARPA, and eligible for the full benefit after ARPA, the family's income would increase by $3,600.

---

[19] The TRIM3 model does not include information on the taxpayer identification number of family members, including children. Instead, the model includes an imputed variable on immigration status. One of the values of this variable is whether an individual is an "unauthorized immigrant." In comparison to the other values of this immigrant status variable, unauthorized immigrants would be less likely to have a social security number (SSN) than other types of immigrants. For more information, see CRS Report R43840, *Federal Income Taxes and Noncitizens: Frequently Asked Questions*.

[20] Prior to the ARPA expansion of the child credit, the Tax Policy Center also estimated that poor families with children were less likely to receive the benefit and received a smaller benefit on average than moderate- and higher- income families with children. See Table 2 in CRS Report R46502, *The Child Tax Credit: Selected Legislative Proposals in the 116th Congress*.

[21] In some cases, larger families with higher incomes may be new recipients of the credit due to the new phaseout formula. For example, consider an unmarried parent (who files as head of household) with three qualifying young children. Pre-ARPA, the parent's maximum child tax credit would have been $6,000 ($2,000 x 3). This $6,000 credit would begin to phase out at $200,000 of income and be entirely phased out at $320,000 of income. In contrast, under ARPA, their $10,800 credit would phase down to zero at $328,500 of income. This implies that between $320,000 and $328,500 of income, they would receive a credit under ARPA that they were not eligible for prior to ARPA. However, as previously discussed, most head of household filers have income below $100,000 and most married couples would not be subject to these different rules. For more details on t he phaseout, see footnote 9.

Change in Average Family Income

CRS estimates that the ARPA expansion of the child credit will almost double the average credit amount, from $2,597 to $5,086 (as illustrated in Figure 3). The largest increase is estimated to occur among the lowest-income families. Prior to ARPA, poor families with children were estimated to receive an average credit of $976. After ARPA, these same families are estimated to receive an average credit of $5,421, a credit amount comparable to that received by all but the highest-income families with children (as illustrated in Figure 3).

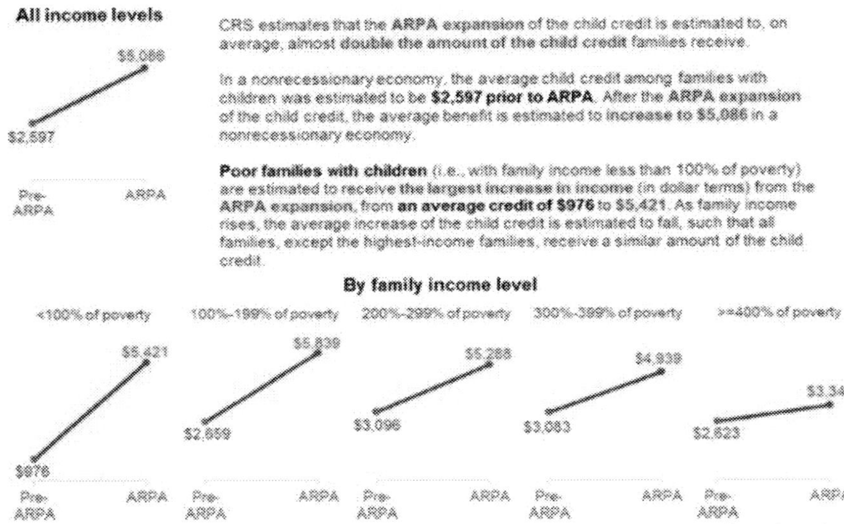

Source: CRS analysis of TRIM3-augmented CPS ASEC files representing data from 2015 to 2017.

Notes: See the notes for Table B-4 and Table C-3. The slopes of the lines in the slope graphs reflect the absolute change before and after ARPA, in dollar terms.

Figure 3. Estimated Child Credit Amount per Family Before and After the ARPA Expansion of the Child Credit, by Family Income Level.

Moderate-income and some higher-income families also tend to receive a larger credit after ARPA, although the estimated increase in the credit amount is smaller compared to poor families, as illustrated in Figure 3. For example, on average a family with income between 200% and 299% of poverty is estimated to see their child credit increase from an average of $3,096 per family to $5,288. Even the highest-income families, those with incomes 400% or more of poverty, are estimated to see their credit increase by about $700 per family (from $2,623 to $3,343).

Because these estimated average credit amounts, before and after ARPA, are calculated per family, differences in family composition (i.e., the number of children and their ages) at different income levels could also affect the estimates in Figure 3. CRS's analysis, however, suggests these effects may not be large.[22]

Poor families with children tended to receive little to no benefit from the child credit prior to ARPA, either because their low levels of income made them ineligible entirely (as previously discussed) or placed them in the credit's phase-in range (see Figure 1). ARPAsubstantially increased the benefit amount for poor families by eliminating the phase-in of the child credit (i.e., making the credit fully refundable), as well as creating a larger maximum benefit available to all low- and moderate-income families with qualifying children ($3,600 for young children and $3,000 for older children). For example, prior to ARPA, a single parent with $10,000 of earned income and one young child could receive a $1,125 child credit, as illustrated in *Figure 1.* After the ARPA credit expansion, they can receive a $3,600 credit, a 220% increase. Generally, the *lower* the family's income, the *larger* the increase from the ARPA expansion. For example, if the same single parent with one young child had no earned income, their credit would increase from $0 before ARPA to $3,600 after the ARPA expansion, as shown in *Figure 1.*

As previously discussed, ARPAalso increased the *share of poor families* receiving the credit *(Figure 2).* Hence, the larger credit for many poor families (primarily due to full refundability and a larger per-child credit amount) and the larger share of poor families eligible for the credit (primarily due to full refundability) are major factors driving a larger average credit among poor families.

Some moderate-income and higher-income families with children also receive a larger credit on average as a result of ARPA. CRS's analysis

---

[22] Alongside changes in eligibility incurred by ARPA, differences in family composition by income level may affect the results displayed in this figure. However, CRS estimates that across income levels, families with children have similar numbers of children on average, although lower-income families may have slightly more young children. Families living at < 100% of poverty have 1.9 children on average (0.6 young children), compared to 2.0 for families at 100%-199% (0.7 young children), 1.8 for families at 200%-299% (0.6 young children) and 1.8 for families at 300%- 399% (0.5 young children), and 1.7 for families living at 400% of the poverty line or greater (0.5 young children).

suggests that among moderate- and higher-income families, the increases in the credit tend to be smaller on average than for lower-income families.

This may be because a significant share of these moderate- and higher-income families are subject to the ARPA phaseout, and thus receive a smaller increase in the credit or no increase at all. For example, as highlighted in *Figure 1*, some moderate- and higher-income families would receive the maximum credit under ARPA (e.g., $3,600 if income was under $112,500 in *Figure 1*). Higher up the income scale, families would receive a smaller maximum credit, as the ARPA expansion phases out (e.g., a $2,725 credit for a family with $130,000 of income in *Figure 1*).

Higher-income families are also more likely to include some families subject to the TCJA phaseout (e.g., a $1,500 credit for a family with $210,000 of income in *Figure 1*), including those who receive no credit (e.g., $0 for a family with $240,000 or more in income in *Figure 1*), further reducing the average credit per family across the highest-income families.[23]

As with low-income families, expanded eligibility for 17-year-olds may increase the credit amount for some moderate- and higher-income families, and hence contribute to a larger average credit per family.[24] Some families higher up the income distribution (i.e., with family income greater than or equal to 200% of poverty) may also include low-income taxpayers eligible for the maximum credit amount under ARPA—for example, a low-income couple with a young child who live with higher-income parents or grandparents.

---

[23] Some larger families with higher incomes may in certain cases actually receive a larger credit due to the new phaseout formula, although existing data from the IRS suggest the number of families would be small. For example, consider an unmarried parent (who files as head of household) with three qualifying young children. Before ARPA, at $200,000 of income, their credit would have been $6,000. At the same level of income, under ARPA their credit would be $6,425, $425 more. IRSdata indicate most head of household filers have income under $100,000. Most married couples would not be subject to these different phaseout rules, unless they had many qualifying children—for example, 8 or more young children and 13 or more older children. For more details on the ph aseout, see footnote 9.

[24] For example, using the TRIM3 microsimulation model, CRS estimates that in about 10% of families with children with income greater than or equal to 400% of poverty, all the children were 17 years old, while lower down the income spectrum, the share of families with only 17 -year-old children was between approximately 3% and 5%. Some families higher up the income distribution (i.e., with family income greater than or equal to 200% of poverty) may also include low-income taxpayers eligible for the maximum credit amount under ARPA (i.e., low-income taxpayers who are part of higher-income multigenerational families).

Change in Poverty

Comparing poverty rates before and after the ARPA expansion of the child credit provides one measure of this policy change's antipoverty impact. If the ARPAchild credit expansion boosts a poor family's income sufficiently to push them above the poverty threshold (an amount of money below which a family is counted as poor), the family and all its members would be counted as nonpoor as a result of this policy.

In contrast to poverty rates, comparing the aggregate poverty gap before and after the ARPA expansion of the child credit is another metric that can be used to understand the antipoverty impact of this policy change. The poverty gap is the difference between the poverty threshold and a family's disposable income. (By definition, the poverty gap for a family with income above the poverty threshold is $0.) Unlike the poverty rate, which is based on whether a family is above or below the poverty threshold, the poverty gap provides a way of examining the degree to which a family is below that threshold. The larger the poverty gap, the poorer the family.[25] For this analysis, poverty gaps are summed together across all poor families to determine the aggregate poverty gap both before and after the ARPA expansion of the child credit.

Change in Poverty Rates

CRS estimates that the ARPA expansion of the child credit will nearly halve the child poverty rate (as illustrated in Figure 4). Similarly, CRS estimates that the ARPA child credit expansion will nearly halve the poverty rate of all individuals (adults and children) who live in families with children (as illustrated with the light pink line in Figure 4).

[25] For example, assume there are two poor families who have the same poverty threshold of $25,000. The first family has $20,000 of disposable income; hence their poverty gap is $5,000. The second family has $10,000 of disposable income—they are poorer than the first family—and their poverty gap is $15,000. Hence, the larger the poverty gap, the poorer the family.

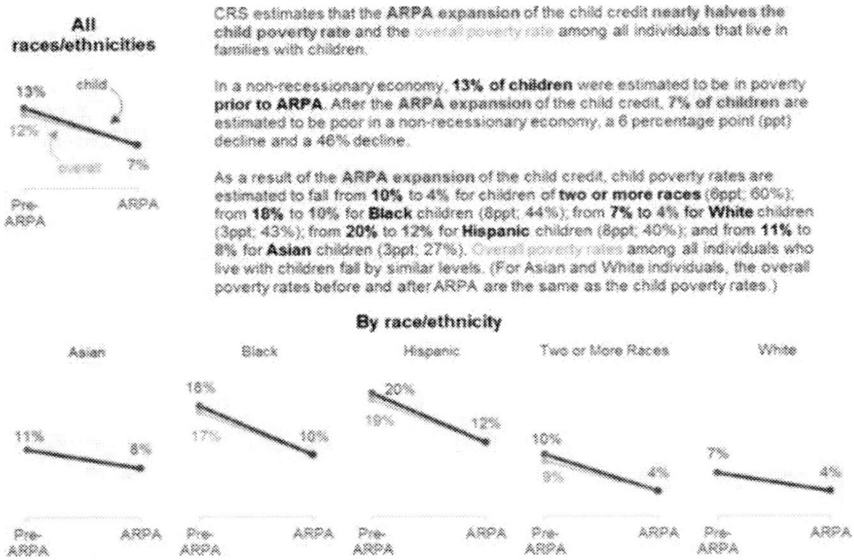

Source: CRS analysis of TRIM3-augmented CPS ASEC files representing data from 2015 to 2017.

Notes: See notes for Table B-6 and Table C-4. The slopes of the lines in the slope graphs reflect the absolute change before and after ARPA, in percentage point terms.

Figure 4. Estimated Child and Overall Poverty Rates Before and After the ARPA Expansion of the Child Credit by Race/Ethnicity.

Prior to ARPA, child poverty rates in the United States were higher among Black and Hispanic children compared to the overall child poverty rate (18% and 20%, respectively, compared to 13% of children overall, as illustrated in Figure 4). As a result of the ARPA child credit expansion, the poverty rates of Black, White, and Hispanic children are estimated to fall in roughly similar proportion to each other and in relation to the rate among children of all races and ethnicities (44%, 43%, and 40%, respectively, compared to 46% overall).[26] Hence, while the ARPA child credit expansion significantly reduces child poverty rates, it does so roughly proportionally

[26] The largest percentage change in poverty rates is estimated to occur among children of two or more races (a 60% reduction), higher than the average rate reduction for children of all races and ethnicities. This population tends to be relatively small (CRS estimates that there are fewer than 300,000 children of two or more races in poverty, see Table B-5) and has a pre-ARPA child credit expansion poverty rate less than the overall rate (10% compared to 13%). The relatively small pre-ARPA poverty rate means the percentage change in poverty rates will be larger, all else being equal.

among White, Black, and Hispanic children, and so disparities in poverty rates remain after this policy change. In contrast, the ARPAexpansion of the child credit has a comparatively modest effect on the poverty rates of Asian children (a 27% decline), which is estimated to increase the disparity in child poverty rates between Asian children and children overall.

Whether and to what degree the ARPA expansion reduces child poverty rates overall and among children of different races and ethnicities is a result of numerous factors, including the share of poor families eligible for the ARPA-expanded credit, the additional benefit from the ARPA expansion, the depth of poverty families are in before the ARPA expansion, and the child poverty rates before the ARPA expansion.

Previous analysis in this report suggests that almost all poor families with children receive the child credit after the ARPA expansion (94% in Figure 2) and that the ARPA expansion provides an average estimated increase in income of $4,445 among poor families with children (Figure 3). Hence, these estimates suggest most poor families will see a substantial income boost from the ARPA expansion. (Some poor families may not receive the benefit even after the ARPA expansion due to restrictions on the eligibility of certain noncitizen children, specifically noncitizen children without SSNs.)[27]

The closer a family is to the poverty threshold pre-ARPA, the more likely it is that the ARPA child credit expansion provides the family with sufficient resources to move them above the poverty threshold and out of poverty. In other words, the deeper a family with children is in poverty, all else being equal, the less likely the ARPA expansion will increase their family income enough so that the family (and all its members, including children) exits poverty.[28]

The depth of poverty compared with the increase in income from the ARPAexpansion may be one reason that, even after ARPA, child poverty rates remain high among children of some racial and ethnic groups. For

---

[27] CRS estimates, using the TRIM3 microsimulation model, that among poor families with children, approximately 2.3% of these families have children who are unauthorized immigrants, and hence may be ineligible for the child credit before and after the ARPA expansion (ultimately, ineligibility of noncitizen children depends on the child's taxpayer ID, which is not modeled in TRIM3). Higher up the income distribution, less than 1% of families (depending on their family income level) have all unauthorized immigrant children. For more information, see footnote 19.

[28] This effect is to be expected, since a family with a poverty gap of $100 (quite near to the threshold) requires much less to move above the poverty threshold than does a family with a poverty gap of $10,000 (relatively far from the threshold).

example, prior CRS research suggests that poor Hispanic families and poor Asian families, tend to be deeper in poverty than poor families of other racial and ethnic groups.[29] Hispanic and Asian child poverty rates may thus be higher than the overall child poverty rate even after the ARPA child credit expansion because many poor Asian and Hispanic families may require a larger benefit in order to exit poverty. Previous research also indicates that poor Asian families may have fewer children compared to other poor families.[30] This would suggest that the ARPA expansion may result in a smaller increase in income per poor Asian family.[31]

High child poverty rates before the ARPA expansion can also be a factor in high child poverty rates after the expansion. For example, among poor Black families with children, CRS estimates suggest a majority receive an increase in the credit after the ARPA expansion (96% see Table C- 2), the average increase in the credit received by poor Black families is large ($4,775 see Table**C-3**), and the depth of poverty is comparable to the all races average.[32] But because child poverty rates are much higher for Black children before ARPA, even a comparable reduction in the prevalence of poverty will still mean a larger share of Black children are in poverty compared to all children after the ARPA expansion.

---

[29] See CRS Report R46825, *Need-Tested Benefits: Impact of Assistance on Poverty Experienced by Low-Income Families and Individuals.* According to this analysis, "After receiving need-tested benefits [excluding the ARPA expanded credit], the typical family in most racial/ethnic groups would have required an amount closer to $5,000 to exit poverty. The exceptions were Hispanic families, with a median poverty gap of $6,169 (roughly $517 per month), and Asian families, with a median poverty gap of $9,911 (roughly $820 per mont h)."

[30] For example, according to the U.S. Census Bureau, poor Asian families with children had on average 1.83 children per family, while all poor families with children had on average 2.28 children per family. U.S. Census Bureau, *POV33: Mean Number of Related Children per Primary Family by Family Structure, Age of Householder and Poverty Status: 2019*, https://www.census.gov/data/tables/time-series/demo/income-poverty/cps-pov/pov-33.html. Note that this definition of poverty is the official poverty measure (OPM).

[31] In the context of the poverty rate, the ratio of the number of children to family size may also be a factor. If a family is large, with many adults and few children, it may need substantial resources to exit poverty. However, this family will receive comparatively less than similarly sized families with similar needs that have more child credit - eligible children.

[32] See Table 6 in CRS Report R46825, *Need-Tested Benefits: Impact of Assistance on Poverty Experienced by Low- Income Families and Individuals*, in which the typical poor black family had a poverty gap of $5,116, compared to $5,644 for all families. These estimates are of the baseline poverty gap after need-tested benefits, excluding the additional benefit from the ARPA-expanded child credit.

Change in the Poverty Gap

CRS estimates that the ARPA expansion of the child credit will reduce the aggregate poverty gap among families with children by $15.4 billion, or by about 40%, as illustrated in Figure 5. The largest proportional reduction in the poverty gap is estimated to occur among Hispanic families with children (46%) and families of two or more races (43%), with comparable although smaller reductions among Black families (40%) and White families (38%). In comparison, according to CRS's analysis, the ARPA expansion's estimated impact is comparatively smaller among Asian families with children (a 22% reduction from $3.2 billion to $2.5 billion).

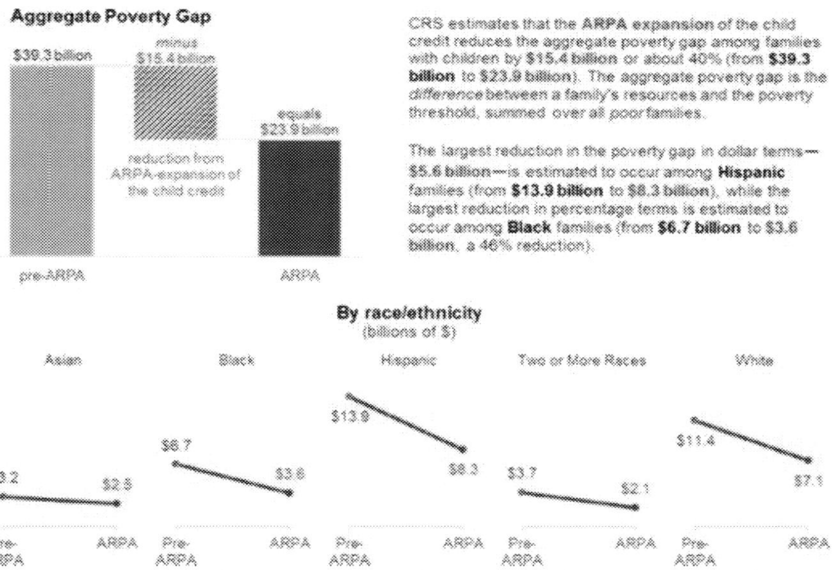

Source: CRS analysis of TRIM3-augmented CPS ASEC files representing data from 2015 to 2017.

Notes: See notes for Table B-7 and Table C-5. The slopes of the lines in the slope graphs reflect the absolute change before and after ARPA, in dollar terms.

Figure 5. Estimated Aggregate Poverty Gap Before and After the ARPA Expansion of the Child Credit by Race/Ethnicity.

As with the ARPA expansion's impact on poverty rates, numerous factors, often in combination, may affect its impact on the aggregate poverty gap. Such factors include the number of families in poverty, the depth of poverty, and the amount of the additional benefit from the ARPA expansion.[33] Differences in these factors may explain some of the differences in the declines in the poverty gap among families of different races and ethnicities. For example, one factor behind the high aggregate poverty gap among White and Hispanic families even after the ARPA expansion may be the large number of poor White and Hispanic families before the ARPA expansion (see Table B-1). Even small poverty gaps per family summed over many families can lead to a large aggregate poverty gap.

The depth of poverty among poor families before they receive the ARPA-expanded credit in comparison to the amount of an increased child credit they receive may also affect the decline in the aggregate poverty gap after the ARPA expansion. For example, as previously discussed, prior CRS research indicates that the typical poor Asian family is significantly poorer than poor families of other races (the typical Hispanic family is also poorer than poor families overall, albeit less so than poor Asian families according to this analysis). Asian families in poverty also tend to receive a smaller credit (perhaps because of fewer or older children or perhaps due to the presence of noncitizen children without SSNs).[34] Combined, this may explain why the ARPA expansion is likely to more modestly reduce the aggregate poverty gap among Asian families compared to all families.

Impact on Budgetary Cost

Available data suggest that the ARPA expansion of the child credit will dramatically increase the budgetary cost of this tax benefit. Prior to the ARPA expansion, the total cost of the child credit was $117.7 billion, according to the IRS's most recent data from 2018 tax returns.[35] Of that amount, $81.5 billion (70%) offset income taxes owed (the nonrefundable portion), while $36.2 billion (30%) was received as the refundable portion of the credit (and hence exceeded income taxes owed).

---

[33] Limitations on child credit eligibility for noncitizen children may also reduce the impact the ARPA expansion has on reducing the poverty gap, by lowering the average credit amount, all else being equal.

[34] Poor families with more children and more young children are likely to receive a bigger benefit in dollar terms than those with fewer (and older) children, all else being equal.

[35] Internal Revenue Service, *Individual Complete Report (Publication 1304), Table 3.3*, Statistics of Income, 2018, https://www.irs.gov/statistics/soi-tax-stats-individual-statistical-tables-by-size-of-adjusted-gross-income.

The Joint Committee on Taxation (JCT) estimates that the total cost of the one-year ARPA expansion is $105.1 billion, of which $84.4 billion is attributed to the refundable portion of the credit.[36] This suggests that the total annual cost of the child credit after the ARPA expansion would increase by almost 90%, potentially to over $200 billion. These estimates also suggest that over $120 billion (60% of the total child credit dollars) could be attributable to the refundable portion of the child credit after the ARPA expansion, a 233% increase in total dollars received as the refundable portion of the credit. By way of comparison, the EITC prior to ARPA was estimated to be about $65 billion in 2018 (changes to the EITC for 2021 will increase its size by about $16 billion).[37]

As previously discussed, low-income families generally have little to no income tax liability, and receive most if not all of their child credit as the refundable portion. Low -income families include both those in poverty and those with income between 100% and 199% of poverty. CRS estimates of the ARPA child credit expansion's impact suggest that about two-thirds of the increase in aggregate credit dollars will go to low -income families (those with income up to 199% of poverty), with about a third of the increase being received by families with income 200% of poverty or more.[38] These

[36] The Joint Committee on Taxation estimates that the total cost of the one-year ARPA expansion of the child credit is $109.5 billion between FY2021 and FY2031, of which $88.8 billion is attributed to the refundable portion of the credit. These estimates, however, also include the cost of the permanent extension of the child credit to residents of the territories. Unlike residents of Puerto Rico, who are to apply directly for the child credit with the IRS, other territorial residents are to apply for and receive the child credit from their territorial tax authority. The Treasury is to provide these territorial governments with funds to cover these payments. This permanent extension to the territories is effective beginning in 2021 and so applies to the ARPA-expanded child credit. The budgetary cost of this permanent extension is $4.4 billion between FY2023 and FY2031, all of which is attributable to the refundable portion of the child credit. This amount is subtracted from the total cost to isolate the budgetary costs of the one-year expansion. See Joint Committee on Taxation, *Estimated Revenue Effects Of H.R. 1319, The "American Rescue Plan Act Of 2021," Scheduled For Consideration By The House Of Representatives On February 26, 2021* , February 12, 2021, JCX-12-21, https://www.jct.gov/publications/2021/jcx-12-21.

[37] See Joint Committee on Taxation, Estimated Revenue Effects Of H.R. 1319, The " American Rescue Plan Act Of 2021," Scheduled For Consideration By The House Of Representatives On February 26, 2021 , February 12, 2021, JCX-12-21, https://www.jct.gov/publications/2021/jcx-12-21; and CRS Insight IN11610, *The "Childless" EITC: Temporary Expansion for 2021 Under the American Rescue Plan Act of 2021 (ARPA; P.L. 117-2).*

[38] CRS estimates that there are 38,779,000 families with children receiving an average credit increase of $2,489. This would result in an estimated increase in aggregate

estimates suggest that if the ARPA child credit expansion were extended, it would likely be, in budgetary terms, the largest cash assistance program for low- income families with children.

Conclusion

The analysis presented in this report suggests the ARPA-expanded child credit is likely to significantly increase incomes of low -income families with children and substantially reduce both the prevalence of child poverty and the depth of poverty among families with children. Research suggests that a child benefit similar to the ARPA-expanded credit could have significant long- term benefits for children's health, education, and future earnings.[39]

These effects could be diminished by other factors that are beyond the scope of this report. For example, some evidence suggests that the ARPA-expanded child credit, which working and nonworking parents alike can receive, may discourage low -income parents from working.

Existing research suggests this impact may be small, but reductions in earned income could reduce the benefit's anti-poverty impact.[40] Some

---

child credit dollars of about $96.5 billion (38,779,000 x $2,487) from the ARPA expansion. Of that, poor families with children would receive an estimated total of $20.9 billion in increased credit dollars (4,706,000 families x $4,445 average increase per family) and near-poor families would receive an estimated total of $42.7 billion in increased credit dollars (13,429,000 families x $3,180 average increase per family). Hence, CRS estimates that poor families receive in total 22% of additional credit dollars from the ARPA expansion, while near-poor families receive about 44% of additional dollars. See Table B-1 and Table C-3.

[39] Irwin Garfinkel, Laurel Sariscsany, and Elizabeth Ananat, et al., *The Costs and Benefits of a Child Allowance*, Center on Poverty and Social Policy at Columbia University, Poverty and Social Policy Discussion Paper, February 23, 2021, https://www.povertycenter.columbia.edu/news-internal/2021/child-allowance/cost-benefit-analysis.

[40] The National Academy of Sciences (NAS) modeled a similar benefit as the ARPA-expanded child credit (child allowance #2) and estimated that this proposal would result in an aggregate reduction in hours of employment of 277.4 million hours (Table CA-2) over 6.079 million workers who were estimated to reduce their work hours and 149,000 who were estimated to stop working entirely (Table CA-3). The NAS study estimates that among low-income individuals (below 200% of poverty), 4.552 million will have decreased earnings as a result of the child allowance #2 proposal modeled. (Worksheet "CA Main Sheet" in Appendix E). Hence, if all of the decrease in earnings occurred among the low-income population, the average per worker per week reduction would be 1.17 hours (277,400,000 divided by 4,552,000, then divided by 52 weeks). Overall, the NAS study finds that this decrease in employment willlessen the child poverty rate reduction by 0.1 percentage points (Table CA-3). See The National Academies of Science, Engineering, and Medicine,

policymakers may be concerned with the administration of the ARPA-expanded child credit. Families with children who have never been required to file a federal income tax return due to their low incomes would need to file a return to receive the credit. Failure to do so would mean that these families would not receive the child credit, which could lessen its antipoverty effectiveness. More broadly, the administration of this expanded credit generally requires that half of the credit be issued monthly during the last six months of 2021. To determine how much to advance, the IRS will be relying on older data—from 2020 or 2019—to estimate eligibility and then issue advance payments. If this information is out of date and not corrected, a taxpayer could receive a benefit they are ineligible for, and in some cases, have to pay it back. This could discourage take-up of the advance payment or result in IRS compliance measures, like audits, that may discourage participation.

Even with these limitations, CRS analysis suggests that the ARPA expansion of the child credit will transform the credit into a near universally available benefit that provides significant financial assistance to many low-income families with children. Many of the poorest families— who received little to no benefit from the credit prior to ARPA—will receive the largest increases from this legislative change, resulting in a substantial reduction in child poverty. For families with the highest levels of financial hardship—those deepest in poverty—the ARPA-expanded credit may reduce the depth of their poverty, but be insufficient on its own to lift them out of poverty.

Appendix A. Methodology and Data

CRS used Version 3 of the Transfer Income Model (TRIM) to calculate the estimates presented in this report. This model applies government program rules onto data from the Census Bureau's Current Population Survey Annual Social and Economic Supplement (ASEC), allowing CRS to simulate how changes in government programs may impact the population. For this report, CRS simulated ARPA's child credit changes in TRIM's Federal Income Tax module, and then examined how these changes affected families using definitions of income and poverty associated with the Supplemental Poverty

---

A Roadmap to Reducing Child Poverty (Washington, DC: The National Academies Press, 2019), https://www.nap.edu/catalog/25246/a-roadmap-to-reducing-child-poverty. Appendix E, https://www.nap.edu/ catalog/25246/a-roadmap-to-reducing-child-poverty#stats.

Measure (SPM). For more information on the standards CRS adheres to in conducting TRIM analysis, the ASEC, and the SPM poverty measure, please see CRS Report R46824, Need-Tested Benefits: Technical Companion to Selected CRS Reports on Need-Tested Benefits Receipt by Families and Individuals.

Several other methods and caveats specific to this report are discussed further below.

Analytical Methodology

Some racial and ethnic groups are smaller in population size (and ASEC sample size) than others. Because CRS divided each racial and ethnic group into several income levels for this report, the sample size for some estimates was too small to draw reliable conclusions about using only one year of data. To reduce error introduced by small sample sizes, CRS chose to average three years of data (the 2016-2018 ASEC surveys, which report income and other data from 2015-2017) to produce these estimates.[41] CRS also conducted standard error analysis[42] on these three-year averages to ensure that the estimates were sufficiently precise. Although averages tend to skew towards extreme values (unlike some other measurements of central tendencies, such as medians), CRS chose to calculate averages in order to conduct standard error analysis consistent with Census Bureau guidance.[43]

---

[41] The Census Bureau recommends using 3-year average estimates for small subgroups. See U.S. Census Bureau, "Source of the Data and Accuracy of the Estimates for the 2018 Annual Social and Economic Supplement Microdata File," 2020, Standard Errors of Data for Combined Years, G-25, Footnote 5. For more information see https://www2. census.gov/programs-surveys/cps/techdocs/cpsmar18.pdf.

[42] All of these estimates are derived from a sample, which is an incomplete measurement of the U.S. population. CRS uses standard errors to characterize just how incomplete these estimates could be. Standard errors are a measure of the extent to which an estimate can be expected to deviate from a true value for the full population. That is, standard errors attempt to estimate how much these specific survey-based calculations might differ from the reality faced by the full population of Americans. However, standard errors derived from one single sample, as in the case of the ASEC in one given year, do not necessarily reflect the true standard error. Therefore, CRS uses replicate weights, which "allow a single sample to simulate multiple samples, thus generating more informed standard error estimates" to estimate standard errors. Replicate weights are the approach the Census Bureau encourages researchers to use when attempting to estimate standard errors. For more information, see https://cps.ipums.org/cps/repwt.shtml.

[43] U.S. Census Bureau. "Source of the Data and Accuracy of the Estimates for the 2018 Annual Social and Economic Supplement Microdata File," 2020, Standard Errors of

Racial and Ethnic Category Methodology

CRS uses responses recorded on the ASEC survey to define racial and ethnic groups. The ASEC asks respondents to self-identify as American Indian or Alaska Native, Asian, Black or African American, Native Hawaiian or Other Pacific Islander, or White.[44] Additionally, respondents may identify as more than one race or as some other race. Hispanic ethnicity is addressed separately in another question. Therefore, persons of any racial identity can also identify as being Hispanic.[45]

CRS combines these two survey questions to categorize individuals according to both their race and Hispanic ethnicity. CRS categorizes Hispanic individuals as being Hispanic, regardless of their racial identity. All non-Hispanic individuals are then categorized according to their respective racial identities. Using this definition, CRS further defines the race or ethnicity of a family by the racial and ethnic composition of the family members. If one member reports a racial or ethnic identity that differs from their other family members, the family is categorized as having two or more races. For example, if one member of the family identifies as Hispanic and Black, and the other two members identify as non-Hispanic Black, the family would be considered of two or more races. If all members of the family share the same racial or ethnic identity, they are categorized as that identity.

By using compositional measures to define families' racial and ethnic group, CRS can evaluate families of multiple racial and ethnic identities. For example, a family comprised entirely of Black individuals, none of whom identify as Hispanic, would be considered Black. A family comprised of both non-Hispanic Black individuals and Hispanic Black individuals would be considered two or more races. Afamily comprised entirely of Hispanic Black individuals would be considered Hispanic. This method of defining an individual's racial and ethnic group preferences Hispanic ethnicity over

---

Data for Combined Years, G-25. For more information see https://www2.census.gov/programs-surveys/cps/techdocs/cpsmar18.pdf.

44 The Census Bureau is required to categorize race in this way to comply with guidance from 1997 issued by OMB. These definitions "reflect a social definition of race recognized in this country and [are] not an attempt to define race biologically, anthropologically, or genetically." For more information, see https://www.census.gov/topics/population/race/about.html.

45 The Census Bureau is required to categorize ethnicity in this way to comply with guidance from 1997 issued by OMB. For more information, see https://www.census.gov/topics/ population/hispanic-origin/about.html.

racial identity, which may not reflect how a respondent views their own racial and ethnic identity.

Exclusion of Small Population Groups from this Analysis

Despite improving overall sample sizes by averaging three years of data, this report does not present results for persons who identify as non-Hispanic American Indian or Alaska Native, or as non-Hispanic Native Hawaiian or Other Pacific Islander, due to their relatively small sample sizes and relatively high standard errors. However, these persons were counted toward the aggregate totals for all analyses present in the report. Additionally, if such individuals lived in a family with two or more racial or ethnic identities present, they were included in that family.

The Family as the Unit of Analysis

Although the ARPA expansion of the child credit affects taxpayers, the impact of these provisions is analyzed in terms of families. A taxpayer is generally composed of all individuals listed on a federal income tax return (IRS Form 1040) and includes an individual, their spouse (if married), and any dependents. In contrast, poverty analysis is done at the family level because families can share many resources and expenses. Hence, in this report analyses of the impact of the ARPA-expanded child credit are generally done at the family level. In this report, a family is composed of people living together related by blood or marriage (the family), cohabiting partners, and foster children. In some cases, like multigenerational families, a family can be composed of multiple taxpayers. In these cases, tax liabilities and/or benefits for all taxpayers are aggregated to determine the impact of the income tax on the family's resources. If a family is determined to be poor, all members of that family are counted as poor.

Family Income Level

This report uses disposable income to categorize the population across separate income levels and compare higher-income families to families living in poverty. Disposable income is defined as the resources available to families under the research Supplemental Poverty Measure (SPM).[46] These resources are calculated as money income (i.e., earned income plus interest and dividends plus cash social insurance benefits [e.g., Social Security, unemployment insurance]); minus taxes, minus work expenditures (e.g., child care), and minus medical expenditures; plus the value of tax credits (including the child credit and the earned income credit [EITC]) and the value of in-kind benefits (such as food and housing subsidies).

Families with the same disposable income may have differing poverty status (under the SPM, there are thousands of different poverty thresholds which depend on a family's composition, geographic location, and housing tenure).[47] To account for this and compare families living in poverty to families with higher income levels, CRS computes the ratio of each family's SPM resources to their respective SPM poverty threshold. From this ratio, CRS created five separate family income levels, delineating those with disposable income 0%-99% of their poverty threshold (i.e., families living in poverty) from families with ratios of 100%-199%, 200%-299%, 300%-399%, or 400% or higher.

Child credit amounts are estimated per taxpayer, and then included in family resources.[48] For example, assume a family includes two taxpayers (e.g., a single parent with her child lives with her sibling and their family). For each taxpayer, TRIM3 estimates their child credit amount (using AGI, if the family is subject to either the ARPA or TCJAphaseout). According to TRIM3 estimates, one taxpayer receives a $500 increase in their child credit from ARPA and the other taxpayer receives a $100 increase in their child credit from the ARPA expansion. The family's resources will thus increase by $600. Because eligibility for the child credit does not affect eligibility for

---

[46] For more information, see CRS Report R45031, The Supplemental Poverty Measure: Its Core Concepts, Development, and Use.

[47] For more information, see CRS Report R46824, Need-Tested Benefits: Technical Companion to Selected CRS Reports on Need-Tested Benefits Receipt by Families and Individuals.

[48] The federal income tax code, TRIM3, and CRS use another measure of income—adjusted gross income (AGI)—to calculate child credit amounts at the taxpayer level. This income concept, used for credit administration purposes, differs from the disposable income measure CRS uses in this report to group families for the purpose of distributional analyses. For example, AGI does not generally include the value of need-tested benefits, like housing assistance and other in-kind benefits, nor does it include the value of tax credits like the EITC and the child credit. In addition, for certain-low-income taxpayers, AGI does not include the value of Social Security benefits. AGI also does not net out the value of taxes paid or net out work expenditures and out of pocket medical expenditures.

other need-tested programs,[49] or tax liabilities (since tax credits are not taxable income), the change in a family's resources before and after ARPAwill be due entirely to the ARPA changes to the child credit.

Limitations

There are several limitations that should be considered when interpreting the results presented in this report. First, because of the data lags in the TRIM3 model and the use of three-year averages in this analysis, the underlying data used in this report (which reflect a nonrecessionary economic period) are not analogous to economic conditions in 2021, nor will they be for the eventual postrecessionary economy.

Second, the results do not account for the fact that some eligible families may not file an income tax return, which is necessary to receive the child tax credit. Instead, the model used by CRS in this analysis assumes that 100% of eligible families will receive the full value of the credit for which they are eligible.[50] This limitation may be particularly important for the ARPA child tax credit expansion, which made families with very low or no earned income eligible for the child tax credit. These families are generally not required to file an income tax return, and as a result may not know that they are required to file a return in 2021 to claim the ARPA-expanded child tax credit.

Third, the results do not include estimates of eligibility in U.S. territories. The model used by CRS in this analysis does not include information on residents of U.S. territories. As a result, CRS is not able to estimate eligibility for the child tax credit in the territories.

Fourth, the results do not attempt to estimate the impact of the requirement in ARPA that the Treasury issue half of the expected 2021 child tax credit in periodic payments to families beginning in July 2021. Although the use of periodic payments may change the timing of when families receive benefits from the child tax credit, this change will not affect the annual amount of the credit for which families are eligible.

Fifth, the categorization of racial and ethnic groups may not reflect the way that persons reporting their race and ethnicity self-identify. A Pew study

---

[49] See Internal Revenue Code §6409.

[50] For more information see The Urban Institute, "TRIM3: Federal Tax Module Version History," https://boreas.urban.org/documentation/federaltax/main.php.

from 2014 found that 67% of persons who identified as Hispanic viewed being Hispanic as part or all of their racial background.[51] The authors noted that this has two implications: (1) that race among Hispanic persons does not fit neatly into the Census Bureau's current racial categorization standard and (2) that many Hispanic individuals actually view themselves as mixed race, and making this distinction would increase the proportion of mixed race persons in the United States by 2 percentage points. However, the complexities of Hispanic identity (or other racial identities) are difficult to understand using the ASEC, due to sample size and survey issues. The method employed in this report attempts to capture those persons who identify as racially Hispanic, and therefore likely incorrectly categorizes some persons whose Hispanic ethnicity does not play a role in their racial identity.

Finally, estimates prepared using survey data (which include these results) tend to underestimate the value of refundable tax credits such as the child tax credit. Research suggests that one cause of this underestimation may be that families with children where multiple adults file an income tax return have an incentive to strategically choose which adult will claim the children on their return.[52] By doing so, families may maximize the amount of the child tax credit they receive in a way that is not fully captured by the model used by CRS in this analysis.

Appendix B. Pre-ARPA Baseline Estimates

Number and Average Income of Families with Children

Table B-1 presents estimates of the number of individuals in families with children, by family income levels and race and ethnicity. For example, these

[51] Kim Parker, Juliana Menasce Horowitz, and Rich Morin, et al., *Multiracial in America: Chapter 7: The Many Dimensions of Hispanic Racial Identity*, Pew Research Center, June 11, 2015, https://www.pewresearch.org/social-trends/2015/06/11/chapter-7-the-many-dimensions-of-hispanic-racial-identity/#asking-hispanics-about-racial-identities-beyond-census-classifications.

[52] For further discussion of this effect, see David Splinter, Jeff Larrimore, and Jacob Mortenson, *Whose Child Is This? Shifting Of Dependents Among EITC Claimants Within The Same Household*, National Tax Journal 2017, 70:4, pp. 737-758, https://doi.org/10.17310/ntj.2017.4.02. See also Maggie R. Jones and Amy B. O'Hara, *Do Doubled-Up Families Minimize Household-Level Tax Burden?* National Tax Journal 2016, 69:3, pp. 613 -640, http://dx.doi.org/10.17310/ntj.2016.3.05.

data indicate there are 264,000 Asian families with children who are living in poverty. These estimates present baseline population counts, before the ARPA child credit expansion.

Table B-1. Baseline estimated number of families with children by family income level & race/ethnicity

	Race/Ethnicity of Family					
Family Income Level	Asian	Black	Hispanic	Two or More Races	White	*All Races/ Ethnicities*
Ratio of Family Income to Poverty Threshold	*Number of families with children, in thousands*					
<100%	264	889	1,599	494	1,405	*4,706*
100%-199%	575	2,303	3,533	1,794	5,087	*13,429*
200%-299%	451	832	1,155	1,247	4,510	*8,235*
300%-399%	311	382	384	753	3,343	*5,205*
>=400%	534	377	399	975	4,889	*7,204*
All Income Levels	*2,135*	*4,784*	*7,070*	*5,263*	*19,233*	*38,779*

Sources: CRS analysis of TRIM3-augmented CPS ASEC files representing data from 2015 to 2017.

Notes: This table presents estimates of the number of families with at least one child under 18. CRS estimates are averaged over three years of data (2015, 2016, and 2017). Estimates are grouped by family income level and race/ethnicity of the family. These estimates cannot be used to construct poverty rates shown later in this report.

Families are defined as anyone living in the same resource unit, per the Supplemental Poverty Measure (SPM). Family Income Level is calculated as the ratio of a family's disposable income, including government tax es and transfers, to their respective SPM poverty thresholds. This allows for families of similar standards of living across the United States to be grouped together. Families are categorized by their family income level before the ARPA expansion (i.e., the pre-ARPA child credit is included in income, but the increase from the ARPA expansion is not included in income for the purposes of categorizing families by family income level). This categorization allows for a comparison of the same families before and after the ARPA expansion of the child tax credit.

Race or ethnicity of a family is defined by the racial composition of the family members. See Appendix A for more details on this method. CRS does not report aggregated sums for families identifying entirely as American Indian, Alaska Native, or Native Hawaiian or Other Pacific Islander due to inadequate sample sizes that would lead to unreliable estimates. For example, according to CRS estimates, there are 294,000 families of all income levels that may identify as either American Indian, Alaska Native, or Native Hawaiian or Other Pacific Islander. Families of these racial identities are not included in this table, but they are included in "All Races and Ethnicities." Hence, because of this (and rounding), cells do not sum to the total.

Table B-2 presents estimates of average family income among families with children, by family income levels and race and ethnicity. For example, these data indicate that among all Asian families with children who are living in poverty, the average family income is $17,427, as defined by their SPM family income. This table presents baseline income before the ARPA child credit expansion.

Grouping families by their ratio of family income to SPM poverty threshold (i.e., "family income level") allows families of similar standards of living across the United States to be grouped together. Families are each characterized by their family income in relation to their appropriate SPM poverty threshold. Afamily's SPM threshold depends on numerous factors, including where they live (i.e., the geographic variability of housing costs), whether a family rents or owns, and the family's size.[53] So, for example, the SPM threshold for a family in an urban area with high housing costs would generally be higher than the SPM threshold for a family living in a rural area with lower housing costs, all else being equal. This could result in a poor family in an urban area with high housing costs having a higher family income than a poor family in a rural area with lower housing costs. Insofar as there are significant differences in poverty thresholds by race or ethnicity—a topic beyond the scope of this report—there hence may be deviations in average family income by race and ethnicity for a given income category.

Families are categorized by their family income level before the ARPA expansion (i.e., the pre-ARPA child credit is included in income, but the increase from the ARPA expansion is not included in income for the purposes of categorizing families by family income level). This categorization allows for a comparison of the same families before and after the ARPA expansion of the child tax credit.[54]

---

[53] For more information, see "Definition of Need in SPM Poverty Thresholds" in CRS Report R45031, *The Supplemental Poverty Measure: Its Core Concepts, Development, and Use*, by Joseph Dalaker.

[54] Note that the average income estimates in *Table B-2* do not contextualize these income levels with the varying needs of families by geography, housing tenure, and family size. For example, despite exhibiting the lowest incomes in this table, White families generally have comparable need to other racial and ethnic groups, as defined by the average pre-ARPA poverty gap. In other words, on average, White families are similarly as close to their respective poverty threshold as families of other races and ethnicities. A further analysis of SPM poverty thresholds by race/ethnicity is beyond the scope of this report.

Table B-2. Baseline estimated average family income for families with children by family income level & race/ethnicity

	Race/Ethnicity of Family					
Family Income Level	Asian	Black	Hispanic	Two or More Races	White	*All Races/ Ethnicities*
Ratio of Family Income to Poverty Threshold	*Average family income ($) among families with children*					
< 100%	$17,427	$16,642	$20,319	$18,197	$13,959	*$17,282*
100%-199%	$48,112	$36,377	$42,080	$40,997	$38,046	*$39,674*
200%-299%	$78,314	$63,930	$71,203	$70,286	$64,325	*$66,919*
300%-399%	$106,776	$90,321	$96,086	$96,412	$89,944	*$92,377*
>=400%	$212,191	$186,101	$231,115	$196,605	$190,310	*$194,838*
All Income Levels	$100,182	$53,613	$55,541	$82,603	$90,257	*$78,687*

Sources: CRS analysis of TRIM3-augmented CPS ASEC files representing data from 2015 to 2017.

Notes: This table presents estimates of family income among families with at least one child under 18. CRS estimates are averaged over three years of data (2015, 2016, and 2017). Estimates are grouped by family income level and race and ethnicity of the family. A companion table, Table C-3, illustrates the estimated change in family income as a result of the ARPA expansion of the child tax credit.

Families are defined as anyone living in the same resource unit, per the Supplemental Poverty Measure (SPM). Family Income Level is calculated as the ratio of a family's disposable income, including government tax es and transfers, to their respective SPM poverty thresholds.

Race or ethnicity of a family is defined by the racial composition of the family members. See Appendix A for more details on this method. CRS does not report aggregated sums for families identifying entirely as American Indian, Alaska Native, or Native Hawaiian or Other Pacific Islander due to inadequate sample sizes that would lead to unreliable estimates. Families of these racial identities are not included in this table, but they are included in "All Races and Ethnicities." Hence, because of this (and rounding), cells do not sum to the total.

Families with Children Receiving Pre-ARPA Child Credit

Table B-3 presents estimates of the percentage of families with children, of a given income level and race and ethnicity, who received the pre-ARPA child tax credit. For example, these data indicate an estimated 57% of all Asian families with children in poverty (family income level <1 00% of poverty) received the pre-ARPAchild tax credit. Table C-1 displays the average post-

ARPA credit across the same income levels and race and ethnicity categories.

Table B-3. Estimated share of families receiving the pre-ARPA child credit by family income level & race/ethnicity

	RACE/ETHNICITY OF FAMILY					
FAMILY INCOME LEVEL	Asian	Black	Hispanic	Two or More Races	White	*All Races/ Ethnicities*
Ratio of Family Income to Poverty Threshold	*% of all families with children in each income level and of each racial/ethnic group who are simulated as receiving the credit*					
< 100%	57%	41%	65%	51%	46%	*52%*
100%-199%	86%	84%	89%	87%	87%	*87%*
200%-299%	85%	92%	91%	94%	93%	*92%*
300%-399%	90%	93%	91%	94%	93%	*93%*
>= 400%	80%	82%	80%	84%	84%	*84%*
All Income Levels	*81%*	*78%*	*83%*	*86%*	*86%*	*84%*

Sources: CRS analysis of TRIM3-augmented CPS ASEC files representing data from 2015 to 2017.

Notes: This table presents estimates of the percentage of families with at least one child under 18, who were receiving the child tax credit before ARPA. CRS estimates are averaged over three years of data (2015, 2016, and 2017). Estimates are grouped by family income level and race and ethnicity of the family. A companion table, Table C-1, illustrates the estimated share of families that receive the child credit after the ARPA expansion of the child tax credit (including families that receive the same credit and a larger credit). Another companion table, Table C-2, illustrates the share of families that receive a larger credit after the ARPA expansion of the child tax credit.

Families are defined as anyone living in the same resource unit, per the Supplemental Poverty Measure (SPM). Family Income Level is calculated as the ratio of a family's disposable income, including government tax es and transfers, to their respective SPM poverty thresholds. This allows for families of similar standards of living across the United States to be grouped together. Families are categorized by their family income level before the ARPA expansion (i.e., the pre-ARPA child credit is included in income, but the increase from the ARPA expansion is not included in income for the purposes of categorizing families by family income level). This categorization allows for a comparison of the same families before and after the ARPA expansion of the child tax credit.

Race or ethnicity of a family is defined by the racial composition of the family members. See Appendix A for more details on this method. CRS does not report aggregated sums for families identifying entirely as American Indian, Alaska Native, or Native Hawaiian or Other Pacific Islander due to inadequate sample sizes that would lead to unreliable estimates. Families of these racial identities are not included in this table, but they are included in "All Races and Ethnicities." Hence, because of this (and rounding), cells do not sum to the total.

Table B-4 presents estimates of the average pre-ARPAchild tax credit received by families with children, by income level and race and ethnicity. For example, these data indicate Asian families with children in poverty received a pre-ARPA child tax credit of $1,167 on average. Table C-3 displays the average post-ARPA credit across the same income levels, and race and ethnicity categories.

Table B-4. Estimated average pre-ARPA child credit by family income level & race/ethnicity

	RACE/ETHNICITY OF FAMILY					
FAMILY INCOME LEVEL	Asian	Black	Hispanic	Two or More Races	White	*All Races/ Ethnicities*
Ratio of Family Income to Poverty Threshold	*Average credit ($) among families with children*					
<100%	$1,167	$620	$1,307	$917	$828	*$976*
100%-199%	$2,652	$2,316	$2,781	$2,703	$2,721	*$2,659*
200%-299%	$2,660	$2,878	$3,017	$3,238	$3,164	*$3,096*
300%-399%	$2,810	$2,828	$2,975	$3,102	$3,147	*$3,083*
>=400%	$2,387	$2,391	$2,482	$2,603	$2,680	*$2,623*
All Income Levels	*$2,425*	*$2,144*	*$2,479*	*$2,699*	*$2,750*	*$2,597*

Sources: CRS analysis of TRIM3-augmented CPS ASEC files representing income from 2015 to 2017.

Notes: This table presents estimates of the average child tax credit for families with at least one child under 18, before ARPA. CRS estimates are averaged over three years of data (2015, 2016, and 2017). Estimates are grouped by family income level and race and ethnicity of the family. A companion table, Table C-3, illustrates the estimated change in family income as a result of the ARPA expansion of the child tax credit. In other words, this companion table illustrates the increase in the child credit as a result of the ARPA expansion.

Families are defined as anyone living in the same resource unit, per the Supplemental Poverty Measure (SPM).

Family Income Level is calculated as the ratio of a family's disposable income, including government tax es and transfers, to their respective SPM poverty thresholds. This allows for families of similar standards of living across the United States to be grouped together. Families are categorized by their family income level before the ARPA expansion (i.e., the pre-ARPA child credit is included in income, but the increase from the ARPA expansion is not included in income for the purposes of categorizing families by family income level). This categorization allows for a comparison of the same families before and after the ARPA expansion of the child tax credit.

Race or ethnicity of a family is defined by the racial composition of the family members. See Appendix A for more details on this method. CRS does not report aggregated sums for families identifying entirely as American Indian, Alaska Native, or Native Hawaiian or Other Pacific Islander due to inadequate sample sizes that would lead to unreliable estimates. Families of these racial identities are not included in this table, but they are included in "All Races and Ethnicities." Hence, because of this (and rounding), cells do not sum to the total.

Poverty

Table B-5 presents estimates of the number of individuals living in poverty in families with children, by work status and individual race and ethnicity. Additionally, the table displays the number of children living in poverty separately. For example, these data indicate there are 1.06 million Asian individuals (adults and children alike) living in families with children who are living in poverty. Of these individuals, 428,000 are children. Additionally, roughly 77% of these individuals (816,000 of 1.06 million) live in families with workers. These estimates present baseline poverty counts, before the ARPA child credit expansion.

Table B-5. Estimated number of individuals in poverty by presence/absence of workers in family & race/ethnicity

	RACE/ETHNICITY OF INDIVIDUAL					
	Asian	Black	Hispanic	Two or More Races	White	*All Races/ Ethnicities*
	Number of individuals living in poverty, in thousands					
All Individuals (Adults & Children) Living in Families with Children	1,060	3,471	7,438	391	5,613	*18,246*
... & Workers	816	2,068	6,109	269	3,754	*13,179*
... & No Workers	244	1,404	1,329	122	1,859	*5,067*
All Children	428	1,857	3,795	285	2,771	*9,267*

Sources: CRS analysis of TRIM3-augmented CPS ASEC files representing income from 2015 to 2017.

Notes: This table presents estimates of the average number of people living in families and in poverty, with at least one child under 18, before ARPA. CRS estimates are averaged over three years of data (2015, 2016, and 2017).

Estimates are grouped by family work status, and presented separately for children.

Families are defined as anyone living in the same resource unit, per the Supplemental Poverty Measure (SPM). Families with workers are defined as families with at least one worker ages 18 or older who worked at least one week during the year. Race or ethnicity of an individual is defined by the racial identity of the individual. See Appendix A for more details on this method. CRS does not report aggregated sums for individuals identifying entirely as American Indian, Alaska Native, or Native Hawaiian or Other Pacific Islander due to inadequate sample sizes that would lead to unreliable estimates. Individuals of these racial identities are not included in this table, but they are included in "All Races and Ethnicities." Hence, because of this (and rounding), cells do not sum to the total.

Table B-6 presents estimates of the percentage of individuals living in poverty in families with children, by work status and individual race and ethnicity. Additionally, the table displays the percentage of children living in poverty separately. For example, these data indicate 11% of Asian individuals (adults and children alike) living in families with children are in poverty. The percentage of Asian children living in poverty is also 11%. These estimates present baseline poverty rates, before the ARPA child credit expansion. Table C-4 illustrates the poverty rate after the ARPA child credit expansion, across the same family categories and race and ethnicity categories.

Table B-6. Estimated poverty rate including the pre-ARPA child credit by presence/absence of workers in family & race/ethnicity

	Race/Ethnicity of Individual					
	Asian	Black	Hispanic	Two or More Races	White	*All Races/ Ethnicities*
	Percentage of individuals living in poverty, in thousands					
All Individuals (Adults & Children) Living in Families with Children	11%	17%	19%	9%	7%	*12%*
... & Workers	9%	11%	17%	7%	5%	*9%*
... & No Workers	76%	63%	72%	54%	58%	*64%*
All Children	11%	18%	20%	10%	7%	*13%*

Sources: CRS analysis of TRIM3-augmented CPS ASEC files representing data from 2015 to 2017.

Notes: This table presents estimates of the average poverty rate of people living in families with at least one child under 18, before ARPA. CRS estimates are averaged over three years of data (2015, 2016, and 2017). Estimates are grouped by family work status, and presented separately for children. A companion table, Table C-4, illustrates the poverty rate after the ARPA expansion of the child tax credit. In other words, this companion table illustrates the impact of the ARPA expansion's child credit provisions on poverty rates.

Families are defined as anyone living in the same resource unit, per the Supplemental Poverty Measure (SPM). Families with workers are defined as families with at least one worker aged 18 or older who worked at least one week during the year. Race or ethnicity of an individual is defined by the racial identity of the individual. See Appendix A for more details on this method. CRS does not report an aggregated sums for individuals identifying entirely as American Indian, Alaska Native, or Native Hawaiian or Other Pacific Islander due to inadequate sample sizes that would lead to unreliable estimates. Individuals of these racial identities are not included in this table, but they are included in "All Races and Ethnicities." Hence, because of this (and rounding), cells do not sum to the total.

Table B-7 presents estimates of the poverty gap among families living in poverty with children, by work status and individual race and ethnicity. For example, these data indicate Asian families living in poverty with children would require $3.2 billion on aggregate to exit poverty. These estimates present baseline poverty gaps, before the ARPA child credit expansion. Table C-5 illustrates the poverty gap after the ARPA child credit expansion, across the same family categories and race and ethnicity categories.

Table B-7. Estimated poverty gap with the pre-ARPA child credit by presence/absence ofworkers in poor family & race/ethnicity of poor family

	Race/Ethnicity of Family					
	Asian	Black	Hispanic	Two or More Races	White	All Races/ Ethnicities
Family Type	Aggregate poverty gap, in billions of dollars					
Families living in poverty with children...	$3.2	$6.7	$13.9	$3.7	$11.4	$39.3
... & Workers	$1.9	$3.4	$10.2	$2.3	$6.5	$24.2
... & No Workers	$1.3	$3.4	$3.7	$1.4	$4.9	$14.6

Sources: CRS analysis of TRIM3-augmented CPS ASEC files representing data from 2015 to 2017.

Notes: This table presents estimates of the average poverty gap of families with at least one child under 18, before ARPA. CRS estimates there are 4.7 million poor families with children, with 3.2 million with workers, and 1.5 million with no workers. CRS estimates are averaged over three years of data (2015, 2016, and 2017). Estimates are grouped by family work status. A companion table, Table C-5, illustrates the poverty gap after the ARPA expansion of the child tax credit. In other words, this companion table illustrates the impact of the ARPA expansion's child credit provisions on poverty gaps.

Families are defined as anyone living in the same resource unit, per the Supplemental Poverty Measure (SPM). Families with workers are defined as families with at least one worker aged 18 or older who worked at least one week during the year. Race or ethnicity of a family is defined by the racial composition of the family members. See Appendix A for more details on this method. CRS does not report an aggregated sums for families identifying entirely as American Indian, Alaska Native, or Native Hawaiian or Other Pacific Islander due to inadequate sample sizes that would lead to unreliable estimates. Families of these racial identities are not included in this table, but they are included in "All Races and Ethnicities." Hence, because of this (and rounding), cells do not sum to the total.

Appendix C. Post-ARPA Expanded Child Credit Estimates

Table C-1. Estimated share of families receiving the child tax credit after ARPA by family income level & race/ethnicity

	RACE/ETHNICITY OF FAMILY					
FAMILY INCOME LEVEL	Asian	Black	Hispanic	Two or More Races	White	*All Races/ Ethnicities*
Ratio of Family Income to Poverty Threshold	*% of all families with children in each income level and of each racial/ethnic group who are simulated as receiving the credit*					
< 100%	84%	96%	94%	96%	93%	*94%*
100%-199%	96%	99%	98%	99%	98%	*98%*
200%-299%	89%	99%	97%	99%	99%	*98%*
300%-399%	93%	99%	97%	99%	99%	*99%*
>= 400%	83%	90%	84%	89%	90%	*89%*
All Income Levels	*89%*	*98%*	*96%*	*97%*	*96%*	*96%*

Sources: CRS analysis of TRIM3-augmented CPS ASEC files representing data from 2015 to 2017.

Notes: This table presents estimates of the percentage of families with at least one child under 18 who were receiving the child tax credit after ARPA. This includes families receiving a larger credit and families receiving the same amount of the credit. CRS estimates are averaged over three years of data (2015, 2016, and 2017). Estimates are grouped by family income level and race and ethnicity of the family. A companion table, Table B-3, illustrates the estimated share of families that receive the child credit before the ARPA expansion of the child tax credit (including families that receive the same credit and a larger credit). Another companion table, Table C-2, illustrates the share of families that receive a larger credit after the ARPA expansion of the child tax credit.

Families are defined as anyone living in the same resource unit, per the Supplemental Poverty Measure (SPM). Family Income Level is calculated as the ratio of a family's disposable income, including government tax and transfers, to their respective SPM poverty thresholds. This allows for families of similar standards of living across the United States to be grouped together. Families are categorized by their family income level before the ARPA expansion (i.e., the pre-ARPA child credit is included in income, but the increase from the ARPA expansion is not included in income for the purposes of categorizing families by family income level). This categorization allows for a comparison of the same families before and after the ARPA expansion of the child tax credit.

Race or ethnicity of a family is defined by the racial composition of the family members. See Appendix A for more details on this method. CRS does not report aggregated sums for families identifying entirely as American Indian, Alaska Native, or Native Hawaiian or Other Pacific Islander due to inadequate sample sizes that would lead to unreliable estimates. Families of these racial identities are not included in this table, but they are included in "All Races and Ethnicities." Hence, because of this (and rounding), cells do not sum to the total.

Table C-1 presents estimates of the percentage of families with children, of a given income level and race and ethnicity, who received the post-ARPA child tax credit. For example, these data indicate an estimated 84% of all Asian families with children in poverty (family income level < 100% of poverty) received the post-ARPAchild tax credit. Table B-3 displays average pre-ARPA credit receipt across the same income levels and race and ethnicity categories.

Families with Children Receiving a Larger Child Credit Under ARPA

Table C-2 presents estimates of the percentage of families with children, of a given income level and race and ethnicity, who received a larger child tax credit due to ARPA. For example, these data indicate an estimated 84% of all Asian families with children in poverty (family income level < 100% of poverty) received a larger child tax credit due to ARPA, defined as an increase of $10 or more. Table B-3 displays the average pre-ARPA credit receipt across the same income levels and race and ethnicity categories.

Table C-2. Estimated share of families receiving a larger child tax credit due to the ARPA child credit expansion by family income level & race/ethnicity

	RACE/ETHNICITY OF FAMILY					
FAMILY INCOME LEVEL	Asian	Black	Hispanic	Two or More Races	White	*All Races/ Ethnicities*
Ratio of Family Income to Poverty Threshold	*% of all families with children in each income level and of each racial/ethnic group who are simulated as receiving a larger credit*					
<100%	84%	96%	94%	96%	92%	*94%*
100%-199%	96%	99%	98%	99%	98%	*98%*
200%-299%	88%	98%	97%	99%	99%	*98%*
300%-399%	79%	96%	93%	94%	96%	*95%*
>=400%	26%	58%	51%	47%	49%	*47%*
All Income Levels	*73%*	*95%*	*94%*	*88%*	*85%*	*88%*

Sources: CRS analysis of TRIM3-augmented CPS ASEC files representing data from 2015 to 2017.

Notes: This table presents estimates of the percentage of families with at least one child under 18 who were receiving a larger child tax credit after ARPA (i.e., a credit that is $10 or more greater than the pre-ARPA credit). CRS estimates are averaged over three years of data (2015, 2016, and 2017). CRS estimates are averaged over three years of data (2015, 2016, and 2017). Estimates are grouped by family income level and race and ethnicity of the family. A companion table, Table B-3, illustrates the estimated share of families that receive the child credit before the ARPA expansion of the child tax credit (including families that receive the same credit and a larger credit).

Another companion table, Table C-1, illustrates the share of families that receive the child credit after the ARPA expansion of the child tax credit (i.e., they receive the same credit or a larger credit).

Families are defined as anyone living in the same resource unit, per the Supplemental Poverty Measure (SPM). Family Income Level is calculated as the ratio of a family's disposable income, including government tax and transfers, to their respective SPM poverty thresholds. This allows for families of similar standards of living across the United States to be grouped together. Families are categorized by their family income level before the ARPA expansion (i.e., the pre-ARPA child credit is included in income, but the increase from the ARPA expansion is not included in income for the purposes of categorizing families by family income level). This categorization allows for a comparison of the same families before and after the ARPA expansion of the child tax credit.

Race or ethnicity of a family is defined by the racial composition of the family members. See Appendix A for more details on this method. CRS does not report aggregated sums for families identifying entirely as American Indian, Alaska Native, or Native Hawaiian or Other Pacific Islander due to inadequate sample sizes that would lead to unreliable estimates. Families of these racial identities are not included in this table, but they are included in "All Races and Ethnicities." Hence, because of this (and rounding), cells do not sum to the total.

Income

Table C-3 presents estimates of the average percentage and dollar increase in income due to ARPA among families with children, categorized by a given pre-ARPA income level and race and ethnicity. For example, Asian families with children in pre-ARPA poverty (family income level < 100%) received an average increase of $3,155, with an average percentage increase of 81%.

The percentage increase in income in Table C-3 may not equal the average increase divided by the pre-ARPA income as reported in Table B-2. For example, the percentage increase in income for poor Asian families in Table C-3 is 81%, which does not equal the average dollar increase ($3,155) divided by the pre-ARPA income of Asian families living in poverty as reported in Table B-2 ($17,427). The reason for this disparity between average percentage increase and average dollar increase is that percentage change, in this case, is more susceptible to skew. Prior to ARPA, the lowest-income families did not qualify for the child credit, or qualified for a reduced credit, because of their low incomes. ARPA does not restrict families with low or no earnings from receiving a full credit. For such families, the ARPA credit will represent a larger increase than for families already receiving the full ACTC. Bec ause of their low initial incomes, the percentage increase reported could be relatively large, significantly skewing the average.[55]

[55] For example, consider a low-income family living in poverty with $8,000 in pre-ARPA income, most of which originates from the value of government benefits. They have one child who qualifies for the credit, but the family does not qualify for the pre-ARPA credit (i.e., their pre-ARPA child credit was zero) because their earned

Table C-3. Estimated average change in family income from ARPA child credit expansion by family income level & race/ethnicity

	Race/Ethnicity of Family					
Family Income level	Asian	Black	Hispanic	Two or More Races	White	All Races/ Ethnicities
Ratio of Family Income to Poverty Threshold	Average $ change in income; average % change income among families with children					
<100%	$3,155; 81%	$4,775; 71%	$4,506; 39%	$4,840; 44%	$4,261; 78%	$4,445; 59%
100%-199%	$2,499; 6%	$3,458; 10%	$3,209; 8%	$3,443; 9%	$2,990; 8%	$3,180; 9%
200%-299%	$1,721; 2%	$2,115; 3%	$2,161; 3%	$2,360; 3%	$2,213; 4%	$2,192; 3%
300%-399%	$1,227; 1%	$1,787; 2%	$1,843; 2%	$1,839; 2%	$1,928; 2%	$1,856; 2%
>=400%	$309; <1%	$947; 1%	$859; 1%	$727; 1%	$734; 1%	$720; 1%
All Income Levels	$1,684; 13%	$3,139; 19%	$3,124; 14%	$2,585; 8%	$2,141; 9%	$2,489; 11%

Sources: CRS analysis of TRIM3-augmented CPS ASEC files representing income from 2015 to 2017.

Notes: This table presents estimates of the average increase in family income from ARPA expansion of the child credit among families with at least one child under 18. Percentage change is not calculated for families with $0 in pre- ARPA resources. CRS estimates are averaged over three years of data (2015, 2016, and 2017). Estimates are grouped by family income level and race and ethnicity of the family. A companion table, Table B-2, illustrates estimated average family income. Another companion table, Table B-4, illustrates the estimated average pre-ARPA child credit.

Families are defined as anyone living in the same resource unit, per the Supplemental Poverty Measure (SPM). Family Income Level is calculated as the ratio of a family's disposable income, including government tax es and transfers, to their respective SPM poverty thresholds.

---

income is less than the minimum requirement of $2,500. After ARPA, they now qualify for the full ARPA credit, resulting in a $3,000 increase in their income. That $3,000 increase represents an increase of 37.5% ($3,000/$8,000). Now, consider a family with $2,000 in pre-ARPA income in the same situation. This family *also* receives an increase of $3,000, but the percentage increase is now 150%. On average, these two families would have income of $5,000 ($2,0 00 plus $8,000 divided by 2) and the average increase of the child credit ($3,000) would thus equal a 60% increase in the credit for families in this income group, but averaging the percentage change in income (150% plus 37.5% divided by 2) would equal 93.75%. The lower a family's initial income, the greater this effect is (skewing the average percentage increase further) despite receiving the same dollar increase as higher-income families. CRS estimates that among all families in poverty before the ARPA expansion of the child credit, 5.2% exhibited percentage increases of greater than 100%.

This allows for families of similar standards of living across the United States to be grouped together. Families are categorized by their family income level before the ARPA expansion (i.e., the pre-ARPA child credit is included in income, but the increase from the ARPA expansion is not included in income for the purposes of categorizing families by family income level). This categorization allows for a comparison of the same families before and after the ARPA expansion of the child tax credit.

Race or ethnicity of a family is defined by the racial composition of the family members. See Appendix A for more details on this method. CRS does not report aggregated sums for families identifying entirely as American Indian, Alaska Native, or Native Hawaiian or Other Pacific Islander due to inadequate sample sizes that would lead to unreliable estimates. Families of these racial identities are not included in this table, but they are included in "All Races and Ethnicities." Hence, because of this (and rounding), cells do not sum to the total.

Poverty

Table C-4 presents estimates of the percentage of individuals living in poverty in families with children after the ARPA child credit expansion, by work status and individual race and ethnicity.

Table C-4. Estimated poverty rate after ARPA child credit expansion by presence/absence of workers in family & race/ethnicity

	Race/Ethnicity of Individual					
	Asian	Black	Hispanic	Two or More Races	White	*All Races/ Ethnicities*
All Individuals (Adults & Children) Living in Families with Children…	8%	10%	12%	4%	4%	*7%*
… & Workers	6%	6%	11%	3%	3%	*5%*
… & No Workers	64%	37%	51%	26%	35%	*42%*
All Children	8%	10%	12%	4%	4%	*7%*

Sources: CRS analysis of TRIM3-augmented CPS ASEC files representing income from 2015 to 2017.

Notes: This table presents estimates of the average poverty rate of people living in families with at least one child under 18, before ARPA. Estimates are grouped by family work status, and presented separately for children. A companion table, Table B-6, illustrates the estimated poverty rate before the ARPA expansion of the child tax credit.

Families are defined as anyone living in the same resource unit, per the Supplemental Poverty Measure (SPM). Families with workers are defined as families with at least one worker aged 18 or older who worked at least one week during the year. Race or ethnicity of an individual is defined by the racial identity of the individual. See Appendix A for more details on this method. CRS does not report aggregated sums for individuals identifying entirely as American Indian, Alaska Native, or Native Hawaiian or Other Pacific Islander due to inadequate sample sizes that would lead to unreliable estimates. Individuals of these racial identities are not included in this ta ble, but they are included in "All Races and Ethnicities." Hence, because of this (and rounding), cells do not sum to the total.

Additionally, the table displays the percentage of children living in poverty separately.[56] For example, these data indicate 8% of Asian individuals (adults and children alike) living in families with children are living in poverty. The percentage of Asian children living in poverty is also 8%. Table B-6 illustrates the poverty rate before the ARPA child credit expansion, across the same family categories and race and ethnicity categories.

Table C-5 presents estimates of the poverty gap among families living in poverty with children after the ARPA child credit expansion, by work status and individual race and ethnicity. For example, these data indicate that after ARPA, Asian families living in poverty with children would require $2.5 billion on aggregate to exit poverty. Table B-7 illustrates the poverty gap before the ARPA child credit expansion, across the same family categories and race and ethnicity categories.

Table C-5. Estimated poverty gap after ARPA child credit expansion by presence/absence of workers in family & race/ethnicity

Family Type	Race/Ethnicity of Family					
	Asian	Black	Hispanic	Two or More Races	White	*All Races/ Ethnicities*
	Billions of Dollars					
Poor Families with Children ...	$2.5	$3.6	$8.3	$2.1	$7.1	*$23.9*
... & Workers	$1.4	$1.8	$6.1	$1.3	$4.1	*$14.8*
... & No Workers	$1.1	$1.8	$2.3	$0.8	$3.0	*$9.1*

Sources: CRS analysis of TRIM3-augmented CPS ASEC files representing income from 2015 to 2017.

Notes: This table presents estimates of the average poverty gap of families with at least one child under 18, after ARPA. CRS estimates there are 3.2 million poor families with children, with 2.1 million with workers and 1.1 million with no workers. Estimates are grouped by family work status. A companion table, Table B-7, illustrates the estimated poverty gap before the ARPA child credit expansion. Families are defined as anyone living in the same resource unit, per the Supplemental Poverty Measure (SPM). Families with workers are defined as families with at least one worker aged 18 or older who worked at least one week during the year. Race or ethnicity of a family is defined by the racial composition of the family members. See Appendix

[56] The share of *all individuals* who are poor (children and adults) and the share of *children* who are poor may differ, if the ratio of children to adults is not one-to-one. For example, consider a universe where there are 2 families. Family A has 2 adults and 2 children and is not poor. Family B has 2 adults and 4 children and is poor. The ratio of children to adults in this universe is 1.5 to 1. Of the 10 individuals (children and adults), 6 are poor (60% poverty rate). However, among children, the child poverty rate is 67%, since 4 of the 6 children are poor.

A for more details on this method. CRS does not report aggregated sums for families identifying entirely as American Indian, Alaska Native, or Native Hawaiian or Other Pacific Islander due to inadequate sample sizes that would lead to unreliable estimates. Families of these racial identities are not included in this table, but they are included in "All Races and Ethnicities." Hence, because of this (and rounding), cells do not sum to the total.

Chapter 2

The Expanded Child Tax Credit for 2021: Frequently Asked Questions (FAQs)*

Margot L. Crandall-Hollick

In March 2021, Congress passed legislation significantly expanding the child tax credit for one year as part of the American Rescue Plan Act of 2021 (ARPA; P.L. 117-2). ARPA expanded the eligibility for and the amount of the credit for 2021, primarily for low- and middle-income taxpayers. The law also directed the Treasury Secretary to establish a program to advance up to half of the total credit amount before 2021 income taxes are filed. This is a departure from most other tax benefits, which are typically delivered annually in a lump sum after federal income tax returns are filed. These changes expired at the end of 2021 and are no longer in effect, although some households may still be receiving some or all of the expanded credit with their 2021 income tax return.

The 117th Congress is considering proposals to extend and/or modify the temporary child credit expansion included in APRA. In April 2021, House Ways and Means Committee Chairman Richard Neal released a discussion draft of the Building an Economy for Families Act that included a provision to permanently extend the ARPA changes to the child credit.[1] The Biden Administration proposed making the full refundability provision included in ARPA permanent, while extending other ARPA provisions

* This is an edited, reformatted and augmented version of Congressional Research Service Publication No. R46900, updated June 14, 2022.

[1] See House Committee on Ways and Means, "Chairman Neal Unveils Groundbreaking Proposal to Reshape the American Economy," press release, April 27, 2021, https://waysandmeans. house.gov/media-center/press-releases/chairman-neal-unveils-groundbreaking-proposal-reshape-american-economy.

In: A Closer Look at the Child Tax Credit
Editor: Philip Palmer
ISBN: 979-8-89113-601-4

through the end of 2025.[2] At the end of September 2021, the House Budget Committee reported the Build Back Better Act (BBBA; H.R. 5376), which would have effectively extended the ARPA-expanded credit for four years through the end of 2025 and permanently made the credit fully refundable.[3] On November 19, 2021, BBBA passed the House of Representatives. Unlike the House Budget Committee version of the BBBA, the House-passed version would have extended the 2021 expansion of the child credit for one year (2022), while also making the credit fully refundable permanently beginning in 2023.[4] On December 11, 2021, the Senate Finance Committee released updated text of the tax provisions of the BBBA. With respect to the child tax credit provisions, the updated Finance Committee text is virtually identical to the House-passed BBBA.[5]

This report provides answers to selected frequently asked questions (FAQs) about the ARPA- expanded child credit for 2021. Additional resources may be found in the report's appendices:

- *Appendix A*: a selected compilation of research studies;
- *Appendix B:* a selected compilation of resources provided by Congress;

---

[2] See U.S. Department of the Treasury, *General Explanations of the Administration's Fiscal Year 2022 Proposals*, May 2021, https://home.treasury.gov/policy-issues/tax-policy/revenue-proposals; and CRS Insight IN11656, *The Child Tax Credit: How Would the Biden Administration's Proposed American Families Plan Change the Child Tax Credit?*

[3] For more information, see CRS Report R46923, *Tax Provisions in the "Build Back Better Act:" The House Ways and Means Committee's Legislative Recommendations*, coordinated by Molly F. Sherlock; and CRS Insight IN11757, *The Child Tax Credit Under the House Ways and Means Committee "Build Back Better" Reconciliation Language: Summary Table of Changes*, by Margot L. Crandall-Hollick.

[4] For more information on the child tax credit provisions in the House-passed BBBA, see CRS Insight IN11786, *The Child Tax Credit in the House-Passed Build Back Better Act: Summary Table*, by Margot L. Crandall-Hollick. Between when the House Budget Committee reported the bill in September and House passage in November, two modified versions of the legislation were posted on the House Rules Committee website on October 28, 2021, and then on November 3, 2021. For the October 28, 2021, modified version of the Build Back Better Act (BBBA; H.R. 5376) see https://docs.house.gov/meetings/RU/RU00/20211028/114202/BILLS-117117-17ih.pdf. This legislative text reflected the Biden Administration's framework released earlier that day. The White House, "President Biden Announces the Build Back Better Framework," October 28, 2021, https://www.whitehouse.gov/briefing-room/statements-releases/2021/10/28/president-biden-announces-the-build-back-better-framework/. For the November 3 modified text, see https://rules.house.gov/sites/democrats.rules.house.gov/files/BILLS-117HR5376RH-RCP117-18.pdf.

[5] For more information, see CRS Insight IN11827, *The Child Tax Credit in the Senate Finance Committee Text of the Build Back Better Act: Summary Table*, by Margot L. Crandall-Hollick.

- *Appendix C*: a selected compilation of resources provided by Treasury and theInternal Revenue Service (IRS);
- *Appendix D:* a detailed explanation of the safe harbor rules; and
- *Appendix E*: a reference table on the child credit in the U.S. territories.

A. American Rescue Plan Act of 2021 (ARPA; P.L. 117-2) Expansion of the Child Credit

A1. How Did the Child Credit Work Before the ARPA Expansion?

Prior to ARPA, the child tax credit allowed eligible taxpayers to reduce their federal income tax liability by up to $2,000 per qualifying child. For example, a family with three qualifying children could reduce their income tax liability by up to $6,000. A qualifying child was generally any dependent child under 17 years old. The credit was reduced in value, or phased out, by $50 for every $1,000 of income over $200,000 ($400,000 for married couples who filed joint tax returns).[6]

If a taxpayer's income tax liability was less than the maximum value of the child tax credit, the taxpayer was generally eligible to receive all or part of the difference as the refundable portion of the credit. The refundable portion—the amount greater than income taxes owed—is referred to as the additional child tax credit (ACTC) and was generally calculated using "the earned income formula."[7] Under the earned income formula, if taxpayers had earned income above $2,500, the ACTC gradually increased at a rate of 15% of earned income up to the maximum ACTC amount. The maximum ACTC

---

[6] For the purposes of phasing out the child credit, income is defined as modified adjusted gross income (MAGI). Priorto *and* after ARPA (P.L. 117-2), MAGI for the child credit equals adjusted gross income (AGI) increased by foreign earned income of U.S. citizens abroad, including income earned in Guam, American Samoa, the Northern Mariana Islands, and Puerto Rico. Hence, for most taxpayers, the income used to phase out their child credit is their AGI.

[7] All families with three or more qualifying children could also calculate the ACTC using an alternative formula. The alternative formula is the amount by which Social Security taxes paid exceed the earned income tax credit (EITC) up to the maximum refundable credit. Taxpayers could claim whichever ACTC was larger—the ACTC calculated under the earned income formula or under the alternative formula. But for most families who can calculate the ACTC under either formula (i.e., families with three or more qualifying children), the ACTC under the earned income formula was larger than the ACTC under the alternative formula.

amount was $1,400 per qualifying child multiplied by the number of qualifying children. Taxpayers with less than $2,500 of earned income were not eligible for the refundable portion of the credit and, due to their low incomes, would generally be ineligible for the nonrefundable portion of the credit as well. CRS estimates that about one in every five taxpayers (19%) with a credit-eligible child had low incomes that resulted in them receiving less than the maximum credit.[8]

After 2021, the ARPA expansion expired. The credit then reverted to the prior-law parameters described above, including those parameters modified by P.L. 115-97, commonly referred to as the Tax Cuts and Jobs Act or TCJA. The TCJA modifications are scheduled to expire at the end of 2025 (see Table 1).[9]

Prior to ARPA, like other tax benefits, the child credit was received once a year after a taxpayer filed their income tax return (i.e., as part of their income tax refund).

A2. How Did ARPA Change the Child Credit?

ARPA made three main changes to the child credit that affect the credit amount, especially for eligible low- and moderate-income taxpayers. The law also temporarily changed how the credit was delivered. These changes are temporary and in effect for one year—2021.

The three changes that affect the credit amount for 2021 are as follows:

- *Expanding eligibility to 17-year-olds:* The law increased the maximum age foran eligible child from 16 to 17.[10]
- *Making the credit fully refundable:* The law eliminated the ACTC phase-in based on earned income and eliminated the ACTC cap of $1,400 per child.[11] Hence, the child credit for 2021 is "fully refundable" and the full value is available to otherwise eligible

---

[8] See Figure 1 in CRS Report R46502, The Child Tax Credit: Selected Legislative Proposals in the 116th Congress.

[9] For more information on the current-law parameters of the child credit after 2025, see CRS Report R41873, The Child Tax Credit: How It Works and Who Receives It.

[10] The age of the child for a given year's child credit is based on their age on December 31 of that year. In other words, for the 2021 child credit, a child who is 17 years old on December 31, 2021, is considered 17 years old for the purposesof the credit.

[11] The law also eliminated the calculation of the ACTC under the alternative formula. See footnote 7.

taxpayers with no earned income (i.e., it is available to taxpayers who do not work). Full refundability is generally only available to taxpayers who live in the United States for at least half of 2021 (this is sometimes referred to as the "principal place of abode requirement").[12]

- *Increasing the maximum credit amount, with larger increases for younger children:* The law increased the maximum amount of the credit from $2,000 perchild to $3,600 per child for a young child (0-5 years old) and $3,000 per child for an older child (6-17 years old).

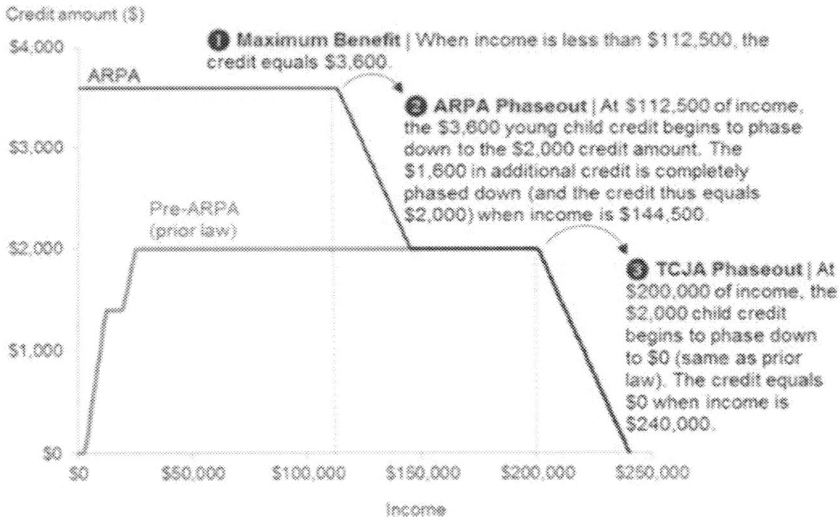

Sources: CRS calculations based on Internal Revenue Code §24 and P.L. 117-2.

Notes: A stylized example assuming the taxpayer has one qualifying child and all income is earned income, with no other sources of income and no above-the-line deductions claimed. Unmarried taxpayers with child credit- qualifying children are assumed in this example to file as head of household. For more examples, see CRS Insight IN11613, The Child Tax Credit: Temporary Expansion for 2021 Under the American Rescue Plan Act of 2021 (ARPA; P.L. 117-2).

Figure 1. Child Credit Amount by Income in 2021 Before and After ARPA Unmarried Taxpayer with One Young Child.

Full refundability and the larger maximum credit will generally increase the credit amount for low- and moderate-income taxpayers, as illustrated in

[12] Full refundability is also available to taxpayers who are bona fide residents of Puerto Rico for 2021.

Figure 1 (low- and moderate-income taxpayers may also receive a larger credit as a result of expanding the eligibility age to include 17-year-olds). Higher-income families will generally receive the same benefit as under prior law (although some with an eligible 17-year-old may also receive a larger credit).

This increase in the maximum child credit—an increase of $1,600 per young child and $1,000 per older child—phases out by $50 for every $1,000 over specified thresholds until the credit amount equals the current-law maximum of $2,000 per child, as illustrated in Figure 1. These thresholds are $112,500 for head of household filers and $150,000 for married joint filers.[13] The thresholds are sometimes referred to as the "first thresholds" or "ARPA thresholds." (The actual income level at which the credit phases down to $2,000 per child depends on the number and age of qualifying children.) For many families, the credit then plateaus at its prior-law level of $2,000 per child and phases out when income exceeds the current-law threshold of $200,000 ($400,000 for married joint filers).[14] These thresholds are sometimes referred to as the "second thresholds" or "TCJA thresholds." (The name is in reference to the law—commonly referred to as the Tax Cuts and Jobs Act [TCJA; P.L. 115-97] that established these thresholds.)

ARPA also temporarily changed the way the credit is delivered, advancing half of the total 2021 credit in six monthly payments between July and December 2021 (see "B. Administration of the ARPA-Expanded Child

---

[13] This threshold also applies to surviving spouses as defined in IRC §2(a). In addition, taxpayers who file as married filing separately or taxpayers who file as singles are subject to a $75,000 threshold. Single filers who can only claim achild tax credit-qualifying child under IRC §152(e), but cannot claim that child under IRC §152(c) (and who have no other dependents for tax purposes) generally may not file as a head of household.

[14] The law states that up until a taxpayer's income reaches $75,000 if single, $112,500 if head of household, and $150,000 if married filing jointly, they will receive the maximum child tax credit amount. This amount is equal to $3,600 multiplied by the number of qualifying children under six years old, plus $3,000 multiplied by the number of qualifying children 6 to 17 years old. After this "first threshold" (i.e., the "ARPA threshold"), the credit amount begins to phase down by $50 for each $1,000 over the threshold. The amount by which the credit phases down is limited to thelesser of (a) the "applicable credit increase amount" (the difference between the ARPA credit and the prior-law credit in 2021) or (b) 5% of the "applicable phaseout range" (the difference between the $200,000 and $400,000 phaseouts enacted under the TCJA and the $75,000, $112,500, and $150,000 phaseouts in ARPA). Notably, 5% of the applicable phaseout range equals $6,250 if single, $4,375 if head of household, and $12,500 if a married joint filer. After the total credit has been phased down by the lesser of (a) or (b), it then remains at its pre-ARPA level until it is phased out againunder the pre-ARPA threshold of $200,000 or $400,000 if married filing jointly (also referred to as the "TCJA threshold").

Credit"). The remaining half of the credit can be claimed on 2021 income tax returns filed in 2022.

A3. What Features of the Credit Were Unchanged by ARPA?

Aside from changing the credit amount for some taxpayers and advancing a portion of the credit (see "A2. How did ARPA change the child credit?"), ARPA generally left other parameters of the credit unchanged. Notably, these include the definition of a qualifying child and the taxpayer ID requirements of a qualifying child. Specifically, a qualifying child must still meet various requirements including being related to the taxpayer (the relationship test) and living with the taxpayer for more than half the year (the residency test). In addition, through 2025, the taxpayer must provide a qualifying child's social security number (SSN) associated with work authorization in order to receive the credit.[15]

A4: Can Americans Living Abroad Receive the Fully Refundable Child Credit?

Generally, no, although if they owe enough in income taxes they may still benefit from other aspects of the ARPA expansion. In order to receive the full amount of the ARPA-expanded credit (and be eligible for the monthly advance payments of the credit in 2021), taxpayers must live in the United States for more than half of 2021 (there is an exception for servicemembers, described in "A5. Are servicemembers stationed overseas eligible for the ARPA-expanded child credit?").[16] Specifically, full refundability applies to taxpayers whose principal place of abode is the United States for over half of 2021. Among married joint filers, only one spouse must fulfill this principal place of abode requirement.[17]

---

[15] For more information, see "Definition of a Qualifying Child" in CRS Report R41873, *The Child Tax Credit: How ItWorks and Who Receives It*.

[16] Full refundability is also available to taxpayers who are bona fide residents of Puerto Rico for 2021. In the case of the advance payments of the 2021 child credit, the IRS will determine if the taxpayer meets the principal place of aboderequirement for the reference year used to calculate the advance amount. In most cases the reference year is 2020, but if a taxpayer has not filed a 2020 return, a 2019 return may be used.

[17] The draft IRS Schedule 8812, *Credits for Qualifying Children and Other Dependents*, includes a question on line 13asking if a taxpayer has a principal place of abode in the

Taxpayers who do not fulfill this requirement (i.e., "expats") but are otherwise eligible to receive the credit may generally calculate and claim the credit when they file their federal income tax return. Insofar as these taxpayers can receive some or all of the credit in the form of the ACTC, they will either calculate the ACTC under the earned income formula (or alternative formula) if they do not claim the foreign earned income exclusion or be ineligible for the ACTC if they do claim the foreign earned income exclusion.[18] (These are the same rules as applied before ARPA.) For example, if an otherwise eligible taxpayer lived outside the United States in 2021 with two qualifying young children, they could be eligible for up to $7,200 in the 2021 child tax credit, if they had sufficient U.S. income tax liability. However, the maximum amount they could claim as the ACTC would be either $2,800 if they did not claim the foreign earned income exclusion, or $0 if they did.

A5. Are Servicemembers Stationed Overseas Eligible for the ARPA-Expanded Child Credit?

Generally, yes. The principal place of abode requirement for the ARPA-expanded credit is defined by reference to Internal Revenue Code (IRC) Section 32(c)(4), including the special military rule:

> the principal place of abode of a member of the Armed Forces of the United States shall betreated as in the United States during any period during which such member is stationed outside the United States while serving on extended active duty with the Armed Forces ofthe United States. For purposes of the preceding sentence, the term "extended active duty"means any period of active duty pursuant to a call or order to such duty for a period in excess of 90 days or for an indefinite period.

United States for more than half of 2021. See https://www.irs.gov/pub/irs-dft/f1040s8—dft.pdf.

[18] See IRC §24(d)(3). Under current law (IRC §911), U.S. citizens and resident aliens who live abroad are generally taxed on their worldwide income. In certain cases, these taxpayers may be eligible to exclude some or all of their foreign earned income when calculating their U.S. federal income tax liability. In 2022, the maximum amount that canbe excluded is $112,000 per person.

A6: Can Noncitizens Receive the ARPA-Expanded Child Credit?

Yes, in certain cases. Eligibility for the child credit is not explicitly based on a taxpayer's citizenship status or on their qualifying child's citizenship status. However, other parameters of the credit may indirectly limit some noncitizens' ability to receive all or some of the ARPA- expanded credit. These parameters are briefly discussed below.

First, all taxpayers—citizens and noncitizens alike—must live in the United States for more than half of 2021 in order to be eligible for the full refundability provision of the credit.[19] (This is sometimes referred to as the "principal place of abode" requirement for full refundability.)[20] Second, under existing law, a qualifying child must be a U.S. citizen or U.S. national, and if not a U.S. citizen or national, the child must be a resident of the United States.[21] Finally, a taxpayer must provide an SSN for each qualifying child in order to claim the benefit.[22] This SSN must be associated with work

---

[19] Full refundability is also available to taxpayers who are bona fide residents of Puerto Rico for 2021. Otherwise eligible taxpayers—citizens and noncitizens alike—who do not satisfy this "principal place of abode" requirement are still eligible for the larger credit (up to $3,600 per young child and $3,000 per older child) and are still eligible to claim the credit for 17-year-olds. Hence, in cases where (1) the principal place of abode requirement is not met; (2) the creditamount exceeds their income tax liability; and (3) the taxpayer is claiming some or all of the credit in the form of the ACTC, then the taxpayer will calculate the ACTC using earned income (they may also calculate under the alternative formula if that yields a larger ACTC). In other words, their ACTC will be calculated as 15% of earned income over $2,500 up to $1,400 child (adjusted for inflation).

[20] Among married taxpayers who file a joint return, this "principal place of abode" requirement must be met by at least one spouse. Taxpayers who participate in the credit's advanced payment program also must fulfill this principal place of abode requirement as documented on their 2020 income tax return (or if those data are not available, their 2019 income tax return).

[21] See IRC §24(c)(2). Children are considered to be a resident of the United States if they pass the tests to be considereda resident alien for tax purposes. For more information, see the answer to question 1 in CRS Report R43840, *Federal Income Taxes and Noncitizens: Frequently Asked Questions*. In addition, whereas all U.S. citizens are considered U.S. nationals, not all nationals are considered citizens. Noncitizen U.S. nationals include persons born in certain U.S. territories, such as American Samoa.

[22] According to a study by the Pew Research Center, "In 2016, 5.6 million children younger than 18 were living with unauthorized immigrant parents. Of these, 675,000 were unauthorized immigrants themselves." It is unclear what shareof those 675,000 children do not have SSNs, nor is it clear how these figures have changed over time. Nonetheless, thisestimate may provide a sense of the number of children who cannot be claimed for the child credit under existing taxpayer ID requirements. Jeffrey Passel and D'Vera Cohn, *U.S. Unauthorized Immigrant Total Dips to Lowest Level in a Decade*, Pew Research Center, November 27, 2018, https://www.pewresearch.org/hispanic/2018/11/27/u-s-unauthorized-immigrant-total-dips-to-lowest-level-in-a-decade/.

authorization, meaning an SSN issued solely to receive a public benefit does not qualify. These types of work-authorized SSNs are generally provided to all U.S. citizen children and certain noncitizen children, including legal permanent residents (i.e., "green card holders"), refugees, and asylees.[23] Eligible taxpayers claiming the credit must provide either an SSN or an individual taxpayer identification number (ITIN) to receive the credit. (Individuals who are not eligible to receive an SSN are required to use an ITIN when filing their tax returns and other documents with the IRS.[24])

Hence, a noncitizen taxpayer who (1) lives in the United States for at least half of 2021; (2) has a taxpayer ID (which can be either an SSN issued from the Social Security Administration or, if ineligible for an SSN, an ITIN issued by the IRS); and (3) has a qualifying child with a work- authorized SSN who is either a U.S. citizen, national, or resident would generally be eligible for the ARPA-expanded child credit.

A7: Can Unauthorized Noncitizens (Sometimes Referred to As "Undocumented Immigrants") Receive the ARPA-Expanded Child Credit?[25]

Yes, in certain cases. For the purposes of the child credit, a taxpayer's eligibility to claim the credit is not based on their immigration status. Instead, any noncitizen, irrespective of their immigration status, may generally be able to claim the ARPA-expanded child credit if

1) their principal place of abode for more than half of 2021 is the United States;
2) the taxpayer has either an SSN, or if they are ineligible for an SSN, an ITIN;
3) the taxpayer's child meets all eligibility requirements including that they are a
4) U.S. citizen, a U.S. national, or a resident of the United States; and

---

[23] For more information, see Congressional Distribution Memorandum CD1321564, *Noncitizen Eligibility for a Work-Authorized Social Security Number (SSN).*

[24] For more information on individual taxpayer identification numbers (ITINs), see CRS Report R43840, *FederalIncome Taxes and Noncitizens: Frequently Asked Questions*.

[25] Unauthorized noncitizens include those who have entered the United States without inspection or have overstayed their period of lawful admission (*overstays*). For more information, see CRS In Focus IF11806, *Citizenship and Immigration Statuses of the U.S. Foreign-Born Population.*

5) the taxpayer's qualifying child has an SSN associated with work authorization.

Hence, there could be cases where a noncitizen taxpayer who is "undocumented" or who is not authorized to work in the United States could be eligible for the ARPA-expanded child credit. For example, an "undocumented" noncitizen living in the United States with a U.S. citizen child could be eligible for the ARPA-expanded child credit.

A8. How Long Are the ARPA Changes in Effect?

The ARPA changes to the child credit were only in effect for 2021 and only affected the credit as claimed on 2021 income tax returns. The ARPA changes to the credit were themselves layered upon other changes in effect from 2018 through 2025, which were enacted by P.L. 115-97 (commonly referred to as the Tax Cuts and Jobs Act or TCJA). Hence, after 2021, the credit reverted to prior-law TCJA parameters until 2025. After 2025, the credit would generally revert to its pre-TCJA parameters under current law, as illustrated in Table 1.

A9. How Much Is the ARPA Expansion of the Child Credit Expected to Cost (I.E., the Budgetary Impact)?

The Joint Committee on Taxation (JCT) estimates that the total cost of the one-year ARPA expansion is $105.1 billion, of which $84.4 billion is attributed to the refundable portion of thecredit (i.e., the ACTC).[26] This is in *addition to* the existing cost of the program before ARPA.

---

[26] The Joint Committee on Taxation estimates that the total cost of the one-year ARPA expansion of the child credit is $109.5 billion between FY2021 and FY2031, of which $88.8 billion is attributed to the refundable portion of the credit.These estimates, however, also include the cost of the permanent extension of the child credit to residents of the territories. Unlike residents of Puerto Rico, who are to apply directly for the child credit with the IRS, other territorial residents are to apply for and receive the child credit from their territorial tax authority. The Treasury is to provide these territorial governments with funds to cover these payments. This permanent extension to the territories is effective beginning in 2021 and so applies to the ARPA-expanded child credit. The budgetary cost of this permanent extension is $4.4 billion between FY2023 and FY2031, all of which is attributable to the refundable portion of the childcredit. This amount is subtracted from the total cost to isolate the budgetary costs of the one-year expansion. See Joint

Prior to the ARPA expansion, the total cost of the child credit was $117.7 billion, according to the IRS's most recent data from 2018 tax returns.[27]

A10: How Do Taxpayers with Children at Different Income Levels Benefit from the ARPA-Expanded Child Credit?

Estimates from the Tax Policy Center compiled in Table 2 suggest that the ARPA-expanded child credit is a near universally available benefit among taxpayers with children and provides the largest benefit to the lowest-income taxpayers. Overall, the share of taxpayers with children eligible for the credit is estimated to increase from 89.1% to 92.0%, with the largest gains occurring among the lowest-income taxpayers (i.e., the share of such taxpayers receiving the credit will increase from 72.6% to 83.2%). In addition, the lowest-income 20% of taxpayers are estimated to see the largest gains in income, both as a share of their after-tax income and in dollar terms. Specifically, the ARPA-expanded child credit is estimated to equal 15.2% of after-tax income for the lowest-income taxpayers ($4,490), compared to 5.6% of their after-tax income prior to ARPA ($1,220).

B. Administration of the ARPA-Expanded Child Credit

B1. How Was the ARPA-Expanded Child Credit Issued?

Unlike most tax benefits, which are received once a year as a lump sum after an income tax return is filed, up to half of the 2021 child credit was issued in advance of 2021 returns being filed.

Committee on Taxation, *Estimated Revenue Effects Of H.R. 1319, The "American Rescue Plan Act Of 2021," Scheduled For Consideration By The House Of Representatives On February 26, 2021*, February 12, 2021, JCX-12-21, https://www.jct.gov/publications/2021/jcx-12-21.

[27] Internal Revenue Service, Individual Complete Report (Publication 1304), Table 3.3, Statistics of Income, 2018, https://www.irs.gov/statistics/soi-tax-stats-individual-statistical-tables-by-size-of-adjusted-gross-income.

Table 1. Selected parameters of the child tax credit under current law

Parameter	Pre-2018 permanent law	2018-2020 permanent law, as amended by the TCJA	2021 permanent law, as amended by the TCJA and ARPA	2022-2025 permanent law, as amended by the TCJA	Post-2025 permanent law
Maximum amount of the credit per child[a]	$1,000 per child 0-16 years old *not adjusted for inflation*	$2,000 per child 0-16 years old *not adjusted for inflation*	$3,600 per child 0- 5 years old $3,000 per child 6- 17 years old *not adjusted for inflation*	$2,000 per child 0-16 years old *not adjusted for inflation*	$1,000 per child 0-16 years old *not adjusted for inflation*
Maximum ACTC per child[a,b] *Maximum amount of the refundable portion of the credit for low-income taxpayers*	$1,000 per child 0-16 years old *not adjusted for inflation*	$1,400 per child 0-16 years old *adjusted for inflation*	$3,600 per child 0- 5 years old $3,000 per child 6- 17 years old *not adjusted for inflation*	$1,400 per child 0-16 years old *adjusted for inflation: $1,500 in 2022 after adjustment.*	$1,000 per child 0-16 years old *not adjusted for inflation*
ACTC calculation	Phased-in amount calculated based on earned income formula: 15% of earned income above $3,000 not to exceed the maximum ACTC.	Phased-in amount calculated based on earned income formula: 15% of earned income above $2,500 not to exceed maximum ACTC.	Fully refundable: The phased-in credit for low-income taxpayers based on earned income is eliminated such that low-income taxpayers can receive the maximum credit amount.	Phased-in amount calculated based on earned income formula: 15% of earned income above $2,500 not to exceed maximum ACTC.	Phased-in amount calculated based on earned income formula: 15% of earned income above $3,000 not to exceed the maximum ACTC.
Phaseout Threshold *MFJ: married filing jointly* *HOH: head of household* *S: single*	$110,000 MFJc $75,000 HOH $75,000 Sd *not adjusted for inflation*	$400,000 MFJ $200,000 HOH $200,000 Se *not adjusted for inflation*	Initial Threshold: Phaseout of Increased Credit $150,000 MFJ[f] $112,500 HOH $75,000 S[g] *not adjusted for inflation*	$400,000 MFJ $200,000 HOH $200,000 S[e] *not adjusted for inflation*	$110,000 MFJ[c] $75,000 HOH $75,000 Sd *not adjusted for inflation*

Table 1. (Continued)

			Second Threshold: Phaseout of pre- ARPA credit $400,000 MFJ $200,000 HOH $200,000 S[e] not adjusted for inflation		
Child ID Requirements	Any taxpayer ID (SSN / ITIN / ATIN)	work-authorized SSN	work-authorized SSN	work-authorized SSN	Any taxpayer ID (SSN / ITIN / ATIN)
Maximum Child Age (at the end of the year)	16	16	17	16	16
Method of Receipt	Claimed on tax return	Claimed on tax return	50% advanced; remainder claimed on tax return	Claimed on tax return	Claimed on tax return

Source: Internal Revenue Code, 26 U.S.C. §24. TCJA refers to P.L. 115-97, commonly referred to as the Tax Cuts and Jobs Act. ARPA refers to P.L. 117-2, the American Rescue Plan Act of 2021.

[a]The maximum credit amount per taxpayer is the maximum amount of the credit per child, multiplied by the number of qualifying children. Similarly, the maximum ACTC per taxpayer is the maximum amount of the ACTC per child, multiplied by the number of qualifying children.

[b]The refundable portion of the child tax credit—the amount that can exceed what a taxpayer owes in cincome taxes—is often referred to as the additional child tax credit or ACTC.

[c]The threshold for married taxpayers who file separately is $55,000.

[d]This includes taxpayers who file as surviving spouses.

[e]This includes married taxpayers who file separately and taxpayers who file as surviving spouses.

[f]This includes taxpayers who file as surviving spouses.

[g]This includes married taxpayers who file separately.

Table 2. Share oftaxpayers with childrenwho receive the child credit and creditamount by income percentile in 2021, before and after ARPA

Before ARPA					After ARPA	
Income Percentile[a]	% of Taxpayers Who Receive the Credit	Benefit as % of After-Tax income	Average Benefit per Taxpayer	% of Taxpayers Who Receive the Credit	Benefit as % of After-Tax income	Average Benefit per Taxpayer
Lowest 20%	72.6%	5.6%	$1,220	83.2%	15.2%	$4,490
Second-Lowest 20%	92.6%	5.8%	$2,560	94.1%	9.6%	$4,940
Middle 20%	97.2%	3.9%	$2,900	97.6%	5.9%	$4,890
Second-Highest 20%	99.2%	2.4%	$2,880	99.2%	3.6%	$4,650
Highest 20%	87.0%	0.7%	$2,140	87.2%	0.8%	$2,720
All	89.1%	2.1%	$2,310	92.0%	3.8%	$4,380

Source: Tax Policy Center Tables T21-0043 and T21-0045; see Appendix A.

Notes: Includes filing and non-filing taxpayers. Includes the $500 nonrefundable tax credit for other dependents. Taxpayers with children are those claiming an exemption for children or with children qualifying for the Child Tax Credit or EITC.

[a] The income percentile classes used in this table are based on the income distribution for the entire population and contain an equal number of people, not tax units. The breaks (in 2020 dollars) are as follows: 20%, $25,500; 40%, $51,000; 60%, $91,100; 80%, $164,300; 90%, $240,900; 95%, $341,700; 99%, $799,100; 99.9%, $3,496,400.

ARPA directed Treasury to issue half of the estimated 2021 credit in periodic payments beginning after July 1, 2021 (these periodic payments will generally be equal in amount).[1] The IRS issued these payments as monthly installments. Taxpayers will claim the remaining half of the total 2021 credit when filing their 2021 income tax return in 2022. In January 2022, the White House launched a website to help taxpayers, including those who are not required to file a tax return due to their low incomes, claim the remainder of their child tax credit. The website——helps taxpayers find resources or services to file their 2021 income tax return.

Like the expansion of the credit amount, the advance payment program was also temporary under current law. Under ARPA, advance payments of the 2021 credit cannot be made before July 1, 2021, or after December 31, 2021.[2]

---

[1] IRC §7527A.

[2] IRC §7527A(f).

B2. How Were the Monthly Advance Payments Calculated?

Advance payments of the 2021 child credit were based on an estimate of the credit taxpayers are eligible to claim on their 2021 income tax return. In order to estimate a taxpayer's 2021 child credit, the IRS used data from their 2020 income tax return, or if that was not available, data from their 2019 income tax return. The year of data used to estimate the 2021 credit is sometimes referred to as the "reference year." Since up to half of the 2021 credit could be issued in advance, the IRS generally calculated 50% of the estimated 2021 credit amount and then issued that in monthly payments.

For example, if a married couple filing jointly listed $75,000 of income and two young children on a 2020 return—and those children were also young in 2021 (i.e., 0-5 years old)—the IRS would have estimated their 2021 credit to be $7,200.[3] The IRS would have issued half of that amount—$3,600—in six monthly payments of $600, beginning July 15, 2021, and ending December 15, 2021.

B3. Could Taxpayers Opt Out of the Advance Payment Program?

Yes, taxpayers could opt out by using the IRS's Child Tax Credit Update Portal (also referred to simply as "the update portal" in this report, or CTC-UP by the IRS).[4] Among married joint filers, both spouses had to opt out in order to stop all advance payments (otherwise half of the monthly advance payments were issued to the spouse who did not opt out).[5] Unless taxpayers opted out, they were automatically enrolled in the advance payment program.

---

[3] See IRC §7527A(b)(1)(D). With respect to estimating the children's ages in 2021 to estimate the advance, "the ages of such children (and the status of such children as qualifying children) are determined for such taxable year by taking into account the passage of time since the reference taxable year." The IRS already receives data from the SSA for tax return processing purposes that includes children's dates of birth, and hence their projected age by December 31, 2021,can be determined.

[4] This tool is available at https://www.irs.gov/credits-deductions/advance-child-tax-credit-payments-in-2021.

[5] See Question J6 "If I'm married filing jointly, does my spouse also need to unenroll?" and Question J7 "If my spouseunenrolls and I don't unenroll, what will happen?" on the IRS's website. Internal Revenue Service, *2021 Child Tax Credit and Advance Child Tax Credit Payments—Topic J: Unenrolling from Advance Payments*, https://www.irs.gov/ credits-deductions/2021-child-tax-credit-and-advance-child-tax-credit-payments-topic-j-unenrolling-from-advance- payments.

Taxpayers may have wanted to opt out of the advance payments if they preferred receiving the benefit as part of their annual income tax refund. Taxpayers may have also wanted to opt out if they were concerned that they might receive more in advance payments than they were actually eligible for. Broadly, this could occur as a result of differences between information used to issue advanced payments (i.e., 2020 or 2019 tax data) and information on their 2021 income tax return. Specifically, it could occur due to changes in a variety of factors between 2021 and the reference year used to calculate the advance payments, including (a) large changes in income, (b) changes in the number of qualifying children (including in cases were children live with a different divorced parent in alternating years), (c) changes in marital status, and (d) changes in principal place of abode, or (e) a combination of these changes.[6]

In cases where the sum of advance payments is greater than the credit the taxpayer is eligible to claim on their 2021 income tax return, taxpayers may need to repay the excess, either by reducing their refund or by remitting payment to the IRS (see "B9. Will taxpayers need to pay back excess amounts of the child credit?").

B4. Were Monthly Payment Amounts Adjusted When the IRS Received New Information?

ARPA allowed the IRS to adjust monthly payments for new information so that the total advance a taxpayer received was 50% of their estimated 2021 credit.[7] For example, if the IRS in August received information that a taxpayer was eligible for a 2021 credit of $7,200 and began issuing advance payments in September, this taxpayer would have generally been issued four

---

[6] If the taxpayer's principal place of abode is not the United States in 2021, but it is in 2020 (or 2019, if 2020 data are not available), then the refundable portion of their 2021 credit amount will be phased in using the earned income formula. Hence, some low-income taxpayers may not be eligible for the full credit amount of $3,600 per young child and $3,000 per older child, and may receive more in advance payments than they are eligible for. See question G6 "I filed my 2020 tax return with a U.S. address although my child and I do not live in the United States. I received Letter 6417 at my U.S. address stating that the IRS will begin to disburse advance Child Tax Credit payments to me. What can I do?" on the IRS's website. Internal Revenue Service, *2021 Child Tax Credit and Advance Child Tax Credit Payments—Topic G: Receiving Advance Child Tax Credit Payments*, https://www. irs.gov/credits-deductions/2021-child-tax-credit-and-advance-child-tax-credit-payments-topic-g-receiving-advance-child-tax-credit-payments.

[7] See IRC §7527A(b)(3), §7527A(a)(3), §7527A(b)(1).

monthly payments of $900, which in total would equal half of their 2021 credit.[8] Alternatively, in certainsituations the IRS issued different amounts of monthly payments such that the sum of all payments issued in 2021 was 50% of their estimated credit amount (i.e., the taxpayer is "madewhole").[9]

Initially, taxpayers could only provide this information via the IRS's Child Tax Credit Non-filerSign-up Tool beginning in mid-June of 2021. By the beginning of September 2021, eligible non- filers could also use the GetCTC tool developed by Code for America in consultation with

[8] If the 2021 credit was estimated to be $7,200, then half of that—$3,600—could be issued in advance. If the taxpayer received six monthly payments, the payments would thus equal $600 each month. If the taxpayer received four monthly payments, the payments would equal $900 each month. According to the IRS, "Families who did not get a July payment and are getting their first monthly payment in August will still receive their total advance payment for the year. This means that the total payment will be spread over five months, rather than six, making each monthly payment larger." Internal Revenue Service, "IRS: Families now receiving August Child Tax Credit payments; still time for low- income families to sign up," press release, August 13, 2021, https://www.irs.gov/newsroom/irs-families-now-receiving-august-child-tax-credit-payments-still-time-for-low-income-families-to-sign-up.

[9] This may be the case, for example, when the IRS made an error in issuing the first payments, as was the case with certain ITIN filers. According to the IRS National Taxpayer Advocate, "Over one million taxpayers who filed their returns with an ITIN did not receive their Child Tax Credit (CTC) monthly payment in July. The IRS has identified the issue, which it fixed prior to issuing the August payments; the issue is not anticipated to occur again. But the fix comes with confusion. Since the IRS erroneously did not make the July payment, it calculated the August payment based uponthe total amount of eligible AdvCTC and then divided it by five months (August-December). Good news: as of August 23, the IRS is retroactively issuing the July payment to these individuals. However, the July payment amount will be based upon the total amount of eligible AdvCTC divided by six months (July-December) and then reduced by the additional amount included in the August payment. I will try to simplify by way of an example: Mary has one child and based upon her 2020 income may have a CTC credit of $3,000. One half of that amount, $1,500, would be eligible to be paid in six monthly payments ($250) as AdvCTC. If Mary filed her 2020 return with an ITIN and did not receive her July payment the IRS calculated her August payment based upon a five-month schedule (August-December) and paid Mary $300 in August ($1,500 divided by five payments). Now that the IRS is retroactively paying Mary her July payment, she will be receiving $250 for the July payment based upon a six-month schedule (July-December, $1,500 divided by six payments) minus the additional $50 she received in August. Her July payment will be $200. Now to add to Mary's confusion, the IRS will be issuing the September payment in the correct amount of $250. All subsequent payments should be $250." Taxpayer Advocate Service, "NTA Blog: Advance Child Tax Credit: What You Should Know: Part II," August 26, 2021, https://www.taxpayeradvocate. irs.gov/news/ nta-blog-advance-child-tax-credit-what-you-should-know-part-ii/.

Treasury.[10] By the end of 2021, the White House was linking directly to the Code for America non-filer tool.[11]

The statute also allowed adjustments that could reduce advance payment amounts. This could have occurred when a taxpayer's advance payments were estimated using 2019 tax data, but their2020 return resulted in a smaller estimated 2021 credit (and hence smaller advance payments) once it was filed and processed.[12] It could have also occurred when a taxpayer updated their information with the IRS using the agency's update portal and that information resulted in a smaller estimated 2021 credit.

The IRS, however, initially stated that it would only be able to accept information on the updateportal that could affect the advance amount in "late summer." The IRS issued a press release at the end of October stating that taxpayers could update their *income* information, which could affect the amount of their November and December payments. However, taxpayers were unableto use the update portal to update the *number of children* they had in 2021.[13]

---

[10] Code for America's non-filer tool can be found at https://www.getctc.org/en.

[11] See, for example, The White House, "Child Tax Credit for Non-Filers," https://www.whitehouse.gov/child-tax-credit/sign-up/.

[12] See, for example, the answer to question E4 "My 2019 tax return was used to determine my advance Child Tax Credit payments. I recently filed my 2020 tax return with a different amount of income. Will the IRS update my advance Child Tax Credit payment amounts?" on the IRS's website. Internal Revenue Service, *2021 Child Tax Credit and Advance Child Tax Credit Payments—Topic E: Advance Payment Process of the Child Tax Credit*, https://www.irs.gov/credits-deductions/2021-child-tax-credit-and-advance-child-tax-credit-payments-topic-e-advance- payment-process-of-the-child-tax-credit#e1#e1.

[13] See Internal Revenue Service, "Child Tax Credit: Families with income changes must enter them in IRS online portalon Monday to impact Nov. 15 payment; Spanish version coming in late November," press release, October 29, 2021, https://www.irs.gov/newsroom/child-tax-credit-families-with-income-changes-must-enter-them-in-irs-online-portal-on-monday-to-impact-nov-15-payment-spanish-version-coming-in-late-november. In late summer, the IRS stated that taxpayers would be able to "make changes to your dependents, marital status and income and re-enroll if you previously unenrolled." Prior to that, the update portal could be used to unenroll from advance payments, make changesto bank information, and update address information. See the answer to question A16 "When will I be able to update my information?" at Internal Revenue Service, *2021 Child Tax Credit and Advance Child Tax Credit Payments—Topic A: General Information*, https://www. irs.gov/credits-deductions/2021-child-tax-credit-and-advance-child-tax-credit- payments-topic-a-general-information#a16#a16.

B5. Was There an Income Threshold Above Which Advance Payments Were Not Issued?

No, the statute did not include an income threshold above which advance payments would not be issued. (Higher-income taxpayers were eligible for a smaller credit compared to low- and moderate-income taxpayers [see Figure 1].) In addition, the IRS never indicated that it would be treating higher-income taxpayers differently than low- and moderate-income taxpayers for purposes of advance payments. Like all taxpayers, higher-income taxpayers could have elected to opt out of receiving advance payments using the update portal (see Appendix C for more information).

B6. Did Otherwise Eligible Households Who, Due to Their Low Incomes, Do Not Normally File a Tax Return, Automatically Receive the Advance Payments?

No, the IRS had to have information from a 2020 or 2019 income tax return in order to calculate the estimated 2021 credit amount, and then issue advance payments.[14] (The IRS also issued payments to taxpayers who used the non-filer portal to receive the first "stimulus check" payment in 2020.)[15] Eligible recipients who were generally not required to file an income tax

---

[14] Existing research suggests eligible households who did not receive advance payments of the credit tended to be low- income. For example, see Natasha Pilkauskas and Katherine Michelmore, "Families with Low Incomes and the Child Tax Credit: Who is Still Missing Out?" *University of Michigan | Poverty Solutions*, December 2021, http://sites.fordschool.umich.edu/poverty2021/files/2021/12/PovertySolutions-Child-Tax-Credit-who-is-still-missing-out-Decembe2021.pdf.

[15] Eligible taxpayers for whom the IRS does not have tax information on file for 2020 or 2019 will not receive the payments. Various outreach activities are under way to enroll these households. The White House, *FACT SHEET: Biden-Harris Administration Whole-of-Government Effort to Ensure Child Tax Credit Reaches All Eligible Families*, September 15, 2021, https://www.whitehouse.gov/briefing-room/statements-releases/2021/09/15/fact-sheet-biden-harris-administration-whole-of-government-effort-to-ensure-child-tax-credit-reaches-all-eligible-families/; and Gabriel Zucker and Maximilian Hell, *Getting the Child Tax Credit to Families With Low or No Incomes Means Using the RightData*, Code for America, September 21, 2021, https://www.codeforamerica.org/news/getting-the-child-tax-credit-to- families-with-low-or-no-incomes-means-using-the-right-data/. Data suggest these families are more likely to be poor. See Aravind Boddupalli, *Where Are Families Most at Risk of Missing Out on the Expanded Child Tax Credit?* Tax Policy Center, October 21, 2021, https://www.taxpolicycenter.org/taxvox/where-are-families-most-risk-missing-out- expanded-child-tax-credit?&utm_source=%20urban_newsletters &utm_medium=news-DD&utm_term=TPC.

return due to their low incomes were encouraged to use the child credit non-filer portal (either the IRS tool or the Code for America tool) to provide the necessary information to issue advance payments.[16] If taxpayers did not receive any advance payments in 2021, but are eligible for the 2021 credit, they will generally receive the entire amount of the credit when they file their 2021 income tax return. (However, if the taxpayer is subject to offset, the credit they receive with their 2021 tax return could be reduced; see "B11. Could the advance payments of the credit and/or the credit claimed on 2021 income tax returns be reduced for child support or other debts?")

B7. Were There Any Limitations on How the Advance Payments of the Credit Could Be Spent?

No, there are no limitations or restrictions on how the advance payments (or the amount received after filing 2021 income tax returns) could be spent. For more information on recent research on how recipients spent the advance payments, see "III. Estimates of How Families/Taxpayers Spent the Child Credit" in Appendix A.

B8: How Will Taxpayers Determine the Amount of the Credit They Can Claim on Their 2021 Income Tax Return?

When a taxpayer files their 2021 return (in 2022), they will first calculate the total amount of the 2021 child credit they are eligible for (based on the number and ages of qualifying children, income, and marital status for 2021). Then, the taxpayer will subtract from their total 2021 credit the sum of advanced child credit payments they received during calendar year 2021. To help with this calculation, the IRS is mailing a year-end summary statement (Letter 6419) to all taxpayers who received advance payments during 2021.

For example, if an unmarried taxpayer had two young children (and filed as a head of household) and less than $112,500 of income in 2020 and 2021,

---

[16] The tool is available at https://www.irs.gov/credits-deductions/child-tax-credit-non-filer-sign-up-tool. Taxpayers canalso use the Code for America non-filer tool at https://www.getctc.org/en. Code for America's tool was developed in consultation with Treasury. Unlike the IRS tool, the Code for American tool works on mobile devices and is available in Spanish.

they would be eligible for a total child credit for 2021 of $7,200. Since they would have received half of their total 2021 credit in advance payments in calendar year 2021 ($3,600), they would ultimately claim the remaining half ($3,600) on their 2021 return. The taxpayer is effectively splitting their total credit between the advance payments they received in 2021 (50% of their total credit) and the remaining 50% of the credit they claim on their 2021 tax return.

In January 2022, the White House launched a website to help taxpayers, including those who are not required to file a tax return due to their low incomes, claim the remainder of their child tax credit. The website—https://www.childtaxcredit.gov/—helps taxpayers find resources or services to file their 2021 income tax return. The site does not itself prepare or file 2021 income tax returns.

B9. Will Taxpayers Need to Pay Back Excess Amounts of the Child Credit?

Potentially, yes, if they received more in advance payments than they are eligible to claim on their 2021 income tax returns. A taxpayer may have excess amounts of the credit due to changes in income, marital status, or number of qualifying children between the year used to estimate the advance (2020 or 2019) and 2021.

For example, if a taxpayer's estimated advance payments totaled $5,400 (based on an estimate of three qualifying young children) but the total 2021 credit they are actually eligible for is $3,600 (because they only had one qualifying young child), they would need to repay up to $1,800 (the difference between $5,400 and $3,600).[17] Excess payments caused by changes in the number of qualifying children generally will not need to be repaid for lower- and moderate-income taxpayers who are protected by a safe harbor (this safe harbor decreases as income rises). For more information on the safe harbor, see "B10. How does the "safe harbor" work?" and Table D-1. Repayment may either reduce a taxpayer's 2021 tax refund or result in the taxpayer being required to remit payment to the IRS (or be subject to offset of a future tax refund).

[17] Three young children x $3,600 per young child = a maximum credit of $10,800. Since up to 50% of the credit can be issued in advance payments, the maximum amount of advance payments equals $5,400.

B10. How Does the "Safe Harbor" Work?

Lower- and moderate-income taxpayers who received excess advance payments of the credit due to changes in the number of qualifying children between 2021 and 2020 (or 2019, if 2020 data are unavailable) may be protected from paying back some or all of these excess payments due to a safe harbor. Effectively, after calculating any excess payments, the taxpayer subtracts from this amount the total safe harbor amount they are eligible for to determine any amount they must ultimately repay (either in terms of reducing their tax refund or remitting payment).

The safe harbor amount is first calculated by multiplying $2,000 times the difference in the number of qualifying children between the reference year (2020 or 2019) and 2021. This is the maximum amount of the safe harbor. The safe harbor amount is then phased down ratably—that is, proportionally—for head of household filers with 2021 income between $50,000 and $100,000 and for married joint filers with 2021 income between $60,000 and $120,000.

For example, if a married taxpayer's advance payments issued in 2021 totaled $5,400 (based on an estimate of three qualifying young children) but the total 2021 credit they are actually eligible for is $3,600 (because they only had one qualifying young child), their excess payments would equal $1,800. If the taxpayer's 2021 income was $75,000, they would be eligible for a $3,000 safe harbor.[18] Since their safe harbor ($3,000) is greater than their excess payment amount ($1,800), the taxpayer would not need to repay the excess amount. For more information on the safe harbor, see Table D-1.

The safe harbor does not apply in cases where excess payments arise from changes in income, marital status, or principal place of abode between the reference year and 2021.

---

[18] The maximum safe harbor they would be eligible for would be $4,000 ($2,000 times the next difference in the number of qualifying children, which is two in this example.) The taxpayer's income places them in the phaseout range of the safe harbor and their maximum safe harbor would be reduced by 25% [= ($75,000-$60,000)/($120,000-$60,000)]from $4,000 to $3,000.

B11. Could the Advance Payments of the Credit and/or the Credit Claimed on 2021 Income Tax Returns Be Reduced for Child Support or Other Debts?

The advance payments of the child credit were generally exempt from offset for certain past-due debts the recipient owed (including past-due child support).[19] In other words, the monthly advance payments issued in 2021 were not reduced for these debts before they were issued by the Treasury. However, the portion of the credit claimed on 2021 income tax returns is subject to offset. In practical terms, that means that when a taxpayer files their 2021 tax return in 2022 and claims the remaining portion of the 2021 child credit, the portion of their 2021 tax refund attributable to the child credit can be offset.

In addition to the offset mechanism—which effectively reduces a government payment before it is issued by Treasury—creditors may also recoup past-due debts through garnishment and levy actions. Practically, these occur after a payment is issued (e.g., deposited in a bank account).

There are no statutory provisions at the federal level that protect the child credit—received either as advance payments or claimed on an income tax return—from garnishment or levy actions.

B12. Does Receipt of the Credit—Either in the Form of Advance Payments or Claimed on a Tax Return—Affect Eligibility for Other Government Programs?

No, receipt of the child credit will not affect eligibility for or the amount of other federally funded government programs. Under a permanent provision of the Internal Revenue Code, tax credits, including the child tax credit—whether received as advance payments or claimed on an income tax return—do not count as income or resources for a 12-month period in determining eligibility for, or the amount of assistance provided by, any federally funded public benefit program.[20]

---

[19] In this report, the term *offset* refers to the Treasury Offset Program, which "collects past-due (delinquent) debts (for example, child support payments) that people owe to state and federal agencies." For more information, see Bureau ofFiscal Service, *Treasury Offset Program*, https://fiscal.treasury.gov/top/.

[20] IRC §6409.

B13. Is the ARPA-Expanded Child Credit—Either in the Form of Advance Payments or Claimed on a Tax Return—Taxable?

No, the child credit is not subject to federal taxation, but in some cases, the expanded credit may affect state liabilities.[21] At the federal level, tax credits, including the ARPA-expanded child credit, are not considered taxable income. This is the case regardless of whether the credit is claimed on a tax return or issued as advance payments.

B14. Did Treasury Update Wage Withholding Schedules to Reflect That up to Half of the Credit Was Issued as Advance Payments Before 2021 Tax Returns Are Filed?

No, Treasury did not automatically update the amount of income taxes withheld from workers' paychecks to take into account that up to half of the 2021 credit was issued in advance (and hence not claimed on 2021 income tax returns). Taxpayers could have manually adjusted their withholding, for example by updating their IRS Form W-4 with their employer.

B15. How Many Advance Payments of the 2021 Credit Were Issued?

Data from Treasury indicate that between 35 million and 36 million families have received a monthly advance payment of the credit between July and

[21] In some cases, the expanded child credit may affect state liabilities, as discussed in a report by Elaine Maag and David Weiner of the Tax Policy Center: "Although Oklahoma is the only state where taxpayers will benefit from its links to the federal CTC, it is not the only state with taxpayers who will be affected by the federal change. About 1 million households across other states will see their state income taxes increase as their federal income taxes drop from the larger CTC. Three-quarters of those taxpayers are in states with a federal income tax deduction. That is, these states allow taxpayers to reduce their taxable income by the amount of their federal income tax bill. If federal taxes drop, more income will be taxed at the state level. Other interactions between federal and state laws cause the state tax increase for other households. For example, some states limit certain state credits to federal tax liability. With lower federal tax liability because of the expanded CTC, households can claim less in state credits. This can occur, for example, in Maryland and New York." Elaine Maag and David Weiner, *How Increasing the Federal EITC and CTC Could Affect State Taxes*, Tax Policy Center, April 22, 2021, p. 7, https://www.taxpolicycenter.org/ publications/how- increasing-federal-eitc-and-ctc-could-affect-state-taxes/full.

December 2021. In total, these payments have equaled over $93 billion, averaging between $423 and $444 per recipient per month.

These numbers were subject to change from month to month as taxpayers enrolled in advance payments, unenrolled from advance payments, or provided information that could change the amounts. Between June 14 and November 15, 2021, taxpayers were able to enroll to receive the payments using a non-filer portal (initially only with the IRS tool, but by September, they could also use the Code for America tool). Beginning in late June of 2021, taxpayers could also opt out of using the update portal (CTC-UP).[22] Taxpayers had until November 29, 2021, to make allowable changes to their information using CTC-UP for remaining advance payments.

Table 3. Advanced payments of the 2021 ARPA-expanded child credit by month

	Total Number of Payments	Number of Qualifying Children	Total Amount of Payments	Average Payment Amount
December 2021	36.1 million	61.2 million	$16.0 billion	$444
November 2021	36.1 million	61.3 million	$15.7 billion	$435
October 2021	36.0 million	61.1 million	$15.5 billion	$430
September 2021	35.5 million	60.0 million	$15.2 billion	$428
August 2021	36.0 million	60.9 million	$15.4 billion	$428
July 2021	35.2 million	59.3 million	$14.9 billion	$423

Sources: U.S. Treasury: Office of Tax Analysis, "Advancing the Child Tax Credit," available at https://home.treasury.gov/policy-issues/tax-policy/office-of-tax-analysis.

Note: The numbers shown reflect advance CTC payments disbursed to eligible recipients based on taxpayer account information and do not account for reversed or undeliverable advance CTC payments.

Excluding the payments disbursed in September 2021, there has generally been a net increase in the number of payments made and number of qualifying children living in families receiving these payments over the past six months. In September, a technical issue resulted in less than 2% of recipients failing to receive their monthly payments, according to the IRS.[23] The IRS issued a statement that these payments were generally issued at the end of September.

---

[22] See White House, "Child Tax Credit for Non-Filers," https://www.whitehouse.gov/child-tax-credit/sign-up/.

[23] Internal Revenue Service, "IRS Statement – Advance Child Tax Credit Payments," press release, September 24, 2021, https://www.irs.gov/newsroom/irs-statement-advance-child-tax-credit-payments.

B16: How Do Low-Income Households That Are Not Required to File a 2021 Income Tax Return Claim the Remainder of the Child Credit?

In order to claim the remainder of the total 2021 credit (or if they received no advance payments, all of the 2021 credit), households must file a 2021 income tax return. Some households' incomes are so low that they do not owe income taxes and are not required to file a tax return in 2021.

Nonetheless, even though these families are not required to file a tax return, they must do so in order to receive the remainder of the 2021 child credit. While some of these eligible nonfilers may have already filed a tax return during the traditional filing season to receive the remainder of the credit, others may have been unaware of this requirement and failed to do so. The traditional filing season for 2021 returns ended April 18, 2022, absent an extension.

Eligible nonfiling households who missed the filing deadline can still file their 2021 returns to receive the remainder of the 2021 child credit using the nonfiler portal created by Code for America at GetCTC.org. This portal opened in 2022 after the traditional filing season for 2021 returns ended.[24]

C. Territorial Residents and the Child Credit

C1. Did Territorial Residents Receive the Child Credit Before ARPA?

It is unclear whether and to what extent residents of territories received the child credit before ARPA. But available information suggests that the credit they received prior to ARPA was generally less than the amount received by residents of the United States in similar circumstances (i.e., same marital status, income, and number of children).

Puerto Rico's income tax does not include a child credit. Prior to ARPA, residents of Puerto Rico with three or more children could receive the additional child credit (ACTC) under the "alternative formula."[25] (The

---

[24] See Brian Faler, "Fearing filing season chaos, IRS hits pause on web tool for Child Tax Credit," *Politico*, March 4, 2022, and Tami Luhby, "Biden administration renews effort to get enhanced child tax credit to low-income families,"*CNN*, May 11, 2022.

[25] Throughout this report, the discussion of residents of U.S. territories will be of *bona fide residents* of these territories.According to the Joint Committee on Taxation, "[a] bona fide

ACTC is the amount of the credit that is greater than income taxes owed, and is also referred to as the "refundable portion" of the credit.) Under the alternative formula, the ACTC effectively equals 7.65% of earned income up to the maximum ACTC per child, which was $1,400 per child before ARPA. Puerto Rican residents applied for the ACTC under the alternative formula directly with the IRS. The alternative formula is, in most cases, less generous than the ACTC calculated under the earned income formula.[26] Because only families with three or more children could receive the ACTC under the alternative formula, Puerto Rican families with one or two children did not receive the ACTC.

While the territorial governments of American Samoa and mirror-code territories may have had child credits under their own internal tax laws, it is unclear whether and to what extent these territorial governments paid out these credits from local funds.[27] Like residents of Puerto Rico, residents of these territories with three or more children could generally receive the ACTC under the alternative formula (and hence families with fewer than three children could not receive the ACTC). Unlike residents of Puerto Rico, residents of American Samoa, Guam, the Commonwealth of the Northern Mariana Islands (CNMI), and the United States Virgin Islands (USVI) applied for the ACTC with their territorial governments, with the IRS issuing aggregate payments to the respective territorial governments to cover the costs of the child credit (sometimes referred to as a "cover-over" payment).[28] (See Table E-1.)

---

resident of a territory for a taxable year is generally an individual (1) who is present for at least 183 days during the taxable year in the territory, and (2) who does not have either a tax home outside the territory or a closer connection to the United States or a foreign country than to the territory. Broadly, a bona fide individual resident of a territory is exempt from U.S. tax on income derived from sources within that territory but is subject to U.S. tax on U.S.-source and non-territory-source income." Further, this discussion generally focuses on territorial residents who are not required to file a federal income tax return, and hencedo not receive the child credit with the federal income tax return.

[26] Under the earned income formula, the ACTC is calculated as 15% of earned income above $2,500, up to the maximum ACTC per child of $1,400 (adjusted for inflation). Beginning in 2026, the formula is scheduled to be 15% ofearned income above $3,000 up to a maximum of $1,000 per child.

[27] A mirror code territory is a territory whose own territorial tax law is effectively the U.S. Internal Revenue Code (IRC) with the territory's name substituted for the United States wherever the term United States is used in the IRC(i.e., it is a "mirror" of the IRC).

[28] The IRS Chief Financial Officer (CFO) made these aggregate payments to territorial governments prior to ARPA.

C2. How Did ARPA Change the Child Credit for Territorial Residents in 2021?

Broadly, ARPA provided clarity on both the amount of the credit territorial residents can receive and the federal funding to cover the cost of this benefit permanently, including for 2021. ARPA generally allowed territorial residents to receive the entire amount of the ARPA-expanded credit.[29] Residents of Puerto Rico are eligible to receive the ARPA-expanded child credit when they file a 2021 tax return directly with the IRS.[30] Residents of American Samoa can receive the full amount of the ARPA-expanded child credit. If American Samoa has an approved plan to distribute these payments, then Treasury is directed to provide the American Samoan government funds to cover their full cost, and the American Samoan government will pay out the benefit to its residents. Otherwise, residents of American Samoa will be able to file a return with the IRS to directly claim the benefit. Residents of mirror-code territories can receive the full benefit of the ARPA-expanded child credit. Residents of mirror-code territories will receive the benefit from their respective territorial governments, with the U.S. Treasury directed to provide each government with a "cover-over" payment for the total cost of the benefit. (See Table E-1.)

C3. Did Territorial Residents Receive the Advance Payments of the 2021 Credit?

No, territorial residents did not receive advance payments from the U.S. Treasury. Residents of Puerto Rico, who receive their child credit payments directly from the IRS, are ineligible to participate in the federal advance payment program. Hence, they will receive the full benefit when they file a 2021 tax return with the IRS in early 2022.

If American Samoa and mirror-code territorial governments elect to advance the 2021 ARPA- expanded credit directly to their residents in a manner similar to the federal advance program, the law provides that Treasury will provide these governments with an additional $300,000 per

---

[29] For more information, see Taxpayer Advocate Service, *TAS Tax Tip: 2021 Advance Child Tax Credit information for U.S. Territory residents*, August 25, 2021, https://www.taxpayer advocate.irs.gov/news/tas-tax-tip-2021-advance-child-tax-credit-information-for-u-s-territory-residents/.

[30] IRS Form 1040-SS or IRS Form 1040-PR.

territory for the associated administrative costs (in addition to the amounts to cover the aggregate costs of the benefit itself).[31]

C4. How Did ARPA Change the Child Credit for Territorial Residents After 2021?

Broadly, ARPA provided clarity on both the amount of the benefit territorial residents can receive and the federal funding to cover the cost of this benefit permanently—that is, after 2021.

Residents of Puerto Rico—irrespective of the number of children they have—will be eligible to receive the ACTC under the alternative formula, applying for this benefit directly with the IRS. If American Samoa has an approved plan to distribute to its residents child credit amounts—both the refundable portion (i.e., the ACTC) and the nonrefundable portion—that reflect those in the Internal Revenue Code (IRC) for a given year, then Treasury is directed to provide the American Samoan government funds to cover the full cost of this credit.[32] If no such plan is in effect, American Samoan residents may apply directly with the IRS like Puerto Rican residents (i.e., they can apply directly with the IRS for the ACTC under the alternative formula, disregarding the limitation for three or more children). Residents of the mirror-code territories can receive child credit amounts—both the refundable portion (i.e., the ACTC) and the nonrefundable portion— that reflect those in the Internal Revenue Code (IRC) for a given year. Treasury is directed to provide these governments funds to cover the full cost of this credit. (See Table E-1.)

---

[31] For example, the governor of the Commonwealth of the Northern Mariana Islands issued a press release stating that its local tax authority, the Department of Finance, Division of Revenue and Taxation (DRT), is implementing a plan. Office of the Governor of the Commonwealth of the Northern Mariana Islands, "DRT planning for advanced payments of the Expanded Child Tax Credit," press release, May 13, 2021, https://governor.gov.mp /news/press-releases/drt-planning-for-advanced-payments-of-the-expanded-child-tax-credit/.

[32] This includes the refundable portion of the child credit—the ACTC—calculated under the earned income formula.

Appendix A. Selected Research on the ARPA-Expanded Child Credit

A variety of research studies have evaluated the effects of the ARPA-expanded child credit, either as a standalone provision or in combination with other provisions.[33] A selection of these studies is provided in this appendix. In some cases, these studies examined the impact of the ARPA-expanded credit if it were to be permanent or extended as part of the Biden Administration's American Families Plan.

I. Poverty and Economic Security

Table A-1 provides a selected list of studies that examine the ARPA-expanded child credit's impact on economic security and poverty as a stand-alone provision. Of note, in 2019, the National Academy of Sciences released a study evaluating the poverty reduction impact of a child allowance similarly structured to the ARPA-expanded child credit.[34]

Table A-1. Selected research on the ARPA-expanded child credit's impact on poverty and economic security

Study	Major Impact/Outcome Evaluated	Notes
Tax Policy Center, *Child Tax Credit Recipients Experienced a Larger Decline in Food Insecurity and a Similar Change in Employment as*	Employment and Material Hardship: Estimates from survey data of changes in material hardship and employment for adults living with children who received advanced CTC payments compared to changes for adults with and without children who did	"The temporary expansion of the child tax credit (CTC) in the American Rescue Plan delivered monthly payments to most families with children from July through December 2021. We use data from the Urban Institute's Well-Being and Basic Needs Survey to compare

[33] For example, see Zachary Parolin et al., *The American Rescue Plan could cut child poverty by more than half*, Centeron Poverty and Social Policy at Columbia University, March 11, 2021, https://www.povertycenter.columbia.edu/news-internal/2021/presidential-policy/biden-economic-relief-proposal-poverty-impact. Or for a comparison of the average value of all child tax benefits in 2021 by proposal, see Table 8 in Alex Brill, Kyle Pomerleau, and Grant M. Seiter, *The Tax Benefits of Parenthood: A History and Analysis of Current Proposals*, American Enterprise Institute, February 2021, https://www.aei.org/research-products/report/the-tax-benefits-of-parenthood-a-history-and-analysis-of-current-proposals/.

[34] National Academies of Sciences, Engineering, and Medicine, *A Roadmap to Reducing Child Poverty*, 2019,https://www.nap.edu/catalog/25246/a-roadmap-to-reducing-child-poverty.

Table A-1. (Continued)

Study	Major Impact/Outcome Evaluated	Notes
Nonrecipients Between 2020 and 2021, Michael Karpman et al. May 9, 2022	not get the payments. Data are from the 2020 and 2021 rounds of the Urban Institute's Well-Being and Basic Needs Survey (WBNS). WBNS is a nationally representative, internet-based survey of adults ages 18 to 64 designed to monitor changes in individual and family well- being as policymakers consider changes to federal safety net programs.	adults ages 18 to 64 that received the payments with those that did not. We find the share of adults who received the payments reporting food insecurity declined more than the share of adults who did not receive the payments. We found no significant differences in the changes in employment between December 2020 and December 2021 for adults who received the payments and adults who did not receive the payments."
Health Affairs, *Patterns of Food Security and Dietary Intake During the First Half of the Child Tax Credit Expansion,* by Elizabeth Adams et al. May 2022	Food Insecurity: Longitudinal patterns of food insecurity and children's dietary intake across the first half of monthly expanded CTC payments among survey participants.	"This study examined food security and children's dietary intake after three months of expanded CTC payments. Parents completed online surveys before and after three months of CTC payments. Among parents participating in the expansion, food and beverage purchases were the most common use of expanded CTC funds (45.9 percent), particularly in households with very low food security (63.0 percent). From before to midway through the CTC expansion, very low food security decreased from 12.7 percent to 5.6 percent, and simultaneously, food security increased from 57.4 percent to 66.4 percent. The CTC expansion was also associated with decreases in children's consumption of added sugar, sugar-sweetened beverages, and sweetened fruit beverages. No changes were observed in children's intake of other dietary components."

Study	Major Impact/Outcome Evaluated	Notes
Washington University in St. Louis Social Policy Institute, *The Impacts of the 2021 Expanded Child Tax Credit on Family Employment, Nutrition, and Financial Well-Being,* by Leah Hamilton et al. April 2022	Variety of Economic and Social Well-Being Outcomes: Researchers surveyed participants about a variety of outcomes including measures of employment, savings, credit usage, well- being, and material hardship (e.g., skipped housing payments, food insecurity).	"We utilized the NORC/Amerispeak probability-based online panel to survey a nationally-representative group of 1,782 American parents eligible for the credit and a comparison group of 2,015 ineligible households ... we find that families used the CTC to cover routine expenses without reducing their employment. Eligible families experienced improved nutrition, decreased reliance on credit cards and other high-risk financial services, and also made long term educational investments for both parents and children. We find that these changes were especially promising for Black, Hispanic, and other minority families, along with low- and moderate-income families, suggesting that the expanded CTC may be an important tool for addressing both racial financial inequality and a widening income gap in the United States."
Washington University in St. Louis Social Policy Institute, Expanded Child Tax Credit Payments Did Not Reduce Employment, by Stephen Roll, Leah Hamilton, and Yung Chun October 2021, Revised January 26, 2022, Revised March 18, 2022	Employment: Estimates of the change in labor supply from child tax credit expansion proposals using Census Household Pulse survey.	"There is no evidence within the Census Household Pulse data—a large, high- quality, nationally-representative data source—that CTC payments led parents to leave the workforce. Our analyses also found no significant differences in employment rates for low-income, middle-income, or high-income families receiving the CTC. We also see no evidence that the CTC is increasing the proportion of parents who are staying home with their children rather than working."
NBER Working Paper, Effects of the Expanded Child Tax Credit on Employment Outcomes: Evidence from Real World Data	Employment: Estimates of the labor supply response using data from the monthly Current Population Survey (CPS) files and the Census Household Pulse Survey microdata from April through December 2021.	"Across both samples and several model specifications, we find very small, inconsistently signed, and statistically insignificant impacts of the CTC both on employment in the prior week and on active participation in the labor force

Table A-1. (Continued)

Study	Major Impact/Outcome Evaluated	Notes
from April to December 2021, by Elizabeth Ananat et al. October 10, 2021, Revised March 2022		among adults living in households with children. Further, labor supply responses to the policy change do not differ for households for whom the CTC's expansion eliminated a previous work incentive. Thus, our analyses of real- world data suggest that the expanded CTC did not have negative short-term employment effects that offset its documented reductions in poverty and hardship."
Columbia's Center on Poverty and Social Policy, 3.7 Million More children in Poverty in January 2022 Without Monthly Child Tax Credit, by Zachary Parolin, Sophie Collyer, and Megan A. Curran. February 17, 2022	Child poverty on a monthly basis: Simulated estimates of child poverty rates and number of children in poverty using the Supplemental Poverty Measure (SPM) in January 2022, after advanced payments of the child tax credit had ended. These estimates are also provided by race/ethnicity.	"The monthly child poverty rate increased from 12.1 percent in December 2021 to 17 percent in January 2022, the highest rate since the end of 2020. The 4.9 percentage point (41 percent) increase in poverty represents 3.7 million more children in poverty due to the expiration of the monthly Child Tax Credit payments. Latino and Black children experienced the largest percentage-point increases in poverty (7.1 percentage points and 5.9 percentage points, respectively)."
[Working Paper], Investigating the Effects of the 2021 Child Tax Credit Expansion on Poverty and Maternal Employment, by Jacob Bastian January 19, 2022	Child and Adult Poverty: Simulated estimates of adult and child poverty (numbers and rates) using both the official poverty measure (plus the child credit amounts) and the Supplemental Poverty Measure (SPM), which already includes these amounts in resources. Employment: Simulated estimates of the labor supply response of parents to the ARPA-expanded child credit using both the American Community Survey (ACS) and the Current Population Survey (CPS).	"Using my preferred approach, I find that the 2021 CTC would lead 413,000 adults—including 325,000 mothers and 96,000 poor adults—to stop working. Over a full year, the CTC would reduce adult and child poverty rates from 11.1% and 17.2%, to 7.4% and 11.2%. Overall, the 2021 CTC reduces adult and child poverty by 33.3% and 34.9%, and reduces deep poverty by 43.5% and 51.3%, larger than the impact of the 2018 CTC and Earned Income Tax Credit combined."

Study	Major Impact/Outcome Evaluated	Notes
Columbia's Center on Poverty and Social Policy, Sixth Child Tax Credit Payment Kept 3.7 Million Children Out of Poverty in December, by Zachary Parolin and Megan A. Curran. January 18, 2022	Child poverty on a monthly basis: Simulated estimates of child poverty rates and number of children in poverty using the Supplemental Poverty Measure (SPM) in December 2021, after the sixth advance payment of the child credit. These estimates are also provided by race/ethnicity.	"The Child Tax Credit reached 61.2 million children in December 2021, an increase of 2 million children over six months from the rollout to 59.3 million children in July. Increasing coverage increased its anti-poverty effects: the first payment kept 3 million children from poverty in July and the sixth Child Tax Credit payment kept 3.7 million children from poverty in December. On its own, the Child Tax Credit reduced monthly child poverty by close to 30 percent. In the absence of a January payment, the monthly child poverty rate could potentially increase from 12.1 percent to at least 17.1 percent—the highest monthly child poverty rate since December 2020."
Journal of the American Medical Association (JAMA) Network Open, Association of the Implementation of Child Tax Credit Advance Payments with Food Insufficiency in US Households, by Paul R. Shafer et al. January 13, 2022	Food Insufficiency: Researchers estimated the impact of the first monthly CTC payment (i.e., the July payment) on food insufficiency based on data from the U.S. Census Bureau's Household Pulse Survey. The survey asks respondents: "In the last 7 days, which of these statements best describes the food eaten in your household?" Respondents who choose the answers "Sometimes not enough to eat" or "Often not enough to eat" are considered to be food insufficient.	"We found that the first round of advance CTC payments in July 2021 was associated with a 26% reduction in food insufficiency in US households with children. Nearly two-thirds of families with children reported receiving an advance CTC payment, likely a considerably lower amount than ultimately will receive it. The small percentage of households without children that reported receiving a CTC payment may have had custody changes or had a child who aged out of eligibility."
Columbia's Center on Poverty and Social Policy, November Child Tax Credit payment kept 3.8 million children from poverty December 15, 2021	Child poverty on a monthly basis: Simulated estimates of child poverty rates and number of children in poverty using the Supplemental Poverty Measure (SPM) in November 2021, after the fifth advance payment of the child credit. These estimates are also provided by race/ethnicity.	"The fifth monthly payment of the expanded Child Tax Credit kept 3.8 million children from poverty in November 2021. The Child Tax Credit reached 61.3 million children in November and, on its own, contributed to a 5.1 percentage point (29.4 percent) reduction in child poverty compared to what the monthly poverty rate in November would have been in its absence."

Table A-1. (Continued)

Study	Major Impact/Outcome Evaluated	Notes
Center on Budget and Policy Priorities (CBPP), If Congress Fails to Act, Monthly Child Tax Credit Payments Will Stop, Child Poverty Reductions Will Be Lost, by Kris Cox, Chuck Marr, Arloc Sherman, and Stephanie Hingtgen December 3, 2021	Child Poverty: Simulated estimates of the number of children who would experience reduced income and fall either into poverty or deeper into poverty if the ARPA-expanded child tax credit were not extended, relative to circumstances if the expansion were extended. Estimates are made using 2018 data and simulate the impact in a nonrecessionary economy. These estimates are provided at the state level.	"An estimated 9.9 million children are at risk of slipping back below the poverty line or deeper into poverty if the [ARPA] expansion is not extended.... These include 3.8 million Latino, 2.9 million white, 2.1 million Black, 426,000 Asian, and 280,000 American Indian or Alaska Native (AIAN) children."
Columbia's Center on Poverty and Social Policy, October Child Tax Credit payment kept 3.6 million children from poverty	Child poverty on a monthly basis: Simulated estimates of child poverty rates and number of children in poverty using the Supplemental Poverty Measure (SPM) in October 2021, after the	"The fourth monthly payment of the expanded Child Tax Credit kept 3.6 million children from poverty in October 2021. The Child Tax Credit reached 61.1 million children in October and,
November 30, 2021	fourth advance payment of the child credit. These estimates are also provided by race/ethnicity.	on its own, contributed to a 4.9 percentage point (28 percent) reduction in child poverty compared to what the monthly poverty rate in October would have been in its absence."
JPMorgan Chase & Co., Household Cash Balance Pulse: Family Edition November 2021	Cash balances: De-identified administrative banking data reporting cash account balances.	"Families who received advanced CTC in 2021 had balances in September that were 70 percent higher than two years prior, while families without kids had balances that were 50 percent higher.... In this sense, advanced CTC payments may be helping families with kids maintain elevated cash balances."
Jain Family Institute, Analysis of Full Refundability of the Child Tax Credit Without Expansion, by Jack Landry and Stephen Nuñez October 28, 2021	Child poverty: Simulated estimates of child poverty rates, number of children in deep poverty, and poverty gap under several scenarios. Those scenarios include the full ARPA expansion of the child credit, full refundability of the pre- ARPA credit (i.e., $2,000 per child), and an increase of the pre-ARPA credit without full refundability.	"Treating the TCJA-era [child credit] as the baseline, we find that the full ARPA expansion reduces child poverty by 40 percent, introducing full refundability alone reduces it by 19 percent, and introducing the dollar amount expansion alone reduces it by only 7 percent. The full ARPA expansion reduces deep child poverty by 49 percent, introducing

Study	Major Impact/Outcome Evaluated	Notes
	Estimates are made using 2018 data and simulate impacts in a nonrecessionary economy. Other Impacts: Simulated estimates of the budgetary cost of the child credit under these different scenarios.	full refundability alone reduces it by 32 percent, and introducing the dollar amount expansion alone reduces it by only 2 percent. The full ARPA expansion reduces the average child poverty gap by $638, introducing full refundability alone reduces it by $363, and introducing the dollar amount expansion alone reduces it by only $73. The TCJA-era CTC costs about $117 billion per year. The full ARPA CTC expansion would raise that to roughly $216 billion (+$ 99 billion); extending full refundability alone would raise it to $134 billion (+ $17 billion); the dollar amount expansion alone would raise it to $162 billion (+$45 billion)."
Columbia's Center on Poverty and Social Policy, Expanded Child Tax Credit Continues to Keep Millions of Children from Poverty in September October 27, 2021	Child poverty on a monthly basis: Simulated estimates of child poverty rates and number of children in poverty using the Supplemental Poverty Measure (SPM) in September 2021, after the third advance payment of the child credit. These estimates are also provided by race/ethnicity.	"The third monthly payment of the expanded Child Tax Credit (CTC) kept 3.4 million children from poverty in September 2021. The monthly child poverty rate increased between August and September, from 11.5 percent to 13.2 percent, due to the expiration of expanded unemployment benefits across the country and the rollback of Supplemental Nutrition Assistance Program (SNAP) emergency allotment benefits in some states. However, the Child Tax Credit contributed to a 4.6 percentage point (26 percent) reduction in child poverty compared to what the monthly poverty rate in September would have been in its absence."
Becker Friedman Institute for Economics at the University of Chicago, The Anti-Poverty, Targeting, and Labor Supply Effects of the Proposed Child Tax Credit Expansion, by	Employment: Simulated estimates of the labor supply response of parents to the ARPA-expanded child credit. These estimates are made using 2016 survey and administrative data included in the Comprehensive Income Dataset (CID). Child Poverty: Simulated estimates of the impact of the.	"By replacing the [prior law child tax credit] TCJA CTC (which contained substantial work incentives akin to the EITC) with a universal basic income-type benefit, the CTC expansion reduces the return to working at all by at least $2,000 per child for most workers with children. Relying on elasticity estimates consistent with

Table A-1. (Continued)

Study	Major Impact/Outcome Evaluated	Notes
Kevin Corinth et al. October 7, 2021	ARPA-expanded child tax credit on child poverty rates incorporating estimates of labor supply responses to the child tax credit. These estimates are made using 2016 survey and administrative data included in CID.	mainstream simulation models and the academic literature, we estimate that this change in policy would lead 1.5 million workers (constituting 2.6% of all working parents) to exit the labor force. The decline in employment and the consequent earnings loss would mean that child poverty would only fall by 22%."
National Bureau of Economic Research (NBER), Estimating the Net Fiscal Cost of a Child Tax Credit Expansion, by Jacob Goldin, Elaine Maag, and Katherine Michelmore	Employment: Estimates of the change in labor supply from child tax credit expansion proposals using 2017 data. Fiscal Cost: Simulated estimates of the direct costs of the child tax credit expansion proposals. These include the costs of increased benefits, changes in tax revenue	"We study the fiscal cost of three such proposals that would expand refundability of the credit to low-income children, increase the maximum credit amount, and/or eliminate the income phase-out to make the credit universal. For each proposal, we use the Current Population Survey to estimate
October 2021, Revised December 2021, Published in 2022	from labor supply responses, and longer-term tax revenue changes attributable to children's future earnings. Simulations are based on 2017 data.	three components of the net fiscal cost: the direct cost (additional tax refunds or lower tax liability), revenue changes due to taxpayers' labor supply responses, and long-term changes in tax revenue due to changes in children's future earnings. We find that direct costs are by far the most important component but that long-term earning changes also play an important role, offsetting 20% of the direct costs of making the credit fully refundable. In contrast, labor supply responses modestly contribute to the fiscal cost of the CTC expansions we model."
Columbia's Center on Poverty and Social Policy, Second Child Tax Credit Payment Keeps 3.5 Million Children Out of Poverty, by Zachary Parolin and Megan Curran September 24, 2021	Child poverty on a monthly basis: Simulated estimates of child poverty rates and number of children in poverty using the Supplemental Poverty Measure (SPM) in August 2021, after the second advance payment of the child credit. These estimates are also provided by race/ethnicity.	"The second monthly payment of the expanded Child Tax Credit (CTC) lifted 3.5 million children out of poverty in August 2021. The child poverty rate declined from 11.9 percent in July 2021 (the month featuring the first CTC payment) to 11.5 percent in August 2021. Without the CTC, the monthly child poverty rate in August 2021 would have been 16.2

Study	Major Impact/Outcome Evaluated	Notes
		percent. The CTC contributed to a 4.7 percentage point (29 percent) reduction in child poverty compared to what the monthly poverty rate in August would have been in its absence."
Center on Budget and Policy Priorities (CBPP), Earnings Requirement Would Undermine Child Tax Credit's Poverty-Reducing Impact While Doing Virtually Nothing to Boost Parents' Employment, by Arloc Sherman, Chuck Marr, and Stephanie Hingtgen September 23, 2021	Child Poverty: Simulated estimates of the number of children in poverty with and without full refundability. Specifically, the authors estimate child poverty rates with the ARPA-expanded child credit and compare them to child poverty rates with the ARPA-expanded child credit with the prior-law earned income formula used to phase-in the credit for low-income taxpayers. Estimates are made using 2018 data and simulate the impact in a nonrecessionary economy. (Note that when simulating the ARPA- expanded child credit with the prior-law earned income formula, the authors eliminate the statutory maximum amount of the refundable portion of the credit of $1,400 per child.)	"The Rescue Plan's Child Tax Credit expansions are expected to cut child poverty by over 40 percent, lifting more than 4 million children out of poverty. More than 80 percent of this effect [3.6 million children] comes from the provision making the full credit available to families even if they have low or no income."
Jain Family Institute, Reducing Refundability of the Child Tax Credit: Assessing Poverty Impact and Trade-offs, by Jack Landry and Stephen Nuñez September 22, 2021	Child Poverty: Simulated estimates of child poverty rates with and without full refundability. Specifically, the authors estimate child poverty rates with the ARPA-expanded child credit and compare them to child poverty rates with the ARPA-expanded child credit with the prior-law earned income formula used to phase-in the credit for low-income taxpayers. Estimates are made using 2018 data and simulate the impact in a nonrecessionary economy. (Note that when simulating the ARPA- expanded child credit with the prior-law earned income formula, the authors set the maximum amount of the refundable portion of the credit at 70% of the maximum credit amount, as opposed to the statutory amount of $1,400 per child.)	"Treating the Biden [ARPA-expanded] CTC as a baseline, limiting the refundability of the CTC would increase child poverty by 53 percent, leaving behind 3.2 million children. The largest impacts would fall on Black children, increasing the Black child poverty rate by 83%."

Table A-1. (Continued)

Study	Major Impact/Outcome Evaluated	Notes
Jain Family Institute, Assessing Non-Filer Rates & Poverty Impact for the American Rescue Plan Act's Expanded CTC, by Jack Landry and Stephen Nuñez September 8, 2021	Child poverty: Simulated estimates of child poverty rates of the ARPA- expanded child credit under different assumptions about how many eligible non-filing households receive the benefit.	"Our analysis conservatively estimates that upwards of 6.4 million eligible children will not receive the benefit, resulting in an estimated child poverty reduction of 11 to 18 percent, and a 92 percent take-up rate. We do not know exactly who these children are, but we find a substantial portion—at least 71 percent—receive other government benefits, meaning that better data sharing between state and federal benefits agencies could offer a crucial avenue for enrollment. Greater enrollment could dramatically increase the child poverty reduction, up to 40 percent."
Columbia's Center on Poverty and Social Policy, The Initial Effects of the Expanded Child Tax Credit on Material Hardship, by Zachary Parolin et al. August 30, 2021	Food Insufficiency: Researchers estimated the impact of the first monthly CTC payment (i.e., the July payment) on food insufficiency based on data from the U.S. Census Bureau's Pulse Survey. The survey asks respondents: "In the last 7 days, which of these statements best describes the food eaten in your household?" Respondents who choose the answers "Sometimes or often not enough to eat" are considered to be food insufficient. Other Material Hardship Indicators: Researchers also estimated the impact the first monthly CTC payment had on other hardship indicators, including difficultly with paying for usual household expenses and whether the household is on time with rent or mortgage payments (See Table 1 of the Columbia Center on Poverty and Social Policy report).	"Our findings offer three primary conclusions regarding the initial effects of the first monthly CTC payment delivered mid-July 2021. First, the July 2021 CTC payment strongly reduced food insufficiency among low-income households with children; a $100 increase in CTC benefits (adjusted for household-size) is associated with a 7- percentage point, or roughly 25 percent, decline in food insufficiency among low- income families who report receipt of the CTC. Second, the effects of the first CTC payment on food insufficiency are concentrated among households with annual incomes of less than $35,000. Third, increasing the coverage rate of the CTC is critical for further reducing material hardship."

Study	Major Impact/Outcome Evaluated	Notes
Columbia's Center on Poverty and Social Policy, Monthly Poverty Rates Among Children after the Expansion of the Child Tax Credit, by Zachary Parolin et al. August 20, 2021	Child poverty on a monthly basis: Simulated estimates of child poverty rates and number of children in poverty using the Supplemental Poverty Measure (SPM) in July 2021, after the first advance payment of the child credit (July 2021). These estimates are also provided by race/ethnicity. Primary estimates assume that about 60 million children live with taxpayers who receive the credit, while the maximum number of children who live in credit- eligible households is estimated to be up to 67 million. The authors also simulate a range of monthly child poverty rates under varying levels of CTC receipt (providing estimates that range from around 56 million to around 67 million children receiving the benefit).	"The monthly child poverty rate fell from 15.8 percent in June to 11.9 percent in July 2021. This drop in child poverty is primarily due to the first payment of the expanded Child Tax Credit, which on its own kept approximately 3 million children from poverty in July; without it, the monthly child poverty rate would have been 4.1 percentage points (or 25.6 percent) higher [i.e., would have been 15.9% in July]."
U.S. Census Bureau, Economic Hardship Declined in Households with Children as Child Tax Credit Payments Arrived, by Daniel J. Perez-Lopex August 11, 2021	Food Insufficiency: The percentage of adults experiencing food insufficiency (sometimes or often not having enough to eat) before and after receipt of the first advance child credit payments in July 2021. Financial Hardship: The percentage of adults having difficulty paying expenses before and after receipt of the first advance child credit payments in July 2021.	"The survey shows introduction of the [advanced] CTC coincided with a drop in food insufficiency in households with children [from 11% to 8.4%]. It also showed that in those households, there was a drop in difficulty paying weekly expenses [from 31.5% to 29.0%]."
Columbia's Center on Poverty and Social Policy, The Benefits and Costs of a U.S. Child Allowance, by Irvin Garfinkel et al. August 2, 2021, Revised March 2022	Variety of Long-Term Outcomes from Increased Family Income: Estimates the current and future benefits of an expanded child credit including future earnings of child beneficiaries; future tax payments of child beneficiaries, neo-natal mortality, children's health and longevity, transfer costs, expenditures on child protection, crime, expenditures on children's and parents' health, and parent tax payments.	"Our estimates indicate that making that expansion permanent would cost $97 billion per year and generate social benefits with net present value of $982 billion per year. Sensitivity analyses indicate that our estimates are robust to alternative assumptions."

Table A-1. (Continued)

Study	Major Impact/Outcome Evaluated	Notes
Urban Institute, How a Permanent Expansion of the Child Tax Credit Could Affect Poverty, by Gregory Acs and Kevin Werner July 29, 2021	Child Poverty: Simulated child poverty rates and the number of children in poverty measured using the SPM during a nonrecessionary economy (2018 data used). Child poverty statistics broken down by race/ethnicity, metropolitan and nonmetropolitan areas, states, race, and ethnicity. Other Impacts: Information on changes in family income is also provided.	"Expanding the CTC would reduce child poverty by 5.9 percentage points, from 14.2 to 8.4 percent (rounded to the nearest tenth), using 2018 as a benchmark for a typical year. That means 4.3 million fewer children would be in poverty in a typical year, representing over a 40 percent decrease in child poverty."
Congressional Research Service, The Child Tax Credit: Impact of the American Rescue Plan Act (ARPA; P.L. 117-2) Expansion on Income and Poverty, by Margot Crandall-Hollick, Jameson Carter, and Conor Boyle July 13, 2021	Child Poverty: Simulated child poverty rates measured using the SPM during a nonrecessionary economy (2016-2018 data used). Child poverty rates are broken down by race/ethnicity. Other Impacts: Information on poverty rates of individuals who live in families with children, changes in family income, and percentage of families receiving the credit is also provided.	"CRS estimates that in a nonrecessionary economy, the ARPA expansion of the child credit will result in nearly all families with children including the lowest-income families with children, receiving the child credit [from 84% of all families with children receiving the credit before ARPA, to 96% after ARPA] the estimates also indicate that the largest share of new recipients will be the poorest families [from 52% of poor families with children receiving the credit before ARPA to 94% after ARPA]. CRS's analysis indicates that the largest increases in income are estimated to occur among poor families with children, substantially reducing the prevalence of child poverty [i.e., the child poverty rate is estimated to fall from 13% to 7%] and the depth of poverty among families with children [i.e., the poverty gap is estimated to fall by 40%]."
Urban Institute, 2021 Poverty Projections: Assessing the Impact of Benefits and Stimulus Measures, by Laura Wheaton, Linda	Poverty: Number of people in 2021 lifted out of poverty by age using the SPM (projected 2021 data). Estimates of the impact of the advanced child credit can be found in Table 6 of the Urban report.	For this analysis, the Urban Institute models only the benefits received in 2021—that is, the advance of the child credit, which is one-half of the total credit amount. This study

Study	Major Impact/Outcome Evaluated	Notes
Giannerelli, and Ilhman Dehry (This is an update of a March 2021 analysis.) July 2021	This study also estimates the poverty impact of COVID-19 policies in combination.	finds that the advanced child credit will lift 1.8 million people out of poverty in 2021, of which 1 million are children (under 18 years old); (see Table 6 of the Urban report).
Center on Budget and Policy Priorities (CBPP), Congress Should Adopt American Families Plan's Permanent Expansion of Child Tax Credit and EITC, Make Additional Provisions Permanent, by Chuck Marr et al. May 24, 2021	Child Poverty: The simulated reduction in child poverty rates measured using the SPM during a nonrecessionary economy (2016-2018 data used). Reductions in child poverty rates are broken down by race/ethnicity for each state. Other Impacts: Number and percentage of children (poor and nonpoor) who would benefit is also provided by race/ethnicity for each state.	"The full Families Plan's Child Tax Credit would lift an estimated 4.1 million children above the poverty line, of whom 1.6 million are Latino, 1.2 million are white, 930,000 are Black, and 132,000 are Asian Of the roughly 9.9 million children it would lift above or closer to the poverty line, 3.8 million are Latino, 2.9 million are white, 2.1 million are Black, and 426,000 are Asian. These changes would reduce the number of children in poverty by more than 40 percent nationally."
American Enterprise Institute (AEI), Unintended consequences: Democrat's child tax credit will cost jobs, by Alex Brill and Kyle Pomerleau April 22, 2021	Employment: Simulated estimates of the impact of the ARPA-expanded child credit on employment.	"We analyzed the impact of a permanent CTC expansion on employment using AEI's Tax-Calculator along with an employment model and set of assumptions from the Congressional Budget Office (CBO). According to our calculation, the likely impact of the CTC expansion on employment will be 296,000 full-time equivalent jobs lost (+/- 155,000). This is due to both the elimination of the phase-in and the phase-out of the larger benefit."

Source: CRS.

II. Estimates of the Number of Children, Families, and Taxpayers Receiving the ARPA-Expanded Child Credit

Children

By State

- The Center on Budget and Policy Priorities (CBPP) has estimated the number of children who would be affected by the permanent extension of the ARPA- expanded child credit: by state (Appendix Table 1) and by state and race/ethnicity (Appendix Table 4). CBPP has also estimated the reduction in child poverty by race and ethnicity from a permanent expansion of the ARPA- expanded child credit (Appendix Table 3).
- CBPP also conducted a comparable analysis of the impact of the temporary ARPA expansion of the child credit.

By Congressional District

- Representative DeLauro's office has provided estimates of the number of children impacted by the ARPA-expanded child credit for selected congressional districts (methodology can be found here).

Families

By State

- The White House has provided state-specific fact sheets on receipt of tax credits expanded by the American Rescue Plan Act, including estimates of the number of families that have benefited from the expanded child credit.
- CRS estimated the number of families eligible for the ARPA-expanded child credit. Families may include more than one taxpayer. See CD1326941, State- Level Estimates of Eligibility for the Expanded Child Tax Credit Included in the American Rescue Plan Act of 2021 (ARPA; P.L. 117-2), by Conor F. Boyle, Jameson A. Carter, and Margot L. Crandall-Hollick, available to congressional clients upon request from the authors.

- The Niskanen Center has also published estimates of the state-level impact of the child credit (in addition, it has provided estimates by metropolitan and nonmetropolitan areas in states, as well as national estimates by households' race and ethnicity). These accompany a report by the Niskanen Center on the economic and community impact of the credit.

By Congressional District

- The Niskanen Center has also published estimates of the county-level impact of the expanded child credit. These accompany a report by the Niskanen Center on the economic and community impact of the credit.

Taxpayers

- The Tax Policy Center (TPC) has estimated the percentage of taxpayers who benefit from the child tax credit in 2021 after the ARPA expansion, by income level (Table T21-0044) and by income percentile (Table T21-0045) at the national level. Note that TPC's analysis is by "tax units" in which a tax unit is everyone listed on an income tax return; includes filing and non-filing units. Tax unit is generally used synonymously with the term taxpayer.
- Estimates in Table T21-0044 can be compared to the benefit from the pre- ARPA credit in 2021 in Table 21-0042 to estimate the impact of the ARPA- expanded credit by income level.
- Estimates in Table 21-0045 can be compared to the benefit from the pre- ARPA credit in 2021 in Table T21-0043 to estimate the impact of the ARPA- expanded credit by income percentile.
- Treasury is providing data on the number of taxpayers receiving the advanced payment of the credit by state as well as the total amount received by taxpayers in each state. See "Treasury Data on Advance Payments" in Appendix C.

III. Estimates of How Families/Taxpayers Spent the Child Credit

- *Center for Law and Social Policy (CLASP) and partners: The Expanded Child Tax Credit is Helping Families, But National Survey Shows Continued Outreach Remains Essential*, April 2022: "This October national survey reached 1,012 families earning under $75,000 yearly and with children under 18 years old living in the household. Survey respondents were weighted statistically to yield nationally representative results. The key survey findings include:
- The CTC monthly payments reached a wide majority of eligible parents. The monthly CTC payments improved reported wellbeing for parents. Families – including Black, Hispanic, and white respondents – are spending their monthly CTC payments on necessities like food, rent, and clothing. The most common reasons respondents reported for not receiving the monthly CTC were confusion or opting for a lump-sum CTC refund at tax time. Very few families accessed the IRS non-filer portal, and those who utilized the tool often reported confusion when using it. Hispanic families, households with the lowest incomes, and eligible taxpayers with lower educational attainment have higher barriers to claim the expanded CTC compared to their counterparts."
- *Bipartisan Policy Center (BPC):* Accessing the Child Tax Credit: Insights from American Parents, March 29, 2022: "BPC and Morning Consult conducted a survey of 1,500 parents from February 17-22, 2022. Nearly two-thirds (63%) of parents who qualified for the CTC in 2021 said that the credit had a large or somewhat large impact on their family's finances. Low-income parents, Black and Hispanic parents, younger parents, and parents in larger households were particularly likely to report that the CTC had a large impact....Most parents who received monthly payments of the CTC during the latter half of 2021 reported spending the credit on basic expenses.While awareness of the CTC is high, administrative challenges prevent some parents from accessing it....Notable income and racial disparities exist in current claim rates low-income parents were more likely than their middle- or high-income counterparts to not know if they qualified or report that they

did not qualify, even though many of these parents would have been eligible."

- *Census: Household Pulse Survey CTC Use Landing Page*: Data and visualizations by state of the percentage of adults in households that received a Child Tax Credit payment in the last four weeks who either mostly spent it or used it to pay down debt.
- *Rapid Assessment of Pandemic Impact on Development-Early Childhood (RAPID-EC) Project, December 2021*: "Since the start of the advance Child Tax Credit payments in July 2021, 76% of parents in our national survey report having received the payments. We have been asking parents how they use these payments and looking at how the payments are affecting families' financial situations and the emotional well-being of parents and children. Over half (55%) of families receiving the Child Tax Credit are using the payments to meet basic needs (e.g., food, housing, utilities, and telecommunications). Fifty-two percent are putting payments toward unpaid bills and other essentials (e.g., vehicle payments, credit card payments, child care); and child care accounts for 37% of the essential costs in this category. Additionally, 38% report putting payments into savings for their children. Moreover, approximately one in five parents who receive the Child Tax Credit payments report using them to pay for household items (e.g., books, items for school, computer) (18%) and recreational activities (e.g., a family outing, vacation, camp for child) (17%) These analyses are based on responses collected from 3,365 caregivers between the dates of July 21st, 2021 and November 16th, 2021 The RAPID-EC project includes a survey of caregivers with children under age 6 and a survey of child care providers and other adults who care for children under age 6."
- *Center for Law and Social Policy (CLASP), November 17, 2021:* "The national survey of 1,012 eligible families with children ages 0-17 living at home was conducted by Ipsos, an international polling firm, with technical guidance from researchers at the University of California, Berkeley. The survey was distributed in the second and third weeks of October, after most eligible families had received up to three rounds of monthly CTC advance payments. The most common way that respondents reported planning to use their CTC refund or monthly payments was towards paying bills, food and

groceries, paying their rent or mortgage, buying clothing and shoes, and paying down credit cards or other debt."

- *Tax Policy Center, November 4, 2021:* "In this brief, we use nationally representative data from the US Census Bureau's Household Pulse Survey collected between July and September 2021 to examine receipt and use of the advance CTC payments among adults living with children under 18, including how these vary by race, ethnicity, and household income. About half of adults (51 percent) reported spending the credit on food. The next most common purchases included clothing (30 percent), utilities (29 percent), and schoolbooks and supplies (25 percent) Compared with adults with incomes of $75,000 or more, adults with incomes below $75,000 were more likely to spend the credit on food, clothing, utilities, schoolbooks and supplies, rent, and vehicle payments and were less likely to save the credit. Nearly 4 in 10 adults who received the credit (39 percent) reported using it mostly to pay off debt, 3 in 10 (30 percent) mostly spent it, and 3 in 10 (30 percent) mostly saved it."
- *Census Bureau, October 26, 2021:* "Three in 10 families that received monthly Advance Child Tax Credit (CTC) payments spent them on kids' school expenses, and 1 in 4 families with young children used them to cover child care costs, according to new results from the U.S. Census Bureau's experimental Household Pulse Survey (HPS). The majority of HPS respondents reported spending their CTC checks on more than one thing."
- *American Enterprise Institute (AEI), October 18, 2021:* "Overall, 62 percent of parents in our sample (n = 1,434) reported receiving the expanded CTC payment, below the roughly 80 percent of households with children who were eligible for the expanded payments. Less than half of these respondents said they mostly spent their payments, although another 20 percent reported using it to pay down debt. Parents in lower-income households were more likely to spend their CTC payments, while higher-income households were more likely to save the money." The survey also asked respondents about the importance of the CTC payments in meeting day-to-day expenses, the effect of receipt on employment, and support for making the expanded credit permanent.

- *University of Michigan Ford School of Public Policy, October 2021:* "To understand more about how the expanded CTC is impacting families and inform strategies to expand access to the credit, we partnered with Propel, the creators of Providers (formerly Fresh EBT), a free mobile application that helps over 5 million families manage their Supplemental Nutrition Assistance Program (SNAP) benefits. This brief discusses findings from two recent surveys with low- income families who use the Providers application, many of whom are eligible for the CTC. We found that while most respondents received the CTC and used it to pay for essential household expenses, a substantial share of CTC-eligible respondents did not receive their first two monthly payments, suggesting more outreach and supports are needed to achieve universal receipt."
- *U.S. Census Bureau, August 11, 2021:* "Many HPS [Household Pulse Survey] respondents reported spending their CTC payments on more than one thing. About 47% reported spending it on food. Nearly 10% of adults in households that received the CTC—and 17% of those with at least one child under age 5—spent their CTC on child care." More details can be found in the Detailed Tables: Child Tax Credit Table.

Appendix B. Congressional Resources

Embedded hyperlinks in the appendices of this report are not visible in the PDF version of this document. Please refer to the HTML version of this report available on crs.gov to view these links.

House Ways and Means Committee

- Subcommittee on Oversight hearing with IRS Commissioner Rettig on the 2022Filing Season, March 17, 2022
- Ways and Means Committee, "One Year Stronger: Neal Hails Tax Cuts forFamilies and Workers," February 22, 2022
- Subcommittee on Oversight hearing with the National Taxpayer Advocate onChallenges Facing Taxpayers, February 8, 2022

- Ways and Means Republicans, "Millions of American Families May FaceSurprise Tax Bills From Child Tax Credit," January 31, 2022
- Ways and Means Republicans, "Debunking Myths About the Child Tax Credit,"December 13, 2021
- Ways and Means roundtable, "Democrats' Welfare Expansion Will Fail the Poorand Threaten Jobs Recovery," on October 20, 2021
- Ways and Means Committee, "Markup of the Build Back Better Act," September9, 2021-September 15, 2021
- One-pager on IRS child tax credit portals, June 10, 2021
- Child tax credit portals FAQs, June 10, 2021
- Subcommittee on Select Revenue Measures hearing, "Funding Our Nation's Priorities: Reforming the Tax Code's Advantageous Treatment of the Wealthy,"May 12, 2021
- Subcommittee on Oversight hearing on the 2021 filing season, March 18, 2021

House Appropriations Committee

- Subcommittee on Financial Services and General Government hearing on Treasury Oversight, May 27, 2021

House Budget Committee

- Full committee hearing, "Ensuring Women Can Thrive in a Post-Pandemic Economy," March 16, 2022

House Financial Services Committee

- Full committee hearing, "The Inflation Equation: Corporate Profiteering, Supply Chain Bottlenecks, and COVID-19," March 8, 2022
- Subcommittee on Consumer Protection and Financial Institutions hearing, "Banking the Unbanked: Exploring Private and Public Efforts to Expand Accessto the Financial System," July 21, 2021

House Oversight and Reform Committee

- Select Subcommittee on the Coronavirus Crisis hearing, "COVID Child Care Challenges: Supporting Families and Caregivers," March 2, 2022
- Select Subcommittee on the Coronavirus Crisis hearing, "Reviewing Pandemic Relief Programs and Charting an Economic Path Forward," September 22, 2021

Senate Appropriations Committee

- Subcommittee on Financial Services and General Government hearing on the fiscal year 2023 budget request from the U.S. Internal Revenue Service, May 3, 2022

Senate Finance Committee

- Full committee hearing, "Spotlighting IRS Customer Service Challenges," February 17, 2022
- Full committee hearing on the President's FY2022 budget, June 16, 2021
- Full committee hearing on the IRS's FY2022 budget, June 8, 2021
- Full committee hearing, "Combating Inequality: The Tax Code and Racial, Ethnic, and Gender Disparities," April 20, 2021
- Full committee hearing, "The 2021 Filing Season and 21st Century IRS," April 13, 2021

Senate Banking, Housing, and Urban Affairs Committee

- Full committee hearing, "The State of the American Economy: A Year of Unprecedented Economic Growth and Future Plans," February 17, 2022
- Full committee hearing, "CARES Act Oversight of the Treasury and Federal Reserve: Supporting an Equitable Pandemic Recovery," September 28, 2021

- Subcommittee on Financial Institutions and Consumer Protection hearing, "Protecting Consumers from Financial Fraud and Scams in the Pandemic Recovery Economy," August 3, 2021
- Full committee hearing, "American Rescue Plan: Shots in Arms and Money in Pockets," March 25, 2021

Joint Economic Committee

- Report, "New Data and Studies Confirm the Enormous Economic Benefits Provided by the Expanded Child Tax Credit," April 14, 2022
- Report, "Update: Six Months of Advance CTC Payments Have Dramatically Reduced Childhood Poverty and Improved Family Finances," December 14, 2021
- Report, "Child Tax Credits Should Promote Work, Not Undermine It," November 2, 2021
- Hearing, "Building Back Better: Raising Revenue to Invest in Shared Prosperity," October 6, 2021

Appendix C. IRS and Treasury Resources on the ARPA-Expanded Child Credit for 2021

Embedded hyperlinks in the appendices of this report are not visible in the PDF version of this document. Please refer to the HTML version of this report available on crs.gov to view these links.

IRS Resources for Taxpayers

- All information from the IRS on the child tax credit and the advance payments of the child tax credit—including Frequently Asked Questions, Tax Tips, Outreach Assistance, and news releases—can be found on the IRS resource page.

- *Non-filer Portal:* Eligible non-filers can use the IRS Child Tax Credit Non-filer Sign Up Tool to receive advance payments.[35]
- Code for America, in partnership with the IRS and Treasury, has launched a simplified portal at GetCTC.org (the portal works on mobile devices and is also available in Spanish).[36] Data on returns processed from this portal can be found on the GetCTC Partner Dashboard.
- *Update Portal*: Eligible taxpayers who want to update information with respect to advance payments or opt out of advance payments can use the IRS Child Tax Credit Update Portal.

Treasury Data on Advance Payments

Treasury has provided data on advance payments of the 2021 child credit by state:

- Advance Child Tax Credit Payments Disbursed December 2021, by State
- Advance Child Tax Credit Payments Disbursed November 2021, by State
- Advance Child Tax Credit Payments Disbursed October 2021, by State
- Advance Child Tax Credit Payments Disbursed September 2021, by State
- Advance Child Tax Credit Payments Disbursed August 2021, by State
- Advance Child Tax Credit Payments Disbursed July 2021, by State

---

[35] Links to all IRS tools for the advanced payment of the 2021 child credit can be found at https://www.irs.gov/credits-deductions/advance-child-tax-credit-payments-in-2021.

[36] See Chris Riotta, "Treasury taps Code for America for tax credit tool," *FCW*, August 13, 2021, https://fcw.com/ articles/2021/08/13/getctc-code-for-america-treasury.aspx?m=1. "Wally Adeyemo, deputy secretary of the Treasury, said in a statement on Friday the agency was working with Congress to create a permanent signup tool allowing America's most vulnerable families—those who do not earn enough income to file taxes annually—to access the expanded CTC program. The administration said it would partner with the civic technology non-profit Code for America to release an initial version of that platform in order to more quickly enroll new families."

Treasury Office of Tax Analysis (OTA) Studies

- Treasury's Office of Tax Analysis (OTA) has estimated the number of taxpayers who would benefit from the child credit in 2022, under current law (i.e., the ARPA changes expiring at the end of 2021), and under the Biden Administration's proposal (i.e., if the ARPA changes were in effect in 2022).

These analyses include estimates of the number of taxpayers that will benefit, the total dollar amount of the benefit, and the average benefit per taxpayer broken down by adjusted gross income (AGI). Detail on the Biden Administration proposal can be found in the FY2022 Treasury Greenbook.

IRS National Taxpayer Advocate

- Annual Report to Congress, 2021 includes assessments of the IRS's administration of the Advance Child Tax Credit ("AdvCTC").
- The IRS National Taxpayer Advocate published three blog posts in late August 2021 on the advanced monthly payments of the ARPA-expanded child credit.
- "Advance Child Tax Credit: What You Should Know: Part I," which "addresse[s] ten things that individuals should know about the Advance Child Tax Credit (AdvCTC)";
- "Advance Child Tax Credit: What You Should Know: Part II," which "focus[es] on issues experienced by taxpayers with Individual Taxpayer Identification Numbers (ITINs) and the issuance of paper checks versus direct deposits for the August payment"; and
- "Advance Child Tax Credit: What You Should Know: Part III," which "explain(s) how AdvCTC tools work, including ID.me, and will discuss the struggles some taxpayers are facing in receiving their AdvCTC."

Treasury Inspector General for Tax Administration

- Report, "The Child Tax Credit Update Portal Was Successfully Deployed, but Security and Process Improvements Are Needed," May 18, 2022

- Report, "American Rescue Plan Act: Implementation of Premium Tax Credit Provisions," May 2, 2022
- Report, "Results of the 2021 Filing Season," March 9, 2022

Treasury and IRS Press Releases

- IR-2022-105, May 6, 2022, "IRS provides guidance for residents of Puerto Rico to claim the Child Tax Credit"
- IR-2022-96, April 27, 2022, "IRS revises Tax Year 2021/Filing Season 2022 frequently asked questions for the Child Tax Credit"
- IR-2022-53, March 8, 2022, "IRS revised 2021 Child Tax Credit and Advance Child Tax Credit Payments frequently asked questions"
- IR-2022-22, February 1, 2022, "IRS revises FAQs for 2021 Child Tax Credit and Advance Child Tax Credit Payments"
- Treasury press release jy0590, February 8, 2022, "Treasury Janet L. Yellen at the White House Child Tax Credit and Earned Income Tax Credit Day of Action"
- Treasury press release jy0567, January 24, 2022, "Treasury and the White House Announce New ChildTaxCredit.gov to Help Families Access the Full Child Tax Credit"
- IR-2022-10, January 11, 2022, "IRS updates FAQs for 2021 Child Tax Credit and Advance Child Tax Credit Payments"
- IR-2021-255, December 22, 2021, "IRS issues information letters to Advance Child Tax Credit recipients and recipients of the third round of Economic Impact Payments; taxpayers should hold onto letters to help the 2022 Filing Season experience"
- IR-2021-249, December 15, 2021, "Families will soon receive their December advance Child tax Credit payment; those not receiving payments may claim any missed payments on the upcoming 2021 tax return"
- Treasury press release jy0533, December 15, 2021, "Treasury and IRS Disburse Sixth Monthly Child Tax Credit to Families of 61 Million Children"
- IR 2021-243, December 7, 2021, "Get ready for taxes: What's new and what to consider when filing in 2022"

- IR-2021-235, November 23, 2021, "Child Tax Credit payments: IRS online portal now available in Spanish; Nov. 29 is last day for families to opt out or make other changes"
- Treasury press release jy0482, November 15, 2021, "Treasury and IRS Disburse Fifth Month of Advance Child Tax Credit Payments"
- IR-2021-222, November 12, 2021, "IRS: Families will soon receive November advance Child Tax Credit payments; time running out to sign up online to get an advance payment in December"
- IR 2021-218, November 9, 2021, "IRS updates 2021 Child Tax Credit and Advance Child Tax Credit Payments Frequently Asked Questions"
- IR-2021-211, October 29, 2021, "Child Tax Credit: Families with income changes must enter them in IRS online portal on Monday to impact Nov. 15 payment; Spanish version coming in late November"
- IR-2021-201, October 15, 2021, "IRS: Families now receiving October Child Tax Credit payments; still time for eligible families to sign up for advance payments"
- Treasury press release jy0411, October 15, 2021, "Treasury and IRS Disburse Fourth Month of Advance Child Tax Credit Payments"
- IR-2021-188, September 15, 2021, "IRS: Families now receiving September Child Tax Credit payments"
- Treasury readout jy0341, September 1, 2021, "Readout: Treasury, White House, and Code for America Host Call to Discuss Collaboration and Launch of New Bilingual and Mobile-Friendly Sign-Up Tool for Advance Child Credit"IR-2021- 171, August 20, 2021, "Child Tax Credit: New update address feature available with IRS online portal; make other changes by August 30 for September payment"
- IR-2021-169, August 13, 2021, "IRS: Families now receiving August Child Tax Credit payments; still time for low-income families to sign up"
- Treasury press release jy0322, August 13, 2021, "Treasury and IRS Disburse Second Month of Advance Child Tax Credit Payments"
- IR-2021-156, July 21, 2021, "IRS holds additional weekend events July 23-24 to help people with Child Tax Credit payments and Economic Impact Payments"

- IR-2021-153, July 15, 2021, "IRS: Monthly Child Tax Credit payments begin"
- Treasury press release jy0274, July 15, 2021, "Treasury and IRS Announce Families of Nearly 60 Million Children Receive $15 Billion in First Payments of Expanded and Newly Advanceable Child Tax Credit"
- IR-2021-150, July 12, 2021, "IRS: Online Child Tax Credit eligibility tool now available in Spanish; other multi-lingual materials help families see if they qualify for advance payments"
- IR-2021-146, July 7, 2021, "IRS holds special weekend events to help people who don't normally file taxes get Child Tax Credit payments and Economic Impact Payments"
- IR-2021-143, June 30, 2021, "IRS: Families receiving monthly Child Tax Credit payments can now update their direct deposit information"
- IR-2021-133, June 24, 2021, "IRS online tool helps families see if they qualify for the Child Tax Credit; one of three tools now available for the upcoming advance payments"
- IR-2021-132, June 23, 2021, "IRS and community partners team up to provide free tax help for families to get advance Child Tax Credit payments and Economic Impact Payments"
- IR-2021-130, June 22, 2021, "IRS announces two new online tools to help families manage Child Tax Credit payments"
- IR-2021-129, June 14, 2021, "IRS unveils online tool to help low-income families register for monthly Child Tax Credit payments"
- Treasury press release jy0227, June 14, 2021, "Treasury and IRS Announce New Online Tool to Help Families Register for Monthly Child Tax Credit"
- IR-2021-124, June 7, 2021, "IRS sending letters to more than 36 million families who may qualify for monthly Child Tax Credits; payments start July 15"
- IR-2021-116, May 19, 2021, "IRS urges groups to share information to help those without permanent addresses get benefits including Economic Impact Payments, upcoming advance Child Tax Credit"
- IR-2021-113, May 17, 2021, "IRS, Treasury announce families of 88 percent of children in the U.S. to automatically receive monthly payment of refundable Child Tax Credit"

- Treasury press release jy0177, May 17, 2021, "Treasury and IRS Announce Families of 88% of Children in the U.S. to Automatically Receive Monthly Payment of Refundable Child Tax Credit"
- IR-2021-106, May 11, 2021, "IRS offers overview of tax provisions in American Rescue Plan; retroactive tax benefits help many people now preparing 2020 returns"
- Treasury press release jy0069, March 18, 2021, "FACT SHEET: The American Rescue Plan Will Deliver Immediate Economic Relief to Families"

Appendix D. Steps to Reconcile Excess Advance Payments of the Child Credit Due to an Incorrect Number of Qualifying Children

Table D-1 outlines the steps a taxpayer would take to reconcile any excess advance payments of the child credit with the credit they are eligible to claim on their 2021 income tax return. In addition, Table D-1 provides an illustration of how the safe harbor would work. ARPA provides a safe harbor in cases where a taxpayer receives excess payments due to a difference in the number of children between the data used to estimate and advance the credit (generally 2020 tax data) and the number of children they claim on their 2021 tax return. In cases where excess payments are due to large changes in income between 2020 and 2021, changes in marital status, or changes in principal place of abode, no safe harbor applies.

Table D-1. Steps for reconciling advance payments of the child credit with theactual credit on 2021 incometax returns

For Excess Payments That Occur Due to an Incorrect Number of Qualifying Children

Steps to Reconcile Excess Advance Payments of the 2021 Child Credit	Example 1 Single parent with 2 qualifying young children in 2020 and 1 young child/0 older children in 2021	Example 2 Single parent with 2 qualifying young children in 2020 and 0 qualifying children in 2021
Step 1: Determine "excess" credit.	For example: If the taxpayer's income is under $112,500 (in 2020 and 2021), then:	For example: If the taxpayer's income is under $112,500 (in 2020 and 2021), then:

Steps to Reconcile Excess Advance Payments of the 2021 Child Credit	Example 1 Single parent with 2 qualifying young children in 2020 and 1 young child/0 older children in 2021	Example 2 Single parent with 2 qualifying young children in 2020 and 0 qualifying children in 2021
A. Calculate the total credit the taxpayer is eligible for on their 2021 return.	A. Total 2021 credit: $3,600	A. Total 2021 credit: $0
B. Calculate the total amount they were advanced in 2021 (based on 2020 information).	B. Total amount advanced: $3,600 (50% of $7,200)	B. Total amount advanced: $3,600 (50% of $7,200)
C. Subtract the advance (B) from the total they are actually eligible for (A). Negative sign indicates excess credit. Positive sign indicates additional amount to be claimed with return. Note that throughout the remainder of the table, excess credit will be displayed as a positive number for ease of calculations.	C. Excess credit: $0 (= $3,600-$3,600)	C. Excess credit: -$3,600 (= $0-$3,600)
If B is greater than A, the taxpayer will have received an excess credit (the difference between A and B). In cases where the taxpayer has received an excess credit, the taxpayer may need to repay some or all of the excess (continue on to the steps below).	The difference between the actual credit they are eligible for in 2021 and the advanced credit is $0. The taxpayer will effectively not receive a credit when they file their 2021 return, because they already received it as the advanced credit.	
Step 2. Determine maximum safe harbor amount.	Not applicable, no excess payment.	
A. Determine net difference between (i) Number of qualifying children used to determine advanced credit and (ii) number eligible for actual credit in 2021.		A. The net difference between (i) the number of qualifying children from a 2020 tax return (2 children) used to determine the advanced credit and (ii) the number of children claimed on a 2021 tax return (0 children) is 2 children.
B. Multiply (A) by $2,000.		B. 2 *children x* $2,000 = **$4,** 000
Step 3: Phaseout maximum safe harbor, if applicable. Depending on income and filing status in 2021, the maximum safe harbor may be subject to reduction.		Not applicable, no excess payment.

Table D-1. (Continued)

Steps to Reconcile Excess Advance Payments of the 2021 Child Credit	Example 1 Single parent with 2 qualifying young children in 2020 and 1 young child/0 older children in 2021	Example 2 Single parent with 2 qualifying young children in 2020 and 0 qualifying children in 2021
No phaseout: If 2021 income is less than or equal to the following thresholds, the safe harbor is not reduced. $40,000 single filers[a] $50,000 head of household filers $60,000 married joint filers[b]		No phaseout: If a single person in 2021 (i.e., single filer in 2021) has income of $40,000 or less, their safe harbor is not reduced (i.e., it equals the maximum safe harbor amount).
Phaseout: The safe harbor is reduced ratably (i.e., proportionally) if 2021 income is between $40,000-$80,000 single filers[a] $50,000-$100,000 head of household filers $60,000-$120,000 married joint filers[b]		Phaseout: If a single person in 2021 has income between $40,000 and $80,000, the maximum safe harbor phases out ratably in relation to income in the phaseout range. For example, if income were $60,000 in 2021, the maximum safe harbor would be reduced by: $60,000−$40,000 [] = 50% $80,000−$40,000 A $4,000 safe harbor reduced by 50% would equal $2,000.
No safe harbor if 2021 income is greater than or equal to $80,000 single filers[a] $100,000 head of household filers $120,000 married joint filers[b]		No safe harbor: If a single person in 2021 has $80,000 or more in income, their safe harbor amount is $0.
Step 4: Calculate the amount of any excess credit that needs to be recaptured (or paid back) on 2021 tax return: Subtract the safe harbor amount (determined after step 3) from the total amount of excess credit (determined in step 1) in 2021.	Not applicable, no excess payment.	If income in 2021 for a single person is: Under $44,000: Payback amount is $0 since the excess credit of $3,600 is less than the $4,000 safe harbor when income is $40,000 or less. Between $40,000 and $44,000 the safe harbor gradually declines but is still greater than or equal to $3,600.

Steps to Reconcile Excess Advance Payments of the 2021 Child Credit	Example 1 Single parent with 2 qualifying young children in 2020 and 1 young child/0 older children in 2021	Example 2 Single parent with 2 qualifying young children in 2020 and 0 qualifying children in 2021
If the safe harbor amount is greater than or equal to excess payment, none of the advanced amount needs to be paid back.		$44,000+: Payback amount equals $3,600 excess credit minus safe harbor until income is $80,000 or more, at which point the total excess credit of $3,600 needs to be repaid. If income was $60,000, the safe harbor would be $2,000, the single person would need to pay back $3,600-$2,000 or $1,600 with their 2021 tax return. If income was $80,000 or more, the safe harbor would be $0, the single person would need to pay back all $3,600 in excess credit with their 2021 return.

Source: CRS analysis of P.L. 117-2.

Notes: Assumes advanced payment that would be received in 2021 would be based on 2020 income and family structure (number of qualifying children and marital status). Broadly, income is assumed to be the same between 2020 and 2021 to isolate the impact of a changing number of qualifying children.

[a] This includes married taxpayers who file separately.

[b] This includes taxpayers who file as surviving spouses.

Appendix E. The Child Credit and Residents of U.S. Territories

Below is a summary comparing child credit receipt among residents of the territories, before ARPA, in 2021 under current law as amended by ARPA, and after 2021 under current law as amended by ARPA.

Table E-1. Child tax credit for residents of the territories

Territory	2021 Under Prior Law (Before ARPA)	2021 Under Current Law (as amended by ARPA)	Post 2021 Under Current Law (as amended by ARPA)
Puerto Rico (PR)	PR did not have a child credit under its own internal revenue laws. PR residents with three or more qualifying children received the ACTC under the alternative formula.[a] Under this formula, the ACTC effectively equaled 7.65% of earned income up to the maximum ACTC of $1,400 per qualifying child. Residents with fewer than three qualifying children did not receive the ACTC. PR residents with three or more children claimed the federal ACTC amount by filing a return with the IRS directly. They did not receive the ACTC via their territorial tax system.	PR does not have a child credit under its own internal revenue laws. PR residents are eligible for the fully refundable ARPA- expanded child credit (up to $3,600 per young child or up to $3,000 per older child). PR residents will claim the total 2021 federal credit amount by filing a 2021 return with the IRS directly.[b] The federal advance payment program of the ARPA- expanded credit does not apply to PR residents.	PR does not have a child credit under its own internal revenue laws. PR residents will be eligible for the ACTC using the alternative formula. The prior- law limitation of the alternative formula to only families with three or more children is eliminated. Effectively, PR residents are eligible for a credit equal to 7.65% of earned income up to the maximum ACTC per child. From 2022-2025 the maximum is $1,400 per qualifying child. Beginning in 2026, the maximum amount of the ACTC is $1,000 per qualifying child. PR residents will claim the federal ACTC amount by filing a return with the IRS directly.
American Samoa (AS)	AS appears to have a child credit under its own internal revenue laws that reflects the parameters of the federal child credit in effect in 2000. (In 2000, the child credit was $500 per qualifying child and refundable for families with three of more children under the alternative formula.) However, it is unclear in practical terms precisely how and to what extent residents of American Samoa received	If AS has a plan approved by the Treasury Secretary to distribute the ARPA-expanded child credit amounts to its residents, Treasury is directed to cover the total cost of the ARPA-expanded child credit as if American Samoa had a mirror-code tax system. In addition, if AS chooses to provide advance payments of the 2021 credit in a manner similar to the federal program to advance the	If AS has a plan approved by the Treasury Secretary to distribute child credit amounts to its residents, Treasury is directed to cover the total cost of child credit—the refundable portion (i.e., the ACTC) and nonrefundable portion—as if American Samoa had a mirror-code tax system. From 2022 to 2025, the maximum child credit amounts are $2,000 per child, of which $1,400 may be received as the refundable portion of the credit (i.e., the

Territory	2021 Under Prior Law (Before ARPA)	2021 Under Current Law (as amended by ARPA)	Post 2021 Under Current Law (as amended by ARPA)
	the child credit under their own territorial tax system.[c] Available information suggests that residents with three or more children received the ACTC as calculated under the alternative formula. The IRS Chief Financial Officer (IRS- CFO) covered the costs of the ACTC under the alternative formula by making an aggregate payment to the territorial government. The exact manner and timing in which the territorial government then made direct payments to its residents is unclear.[d]	2021 credit, Treasury will provide an additional $300,000 for administrative costs. If no such plan is established and approved, AS residents can apply for the ARPA-expanded credit by filing a tax return directly with the IRS, like residents of PR.	ACTC). From 2026 and thereafter, the amounts are $1,000 per qualifying child, of which $1,000 per qualifying child may be received as the ACTC. For these purposes, the ACTC may be calculated under the earned income formula, which is generally more generous than the alternative formula.[e] If no such plan is established and approved, AS residents can apply directly with the IRS for the ACTC calculated under the alternative formula, like residents of PR. In this case, the prior-law limitation of the alternative formula to only families with three or more qualifying children does not apply (i.e., the same treatment as residents of Puerto Rico).
Mirror- Code Territories (CNMI, Guam, USVI).	Mirror-code territories by definition have a child tax credit identical to the federal child tax credit in their own territorial tax code. Hence, residents of mirror-code territories may be eligible for a child credit identical to the credit in the Internal Revenue Code (IRC). However, it is unclear in practical terms whether and to what extent residents of mirror-code territories actually receive a credit under their own territorial tax laws.[f] Available information suggests that residents with three or more children received the ACTC under the alternative formula. The IRS-CFO covered the total cost of the ACTC	Mirror-code territories by definition have a child tax credit identical to the federal child tax credit in their own territorial tax code. Residents of mirror-code territories are eligible for the fully refundable ARPA-expanded child credit (up to $3,600 per young child or $3,000 per older child). Residents of the mirror-code territories will claim the benefit on their territorial tax return. The law directs Treasury to cover the total cost of the ARPA-expanded child credit as paid out by territorial governments In addition, if a mirror-code territory chooses to provide advance payments of the 2021 credit	Mirror-code territories by definition have a child tax credit identical to the federal child tax credit in their own territorial tax code. Hence, residents of mirror- code territories may be eligible for a child credit identical to the credit in the Internal Revenue Code (IRC). From 2022 to 2025, the maximum child credit amounts are $2,000 per qualifying child, of which $1,400 may be received as the refundable portion of the credit (i.e., the ACTC). From 2026 and thereafter, the amounts are $1,000 per qualifying child, of which $1,000 per qualifying child may be received as the ACTC. The ACTC may be

Table E-1. (Continued)

Territory	2021 Under Prior Law (Before ARPA)	2021 Under Current Law (as amended by ARPA)	Post 2021 Under Current Law (as amended by ARPA)
	under the alternative formula by making aggregate payments to the territorial governments. The exact manner and timing in which the territorial governments then made direct payments to their residents is unclear.	in a manner similar to the federal program to advance the credit, Treasury will provide an additional $300,000 for administrative costs.	calculated under the earned income formula, which his generally more generous than the alternative formula.[e] Residents of the mirror-code territories will claim the benefit on their territorial tax return. The law directs Treasury to cover the total cost of the child credit (both refundable portion [i.e., the ACTC] and nonrefundable portion) as paid out by the territorial government.

Sources: CRS Analysis of Internal Revenue Code (IRC) §24, P.L. 117-2, and JCX-3-21.

Notes: This reflects current law and practice and is subject to change for legislative activity, as well as additional information. These summaries assume that residents of these territories generally only file a territorial tax return with their local tax authority, and aside from claiming the ACTC, are not required to file a U.S. federal income tax return. In cases where taxpayers are required to file a U.S. federal income tax return, they may be eligible to claim the child credit on that return.

[a] Under IRC §24(d)(1)(B)(ii), the alternative formula available to taxpayers with three or more qualifying children is equal to the difference in the employee's share of Social Security taxes and Medicare taxes and their EITC. Since territorial residents are generally ineligible for the EITC, the alternative formula is effectively 7.65% of earned income (i.e., W-2 wages, railroad retirement compensation, and self- employment income) up to the maximum ACTC. The maximum ACTC in 2021 before ARPA was $1,400 per qualifying child and is scheduled to remain at that level from 2022 to 2025. Beginning in 2026, the maximum ACTC is scheduled to be $1,000 per qualifying child.

[b] IRS Form 1040-SS or Form 1040-PR.

[c] While American Samoa's internal revenue laws may reflect the credit in place in the Internal Revenue Code for 2000, other forms available on the American Samoan website indicate that eligible residents may be able to claim the ACTC under the alternative formula if they have three or more children. See IRS, Bona Fide Residents of American Samoa—Tax Credits, https://www.irs.gov/ individuals/bona-fide-residents-of-american- samoa-tax-credits, and see schedule 8812 for AS Form 390 for 2020, available at https://www.americansamoa.gov/tax-office. In addition, a 2019 local news article reported that the maximum amount of the ACTC increased to $1,400 per child beginning in 2018, up from $1,000 per child, reflecting changes made to the child credit as

part of P.L. 115-97. See Talanei, "Additional Child Tax Credit is now $1,400," January 31, 2019, https://www.talanei.com/2019/01/31/additional-child-tax-credit-is-now- 1400/.

[d] For example, an April 2019 American Samoan news article about delays in receiving American Samoan tax refunds from 2018 returns stated, "Just in time for Flag Day and Easter, tax refund checks—for those who qualify—will be released today; but only the locally funded ones, it does not include the Additional Child Tax Credit (ACTC), which is funded by the U.S. Internal Revenue Service For taxpayers expecting tax refunds including the ACTC, 'please be informed that all are on hold for now as we await a decision' from the IRS and the US Treasury Department." Fili Sagapolutele, "Tax refunds to be issued today—but no Additional Child Tax Credit yet," Samoa News, April 12, 2019, https://www.samoanews.com/local-news/tax- refunds-be-issued-today-no-additional-child-tax-credit.

[e] Under current law, the earned income formula is 15% of earned income above $2,500 up to a maximum of $1,400 per child (this amount is adjusted for inflation). This formula is in effect from 2022 through 2025. Beginning in 2026, the formula is scheduled to be 15% of earned income above $3,000 up to a maximum of $1,000 per child.

[f] For example, even if a territorial resident were eligible for the full value of the child credit (both the refundable portion [i.e., ACTC] and the nonrefundable portion) under their own territorial income tax law, the territorial government may have recaptured some or all that credit by enacting an excise tax credit.

Chapter 3

How Would the Child Credit Be Calculated for 2023 Under H.R. 7024?*

Margot L. Crandall-Hollick

H.R. 7024, ordered to be reported by the House Ways and Means committee on January 19, includes several provisions that would expand the child tax credit for low-income families by increasing the refundable portion of the credit. The refundable portion of the child credit is sometimes called the additional child tax credit or ACTC. These changes include the following:

1) The ACTC would be calculated per child: After the ACTC amount is calculated undercurrent law (15% of earned income above $2,500), it would then be multiplied by the number of children, effectively phasing in the credit faster for families with more children (i.e., a 30% phase-in rate for two children), capped by the maximum ACTC (seebelow).
2) The maximum amount of the ACTC would increase: The ACTC maximum would rise from $1,600 to $1,800 per child in 2023 and from $1,700 to $1,900 per child in 2024 and equal $2,000 (adjusted for inflation) in 2025.
3) Taxpayers could use prior-year earned income to calculate the ACTC: Taxpayers could calculate the ACTC using their prior-year earned income if their current-year earned income was less than their prior-year earned income. This would apply for 2024 and 2025. Hence, in 2024, a taxpayer could elect to use their earned income for

* This is an edited, reformatted and augmented version of Congressional Research Service Publication No. IN12306, dated January 23, 2024.

In: A Closer Look at the Child Tax Credit
Editor: Philip Palmer
ISBN: 979-8-89113-601-4

2023 to calculate their ACTC if that amount was more than their 2024 earned income (under current law, they could only use their 2024 earned income for this calculation).

Selected Child Credit Parameters

Under Current Law and H.R. 7024

Parameter	Current Law	H.R. 7024
Maximum credit	**$2,000** per child 0-16 years old	**$2,000** per child 0-16 years old (adjusted for inflation for 2024 & 2025)
Maximum ACTC The additional child tax credit (ACTC) is the refundable portion of the credit available to those with no income tax liability. The ACTC is the primary mode by which many low-income taxpayers receive some or all of the child credit.	**$1,600** per child 0-16 years old for 2023 **$1,700** per child 0-16 years old for 2024 *This amount is statutorily $1,400, adjusted for inflation*	**$1,800** per child 0-16 years old for 2023 **$1,900** per child 0-16 years old for 2024 **$2,000** per child 0-16 years old for 2025 (this amount would be adjusted for inflation for 2025)
ACTC formula	**15%** of earned income above **$2,500** capped at the **maximum ACTC** per child x number of children	**15%** of earned income above **$2,500 multiplied by the number of children** capped at the **maximum ACTC** per child x number of children

Source: CRS based on IRC Section 24 and H.R. 7024 (as introduced)

Notes: Current law reflects temporary changes to the child credit made by P.L. 115-97, commonly referred to as the Tax Cuts and Jobs Act (TCJA). In addition, under H.R. 7024, taxpayers could calculate the ACTC in 2024 and 2025 using their prior-year earned income if their current-year earned income was less than their prior-year earned income.

To illustrate the potential impact of these changes, Tables 1-3 provide examples of how the credit would be calculated under current law and H.R. 7024 for hypothetical low-income taxpayers for 2023 (i.e., on 2023 tax returns). Broadly, these illustrate that the lowest-income taxpayers with one child and moderate- income families will likely see no additional benefit for 2023 (Table 2 and Table 3), and that low-income families with two or more children and sufficient earnings are likely to receive a larger credit for 2023 (Table 1).

Table 1. Example 1 of child creditamounts for 2023 under H.R. 7024

Calculation Step	Current Law	H.R. 7024
Married couple (joint filers) with $20,000 of earned income and two children		
1. Calculate the maximum child creditper taxpayer. This is the overall child credit cap.	$4,000 = $2,000 x 2 children	Same as current law
2. Calculate the maximum amount of the child credit that can be received by low-income taxpayers who owe $0 in taxes. This is the additional child tax credit (ACTC) cap.	$3,200 = $1,600 x 2 children	$3,600 = $1,800 x 2 children
3. Calculate the ACTC under the earned income formula.	$2,625 = 15% of earned income greater than $2,500	$5,250 = 15% of earned income greater than $2,500 multiplied by the number of children (i.e., multiplied by 2)
4. Pick the lesser of the amounts calculated in steps 2 and 3.	$2,625 because $2,625 < $3,200	$3,600 because $3,600 < $5,250
5. If the taxpayer has any income tax liability, increase the total credit amount by that liability until it reaches the cap in step 1. If income tax liability + ACTC exceeds the cap in step 1, the credit will equal the max credit in step 1, with the refundable portion of the credit (ACTC) recalculated as the total	Not applicable. $0 in income tax liability so all of the child credit is received as the ACTC.	Same as current law
credit minus income tax liability.		
6. Final credit amount	$2,625 (all as the ACTC)	$3,600 (all as the ACTC)

Source: IRC Section 24 and H.R. 7024 (as introduced).

Notes: All income is assumed to be earned income and earned income is assumed to equal adjusted gross income (i.e., no above-the-line deductions). The taxpayer is assumed to claim the standard deduction and no other nonrefundable credits aside from the child tax credit. Taxpayers and children are assumed to meet all eligibility requirements.

Table 2. Example 2 of child credit amounts for 2023 under H.R. 7024

Calculation Step	Current Law	H.R. 7024
Single parent (head of household filer) with $10,000 of earned income and one child		
1. Calculate the maximum child creditper taxpayer. This is the overall child credit cap.	$2,000=$2,000 x 1 child	Same as current law
2. Calculate the maximum amount of the child credit that can be received bylow-income taxpayers who owe $0 in taxes. This is the additional child tax credit (ACTC) cap.	$1,600 = $1,600 x 1 child	$1,800 = $1,800 x 1 child
3. Calculate the ACTC under theearned income formula	$1,125 = 15% of earned income greaterthan $2,500	$1,125 = 15% of earned income greaterthan $2,500 multiplied by the number of children (i.e., multiplied by 1)
4. Pick the lesser of the amounts calculated in steps 2 and 3	$1,125 because $1,125 < $1,600	$1,125 because $1,125 < $1,800
5. If the taxpayer has any income tax liability, increase the total credit amount by that liability until it reaches the cap in step 1. If income tax liability + ACTC exceeds the cap in step 1, the credit will equal the max credit in step 1, with the refundable portion of the credit (ACTC) recalculated as the total credit minus income tax liability.	Not applicable. $0 in income tax liability so all of the child credit is received as the ACTC.	Same as current law
6. Final credit amount	$1,125 (all as the ACTC)	$1,125 (all as the ACTC)

Source: IRC Section 24 and H.R. 7024 (as introduced).

Notes: All income is assumed to be earned income and earned income is assumed to equal adjusted gross income (i.e., no above-the-line deductions). The taxpayer is assumed to claim the standard deduction and no other nonrefundable credits aside from the child tax credit. Taxpayers and children are assumed to meet all eligibility requirements.

Table 3. Example 3 of child credit amounts for 2023 under H.R. 7024

Calculation Step	Current Law	H.R. 7024
Married couple (married filing jointly) with $40,000 of earned income and three children		
1. Calculate the maximum child creditper taxpayer. This is the overall child credit cap.	$6,000=$2,000 x 3 children	Same as current law
2. Calculate the maximum amount of the child credit that can be received bylow-income	$4,800=$1,600 x 3 children	$5,400=$1,800 x 3 children
taxpayers who owe $0 in taxes. This is the additional child tax credit (ACTC) cap.		
3. Calculate the ACTC under theearned income formula	$5,625=15% of earned income greaterthan $2,500	$16,875=15% of earned income greater than $2,500 multiplied by the number of children (i.e., multiplied by 3)
4. Pick the lesser of the amounts calculated in steps 2 and 3	$4,800 because $4,800 < $5,625	$5,400 because $5,400 < $16,875
5. If the taxpayer has any income tax liability, increase the total credit amount by that liability until it reaches the cap in step 1. If income tax liability + ACTC exceeds the cap in step 1, the credit will equal the max credit in step 1, with the refundable portion of the credit (ACTC) recalculated as the total credit minus income tax liability.	$1,230 in income tax liability (calculated by CRS based on income and other characteristics of example tax unit). Hence, the taxpayer will receive a $6,000 credit of which $1,230 will offset income taxes (nonrefundable portion) and $4,770 will be received as the ACTC (refundable portion).	Same as current law
6. Final credit amount	$6,000 ($1,230 as nonrefundable portion, $4,770 as ACTC)	$6,000 ($1,230 as nonrefundable portion, $4,770 as ACTC)

Source: IRC Section 24 and H.R. 7024 (as introduced).

Notes: All income is assumed to be earned income and earned income is assumed to equal adjusted gross income (i.e., no above-the-line deductions). The taxpayer is assumed to claim the standard deduction and no other nonrefundable credits aside from the child tax credit. Taxpayers and children are assumed to meet all eligibility requirements.

Chapter 4

The Child Tax Credit: How It Works and Who Receives It*

Margot L. Crandall-Hollick

Summary

This report provides an overview of the child taxcredit under current law, including a review of temporary changes made to the credit by P.L. 115-97 (often referred to as the TaxCuts and Jobs Act or TCJA).

The child tax credit allows eligible taxpayers to reduce their federal income taxliability by up to$2,000 per qualifying child. The maximum amount of the credit is equal to the number of qualifying children a taxpayer has multiplied by $2,000. If their tax liability is less than the value of their child tax credit, they may be eligible for a refundable credit calculated using the earned income formula. Under this formula, a family is eligible for a refund equal to 15% of their earnings in excess of $2,500, up to $1,400 per child, the maximum amount of the refundable portion of the credit. The credit phases out for unmarried parents with income over $200,000 and married couples with income over $400,000. Many of these parameters are scheduled to expire at the end of 2025 under P.L. 115-97. The amount of the credit by income for a taxpayer with one qualifying child is illustrated below.

* This is an edited, reformatted and augmented version of Congressional Research Service Publication No. R41873, updated January 12, 2021.

In: A Closer Look at the Child Tax Credit
Editor: Philip Palmer
ISBN: 979-8-89113-601-4

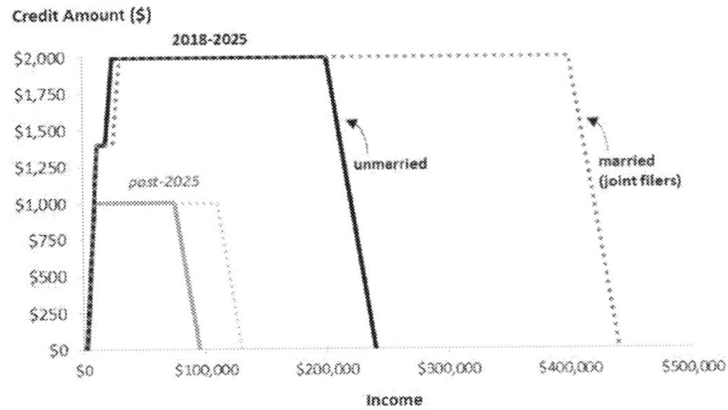

Source: See Figure 1.

The child tax credit was created in 1997 by the Taxpayer Relief Act of 1997 (P.L. 105-34) to help ease the financial burden that families incur when they have children. Like other taxcredits, the child taxcredit reduces taxliability dollar for dollar of the value of the credit. Initially the child taxcredit was a nonrefundable credit for most families. A nonrefundable taxcre dit can only reduce a taxpayer's income taxliability to zero. In contrast, a refundable taxcredit can exceed a taxpayer's income tax liability, providing a cash payment to low- and some moderate-income taxpayers who owe little or no income tax.

The child tax credit has undergone significant changes over time. Most recently, at the end of 2017, Congress expanded thecredit as part of the TCJA (P.L. 115-97). The TCJA doubled the maximum credit amount and more than tripled the income level at which the credit begins to phase out. Additionally, although comparatively more modest, changes were made to the refundable portion of the credit as well, including increasing the refundable credit amount from$1,000 to $1,400 per child and lowering the refundability threshold from$3,000 to $2,500. These changes are scheduled to be in effect from 2018 through the end of2025.

Data from the IRS indicate that the total dollar amount of the child taxcredit has increased significantly since enactment from approximately $23 billion in 1998 to $118 billion in 2018, with the largest increase coming after the TCJA expansions, as illustrated below.

The Tax Policy Center (TPC) estimated the distribution of the child taxcredit by income level for 2019 under current law (including the changes made by the TCJA, as illustrated in the table below). As illustrated in these estimates, the majority of taxpayers with children receivedthe child taxcredit. Slightly less than half of the lowest-income taxpayers with children received the credit and about a quarter of the highest-income taxpayers with children received the credit. TPC estimated that taxpayers with income between $100,000 and $200,000 received the largest credit on average, of more than $3,000.

Taxpayers with children and income under $20,000 received a credit of less than $1,000 on average.

Total Real Child Tax Credit Dollars, 1998-2018

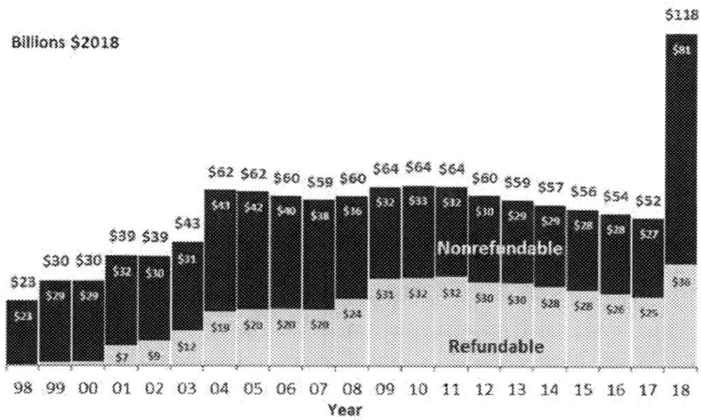

Source: See Figure 2.

Taxpayers with children, by income level in 2019

Income Level	% of All Taxpayers	% of Taxpayers whoReceive theChild Credit	Child Tax Credit as % of After-Tax Income	Average ChildCredit per Taxpayer
Less than $10,000	2.4	47.8	3.5	$250
$10,000-$20,000	8.5	68.0	4.8	$850
$20,000-$30,000	10.4	84.8	5.7	$1,520
$30,000-$40,000	8.6	90.8	6.2	$2,160
$40,000-$50,000	6.9	94.3	5.7	$2,450
$50,000-$75,000	13.6	96.4	5.0	$2,790
$75,000-$100,000	9.7	98.8	3.9	$2,980
$100,000-$200,000	23.7	99.5	2.6	$3,040
$200,000-$500,000	13.2	98.2	1.2	$2,790
More than $500,000	2.5	26.9	0.1	$649
All	100	90.2	2.2	$2,370

Source: See Figures 4 and 5.

Introduction

The child tax credit was created in 1997 by the Taxpayer Relief Act of 1997 (P.L. 105-34) to help ease the financial burden that families incur when they have children. Like other tax credits, the child tax credit reduces tax liability dollar for dollar of the value of the credit. Initially the child tax credit was a nonrefundable credit for most families. A nonrefundable tax credit can only reduce a taxpayer's income tax liability to zero, while a refundable tax credit can exceed a taxpayer's income tax liability, providing a cash payment primarily to low-income taxpayers who owe little or no income tax. Over the past 20 years, legislative changes have significantly changed the credit, transforming it from a generally nonrefundable credit available only to the middle and upper-middle class, to a refundable credit that more low-income families are eligible to claim.

Most recently, at the end of 2017, Congress significantly expanded the credit as part of P.L. 115- 97, often referred to as the Tax Cuts and Jobs Act or TCJA.[1] The law significantly expanded eligibility for and the amount of the credit for many higher-income taxpayers, with a more modest expansion for lower-income taxpayers.

This report provides an overview of the credit under current law and also provides some summary data on these benefits. For a complete legislative history of the credit, see CRS Report R45124, The Child Tax Credit: Legislative History, by Margot L. Crandall-Hollick.

Current Law

The child tax credit allows taxpayers to reduce their federal income tax liability (the income taxes owed before tax credits are applied) by up to $2,000 per qualifying child.[2] If the value of the credit exceeds the amount of

---

[1] The original title of the law, the Tax Cuts and Jobs Act, was stricken before final passage because it violated what is known as the Byrd rule, a procedural rule that can be raised in the Senate when bills, like the tax bill, are considered under the process of reconciliation. The actual title of the law is "To provide for reconciliation pursuant to titles II and V of the concurrent resolution on the budget for fiscal year 2018." For more information on the Byrd rule, see CRS Report RL30862, *The Budget Reconciliation Process: The Senate's "Byrd Rule"*, by Bill Heniff Jr., The Budget Reconciliation Process: The Senate's "Byrd Rule", by Bill Heniff Jr.

[2] The child tax credit can be found in Section 24 of the Internal Revenue Code (26 U.S.C. §24).

tax a family owes, the family may be eligible to receive a full or partial refund of the difference. The refundable portion of the credit is sometimes referred to as the additional child tax credit or ACTC. The total amount of their refund is calculated as 15% (the refundability rate) of earnings that exceed $2,500 (the refundability threshold), up to the maximum amount of the refundable portion of the credit ($1,400 per child).

The credit phases out for higher-income taxpayers. The child tax credit can offset a taxpayer's Alternative Minimum Tax (AMT) liability. Currently, the maximum credit per child, refundability threshold, and phaseout thresholds are not indexed for inflation. From 2018 to 2025, the maximum amount of the ACTC is indexed for inflation.

Residents of the U.S. territories generally do not receive the federal child credit, although families residing in the territories with three or more children may receive the ACTC using an alternative formula.[3]

Table 1 provides an overview of key provisions of the child tax credit under current law and howthey will change beginning in 2026, as scheduled under P.L. 115-97.

---

[3] All families (including those in U.S. territories) with three or more qualifying children can calculate the ACTC using an alternative formula. The alternative formula is the amount by which Social Security taxes paid exceed the earned income tax credit (EITC) up to the maximum refundable credit. For most families, the ACTC under the earned income formula will be larger than the ACTC under the alternative formula. However, because residents of U.S. territories are generally ineligible for the EITC, the formula effectively equals the lesser of their Social Security taxes paid or their maximum ACTC. Under the alternative formula, taxpayers with one or two qualifying children are effectively ineligible for the ACTC.

Residents of American Samoa who file an American Samoan tax return may claim the nonrefundable portion of the child tax credit against their America Samoan income taxes. Residents of American Samoa who have three or more qualifying children may also claim the ACTC, but only under the alternative formula. The Treasury covers the cost of any amount of the ACTC provided to America Samoan residents under the alternative formula. Puerto Rico has no child tax credit under Puerto Rican tax law. Puerto Rican residents with three or more qualifying children may claim the federal ACTC under the alternative formula, but only if they file Form 1040 -SS with the Internal Revenue Service (IRS). Residents of mirror-code territories (Guam, the Commonwealth of the Northern Mariana Islands, and the U.S. Virgin Islands) may claim the child credit (including the ACTC) under both the earned income formula and the alternative formula as part of their respective territorial systems. The Treasury covers the cost of any amount of the ACTC provided to mirror-code territory residents under the alternative formula (it is unclear if the Treasury also covers the cost of the ACTC under the earned income formula).

Table 1. Child tax credit parameters under current law

Parameter	(2018-2025)	(2026-)
	Credit Amount	
Maximum Credit Amount	$2,000 per child 0-16 years old.	$1,000 per child 0-16 years old.
Maximum Additional Child Tax Credit (ACTC)	$1,400[a] per child aged 0-16 years old.	$1,000 per child aged 0-16 years old.
Refundability Formula for ACTC	15% of earnings above $2,500, not to exceed the maximum of $1,400 per child.	15% of earnings above $3,000, not to exceed the maximum of $1,000 per child.
Phaseout Threshold	$400,000 married filing jointly $200,000 head of household & single $200,000 married filing separately	$110,000 married filing jointly $75,000 head of household & single $55,000 married filing separately
Phaseout Rate	Credit is reduced by $50 for every $1,000 (or fraction thereof) above the phaseout threshold.	Credit is reduced by $50 for every $1,000 (or fraction thereof) above the phaseout threshold.
	Other Provisions	
Qualifying Child ID Requirements	Social Security Number (SSN).	SSN or individual taxpayer identification number (ITIN).
Eligibility to Residents of Puerto Rico and Other Territories	Residents of the territories generally do not receive the federal child credit, although families in territories with three or more children may receive the ACTC using an alternative formula.[b]	Same as 2018-2025.

Source: CRS analysis of IRC Section 24, P.L. 115-97, and Joint Committee on Taxation, JCX-17-20.

Notes:

[a]Annually adjusted for inflation.

[b]The alternative formula is the amount by which Social Security taxes paid exceed the earned income tax credit (EITC) up to the maximum refundable credit. Because residents of territories are generally ineligible for the EITC, the formula effectively equals the lesser of their Social Security taxes paid or their maximum ACTC. For more information, see Joint Committee on Taxation, JCX-17-20.

Overview of Current Credit

Each of the key parameters of the child tax credit as in effect from 2018 through 2025 is described in more detail below. The legislative changes made to the child tax credit by P.L. 115-97 have significantly expanded the child tax credit, especially for upper-income taxpayers, as illustrated in *Figure 1.*

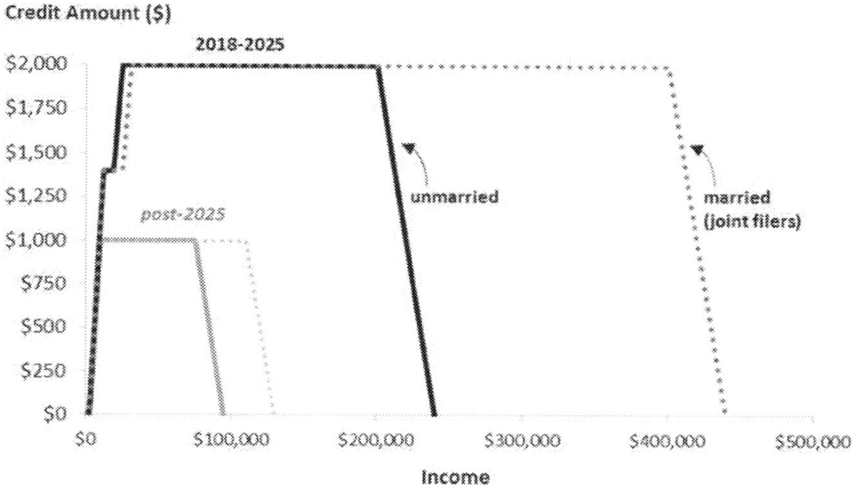

Source: Internal Revenue Code (IRC) Section 24.

Notes: This is a stylized example assuming the taxpayer has one qualifying child. In actuality, the ACTC is calculated based on earned income and the credit is phased down based on modified adjusted gross income (MAGI). Married refers to married taxpayers filing joint returns. The "notch" in the graph when the credit amount equals $1,400 (the vertical axis) occurs when the maximum ACTC amount has been reached.

Figure 1. Child Tax Credit Amount by Income Level.

Maximum Credit per Child

Eligible taxpayers can claim a child tax credit and reduce their federal income tax liability by up to $2,000 per qualifying child. The maximum credit a taxpayer can receive is equal to the number of qualifying children a taxpayer has, multiplied by $2,000. For example, a taxpayer with two qualifying children may be eligible for a $4,000 credit. Taxpayers may receive the child tax credit as a reduction in tax liability (the nonrefundable portion of the credit), a refundable credit (the amount of the credit in excess of income tax liability), or a combination of both.[4] The refundable portion of the credit—the ACTC—is discussed in the subsequent section.

[4] Importantly, even if the credit both reduces tax liability and then is received as a refund, the total value of the nonrefundable and refundable portion of the credit cannot exceed $ 2,000 per child multiplied by the number of qualifying children. Hence, if a family with two children and a $1,500 tax liability is eligible for a $2,000 child tax credit, $1,500

Beginning in 2026, the maximum amount of the credit is scheduled to revert to $1,000 perqualifying child.

Maximum Additional Child Tax Credit (ACTC) per Child, the RefundabilityThreshold, and Refundability Rate

For taxpayers with little or no federal income tax liability, they will be eligible for little if any of the nonrefundable portion of the child tax credit. Instead, they may be eligible to receive the refundable portion of child tax credit. The refundable portion of the child tax credit is often referred to as the additional child tax credit or ACTC. The amount of the refundable child tax credit is generally calculated using the "earned income formula"[5] up to the maximum ACTC amount of $1,400 per qualifying child.

Under the earned income formula, a taxpayer may claim an ACTC equal to 15% of the family's earned income in excess of $2,500, up to the maximum ACTC amount (i.e., up to $1,400 multiplied by the number of qualifying children).[6] The $2,500 amount is referred to as the refundability threshold; the 15% is referred to as the refundability rate. If a taxpayer's earnings are below the refundability threshold, they are ineligible for the ACTC. For every dollar of earnings above this amount, the value of the taxpayer's ACTC increases by 15 cents, up to the maximum amount of the

---

of their credit will reduce their tax liability to zero (the nonrefundable portion) and the family may receive up to $500 of child tax credit as a refundable credit, depending on their income.

[5] Families with three or more children may choose to calculate the refundable portion of the child tax credit using an alternative formula. If the amount calculated under the alternative formula is larger than the refundable credit calculated under the earned income formula, the larger credit can be claimed. The alternative formula is calculated as the excess of a taxpayer's payroll taxes (including one-half of any self-employment taxes) over their earned income tax credit (EITC), not to exceed the maximum credit amount. However, lower-income taxpayers will often pay less in payroll taxes than they will receive in the EITC. This is because payroll taxes are equal to 7.65% of earnings, while the EITC equals up to 45% of earnings.

[6] Congress has sometimes allowed certain taxpayers to elect to use older earned income in computing their ACTC (andearned income tax credit or EITC). In other words, if the most recent earned income results in a smaller credit than the previous year's earned income, taxpayers may use that older earned income to calculate the ACTC and EITC. For a discussion, see "EITC/CTC Credit Computation Look-Back" in CRS Report R45864, *Tax Policy and Disaster Recovery*, by Molly F. Sherlock and Jennifer Teefy. Most recently, P.L. 116-260 included a provision allowing taxpayers to use 2019 earned income (as opposed to 2020 earned income) in calculating their 2020 EITC and ACTC.

credit ($1,400 per qualifying child). For purposes of calculating the ACTC, earned income is defined as wages, tips, and other compensation included in gross income. It also includes net self-employment income (self-employment income after deduction of one-half of Social Security payroll taxes paid by a self-employed individual).

Beginning in 2026, the refundability threshold is scheduled to increase to $3,000 and the maximum ACTC per child (the amount that exceeds income tax liability) is scheduled to decrease to $1,000 per child.

The Phaseout Threshold and Phaseout Rate

The child tax credit phases out for higher-income families. The $2,000-per-child value of the credit falls by a certain amount as a family's income rises. Specifically, for every $1,000 of modified adjusted gross income (MAGI)[7] above a threshold amount, the credit falls by $50—or effectively by 5% of MAGI above the threshold. The threshold amount depends on a taxpayer's filing status, and equals $200,000 for single parents and married taxpayers filing separate returns, and $400,000 for married taxpayers filing joint returns. The actual income level at which the credit is entirely phased out (i.e., equals zero) depends on the number of qualifying children a taxpayer has. Generally, it takes $40,000 of MAGI above the phaseout threshold to completely phase out $2,000 of credit. For example, the credit will completely phase out for a married couple with two children if their MAGI exceeds $480,000.

The Nonrefundable $500 Credit for Non-Child-Tax-Credit Dependents

At the end of 2017, President Trump signed into law P.L. 115-97, which made numerous changes to the federal income tax for individuals and businesses.[8] One of these changes was the creation of a new temporary credit for non-child-tax-credit-

---

[7] With respect to the child tax credit, modified adjusted gross income (MAGI) is equal to Adjusted Gross Income (AGI) increased by foreign earned income of U.S. Citizens abroad, including income earned in Guam, American Samoa, the Northern Mariana Islands, and Puerto Rico. For more information on AGI see CRS Report RL30110, *Federal Individual Income Tax Terms: An Explanation* , by Mark P. Keightley and CRS Report R45145, *Overview of the Federal Tax System in 2020*, by Molly F. Sherlock and Donald J. Marples.

[8] For more information on the changes made to the tax code by P.L. 115-97, see CRS Report R45092, *The 2017 Tax Revision (P.L. 115-97): Comparison to 2017 Tax Law*, coordinated by Molly F. Sherlock and Donald J. Marples.

eligible dependents. The credit is referred to by the IRS as the "credit for other dependents."

This credit is equal to $500 per non-child-credit-eligible dependent. The amount is not annually adjusted for inflation. The phaseout parameters of the child credit (e.g., phaseout thresholds of $400,000 married filing jointly, $200,000 other taxpayers, 5% phaseout rate) apply to the family credit. As discussed below, while P.L. 115-97 imposes a new Social Security number (SSN) requirement for qualifying children being claimed under the child tax credit, the law does not statutorily impose a similar requirement on non-child-credit-eligible dependents.

This credit is generally available for dependents not eligible for the child tax credit. Non-child-credit-eligible dependents excludes otherwise eligible dependents who are not U.S. citizens and are residents of Mexico or Canada.

This provision is scheduled to be in effect from 2018 through the end of 2025.

Definition of a Qualifying Child

In order to claim the child tax credit, a taxpayer's child must be considered "a qualifying child" of the taxpayer and meet several requirements, which may differ from eligibility requirements for other child-related tax benefits:

1. The child must be under 17 years of age by the end of the year. (In other words, if the child turns 17 years old on December 31, 2020, the taxpayer cannot claim them as a qualifying child for the child tax credit on their 2020 income tax return.)
2. The child must be eligible to be claimed as a dependent on the taxpayer's return.[9] Specifically:
   - o The child must be the taxpayer's son, daughter, grandson, granddaughter, stepson, stepdaughter, niece, nephew, or an eligible foster child of the taxpayer.
   - o The child must live at the same principal residence as the taxpayer for more than half the year for which the taxpayer wishes to claim the credit.

[9] See the definition of a qualifying child for the dependent exemption in IRC §152(c). From 2018 to 2025, due to the temporary suspension of the dependent exemption enacted as part of P.L. 115-97, taxpayers may no longer claim theirchildren as dependents for purposes of the dependent exemption, although this does not affect eligibility for the credit and the definition of a dependent remains unchanged by the law. IRC §151(d)(5)(B).

- The child cannot provide more than half of their own support during the tax year.

3. The child must be a U.S. citizen or national. If they are not a U.S. citizen or national, they must be a resident of the United States.[10]

The age and citizenship requirements for a qualifying child for the child tax credit differ from the definition of qualifying child used for other tax benefits and can cause confusion among taxpayers. For example, a taxpayer's 18-year-old child may meet all the requirements for a qualifying child for the EITC, but will be too old to be eligible for the child tax credit.

ID Requirements to Claim the Child Tax Credit

The statute requires that taxpayers who intend to claim the child tax credit provide a valid taxpayer identification number (TIN) for each qualifying child on their federal income tax return. Under a temporary change in effect from 2018 through the end of 2025, the child's TIN must be a work-authorized Social Security number (SSN). The SSN must be issued before the due date of the tax return. Failure to provide the child's SSN may result in the taxpayer being denied the credit (both the nonrefundable and refundable portions of the credit).

Absent any legislative changes, beginning in 2026, a valid TIN for qualifying children will include individual taxpayer identification numbers (ITINs) and Social Security numbers (SSNs). ITINs are issued by the Internal Revenue Service (IRS) to noncitizens who do not have and are not eligible to receive SSNs. ITINs are supplied solely so that noncitizens are able to comply with federal tax law, and do not affect immigration status.

In addition, in order to claim the child tax credit in a given tax year, the taxpayer must also provide their own taxpayer identification number that must be issued before the due date of the tax return. This is a permanent ID requirement that is not scheduled to expire.

---

[10] See IRC §24(c)(2).

Disallowance of the Credit Due to Fraud or Reckless Disregard of the Rules

A tax filer is barred from claiming the child tax credit for a period of 10 years after the IRS makes a final determination to reduce or disallow a tax filer's child tax credit because that individual made a fraudulent child tax credit claim. A tax filer is barred from claiming the child tax credit for a period of two years after the IRS determines that the individual made a child tax credit claim "due to reckless and intentional disregard of [the] rules" of the child tax credit, but that disregard was not found to be due to fraud.[11]

Data on the Child Tax Credit

Estimates from the Internal Revenue Service (IRS) and Tax Policy Center highlight several key aspects of the child tax credit:

- The total dollar amount of the child tax credit has grown over time with the largest increase to date occurring in 2018: Data from the IRS indicate that the total dollar amount of the child tax credit in real terms has increased fivefold since enactment, with the largest increase occurring between 2017 and 2018, after the TCJA; see Figure 2. Initially, the total dollar amount of the credit grew modestly between 1998 and 2003 in real terms, with increases reflecting, in part, legislative expansions of the credit. More recently, prior to the TCJA, the total credit amount fell in real terms. Then, between 2017 and 2018, total credit dollars more than doubled.
- In 2018, the majority of aggregate credit dollars were received by taxpayers with income between $50,000 and $500,000: IRS data indicate that in 2018, the majority (60%) of total credit dollars went to taxpayers with income over $50,000, with nearly one-quarter of all child tax credit dollars (22%) received by taxpayers with income between $100,000 and $200,000; see Figure 3. In comparison, a relatively small share went to the lowest-income or highest- income taxpayers.

---

[11] See IRC §24(g).

- In 2019, more than 90% of taxpayers with children and income between $30,000 and $500,000 received the child tax credit, with lower shares for the lowest- and highest-income taxpayers. The Tax Policy Center (TPC) estimates that across most income groups, the majority of taxpayers with children received the child tax credit in 2019; see Figure 4.[12] About half of the lowest-income taxpayers with children received the credit and about a quarter of taxpayers with children who have income over $500,000 received the credit.
- In 2019, taxpayers with income between $100,000 and $200,000 received the largest credit on average. The Tax Policy Center (TPC) estimates that taxpayers with children and income between $100,000 and $200,000 received a credit of over $3,000 on average in 2019; see Figure 5. Taxpayers with children with income under $20,000 received a credit of less than $1,000 on average, while the highest-income taxpayers with children received a credit of $649 on average.

Total Child Tax Credit Dollars, 1998-2018

The IRS provides estimates of the total child tax credit dollars from 1998 through 2018 (the most recent year available). These data, inflation adjusted to 2018 dollars, indicate that the value of this tax benefit has increased fivefold since enactment, from a total of $23 billion in 1998 to approximately $118 billion in 2018, with the largest increase occurring in 2018, as illustrated in Figure 2. Initially, the credit grew modestly between 1998 and 2003 in real terms, with increases reflecting, in part, legislative expansions to the credit. More recently, prior to the TCJA, the total credit amount fell in real terms. Between 2017 and 2018, total credit dollars more than doubled from $52 billion to $118 billion between 2017 and 2018.

The ACTC expansions under the TCJAresulted in the total amount of the refundable portion of the credit growing from $25 billion to $36 billion (a 44% increase) between 2017 and 2018. The increased credit amount and

[12] The Tax Policy Center measure of income used in its analysis is expanded cash income (ECI), which is defined as cash income plus (1) tax-exempt employee and employer contributions to health insurance and other fringe benefits, (2) employer contributions to tax-preferred retirement accounts, (3) income earned within retirement accounts, and (4) food stamps. For more information, see http://www.taxpolicycenter.org/ resources/ income-measure-used-distributional- analyses-tax-policy-center.

increased phaseout amount under the law contributed to a substantial expansion of the nonrefundable portion of the credit. Aggregate dollars of the nonrefundable portion of the credit tripled from $27 billion in 2017 to $81 billion in 2018. The $500 credit for non-child-credit-eligible dependents also contributed to the increase in the nonrefundable amount estimated by the IRS, although less so than the expansions to the child credit. (The IRS refers to this benefit as the nonrefundable credit for other dependents.) Data on the breakdown of the nonrefundable portion between the child credit and the credit for other dependents are not available. However, estimates from the Tax Policy Center suggest that most dependents—nearly four out of five—would be child-credit-eligible dependents.[13] In addition, the value of the other dependent credit itself is smaller than the child credit ($500 as compared to $2,000). These data suggest that the majority of the $81 billion nonrefundable portion is from the child credit.

Total Child Tax Credit Dollars by Income Level

The IRS also provides estimates of the child credit by taxpayers' income level (in terms of adjusted gross income, or AGI) in 2018. These figures include the $500 credit for non-child-tax- credit-eligible dependents. The majority (60%) of total credit dollars were received by taxpayers with income over $50,000, with nearly one-quarter of all child tax credit dollars (22%) received by taxpayers with income between $100,000 and $200,000, as illustrated in Figure 3. Four in ten child credit dollars (40%) were received by taxpayers with income under $50,000, with almost 10% of total credit dollars received by those with income under $20,000.

Lower-income taxpayers generally receive a credit of $1,400 or less per child, depending on theirearnings. In contrast, higher-income taxpayers with sufficient income tax liability receive a credit of $2,000 per child. For example, a single parent with two children and $15,000 of income is eligible for a $1,875 credit (received entirely as the refundable child credit, or ACTC), less than the maximum ACTC for two children of $2,800 (2 x $1,400) and less than the maximum credit for two children of $4,000 (2 x $2,000). The highest-income taxpayers do not receive a credit due to the credit phaseout.

[13] The Tax Policy Center estimated that in 2019, there were about 95 million dependents of taxpayers with income.

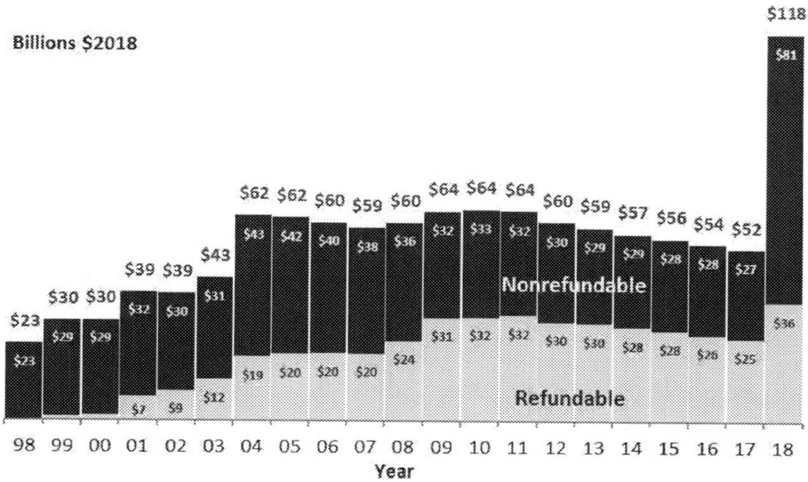

Source: IRS Statistics of Income Table 3.3 and the Bureau of Labor Statistics CPI-U.

Note: Items may not sum to total due to rounding. The data for the nonrefundable portion of the child tax credit also includes the amount of the $500 nonrefundable credit for non-child-tax-credit-eligible dependents.

Figure 2. Total Real Child Tax Credit Dollars, 1998-2018.

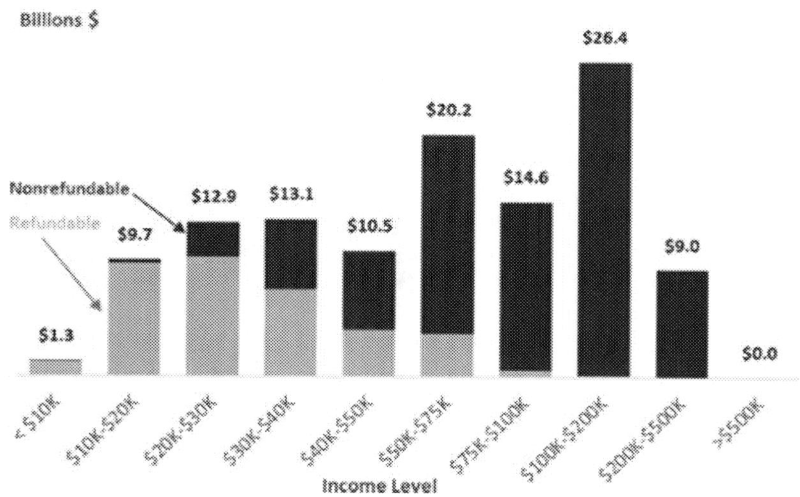

Source: IRS Statistics of Income Table 3.3.

Note: The data for the nonrefundable portion of the child tax credit also includes the amount of the $500 nonrefundable credit for non-child-tax-credit-eligible dependents. Income is adjusted gross income (AGI).

Figure 3. Share of Total Child Tax Credit Dollars by Income, 2018.

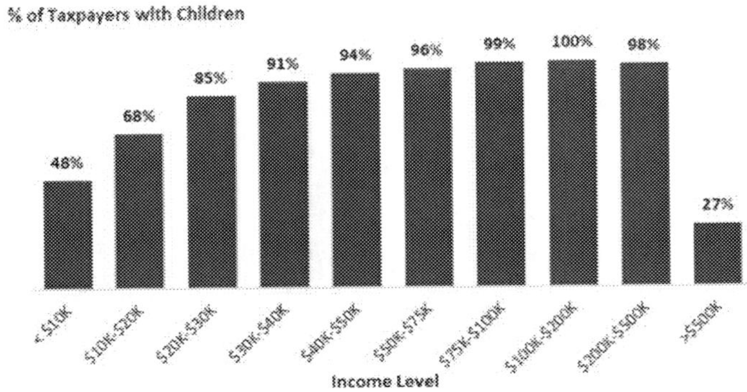

Source: Tax Policy Center Model T20-0091.

Notes: Taxpayers include both filers and nonfilers. Income is defined as expanded cash income (ECI), which equals cash income plus certain other tax-exempt forms of income and benefits like food stamps. These estimates include the $500 credit for non-child-tax-credit-eligible dependents. Taxpayers with children are those claiming an exemption for children at home or away from home or with children qualifying for the child tax credit or earned income tax credit (EITC).

Figure 4. Estimated Share ofTaxpayers with Children Receiving the ChildTax Credit by Income,2019.

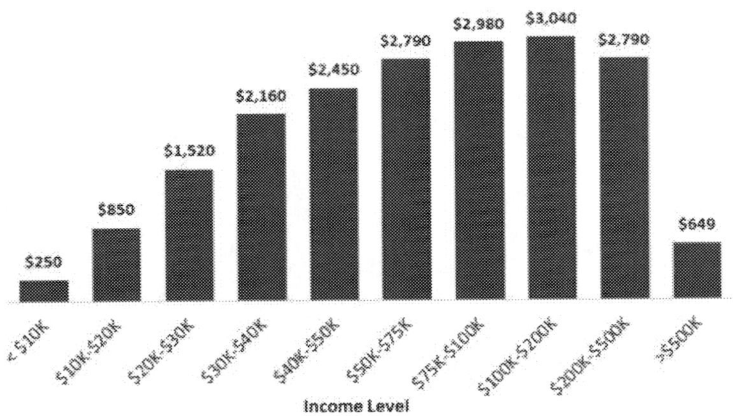

Source: Tax Policy Center Model T20-0091.

Notes: Taxpayers include both filers and nonfilers. Income is defined as expanded cash income (ECI), which equals cash income plus certain other tax-exempt forms of income and benefits like food stamps. These estimates include the $500 credit for non-child-tax-credit-eligible dependents. Taxpayers with children are those claiming an exemption for children at home or away from home or with children qualifying for the child tax credit or earned income tax credit (EITC).

Figure 5. Average Child Tax Credit for Taxpayers with Children by Income, 2019.

Share of Taxpayers with Children Receiving the Child Tax Credit

The Tax Policy Center provides estimates on the share of taxpayers with children that received the child tax credit in 2019. The estimates indicate that among taxpayers with children, almost all—90%—received the child tax credit. More than 90% of taxpayers with children who had income between $30,000 and $500,000 received the child tax credit. In contrast, less than half (48%) of taxpayers with children who had income under $10,000 received the child tax credit in 2019. About one-quarter (27%) of taxpayers with children who had income greater than $500,000 received the credit, as illustrated in Figure 4.

Fewer low-income families with children receive the child tax credit since taxpayers with income under $2,500 (the refundability threshold) are not eligible for the refundable portion of the credit. Due to the phaseout of the credit at higher income levels, about a quarter (27%) of taxpayers with children who have income over $500,000 receive the credit.

Average Child Tax Credit Amount

TPC estimates the average child tax credit amount for taxpayers with children was $2,370 in 2019.[14] Estimates indicate that taxpayers with children and income between $100,000 and $200,000 received the largest credit on average—an estimated $3,040. Taxpayers with children and income under $20,000 received a credit of less than $1,000 on average, while the wealthiest taxpayers with children (income over $500,000) received a credit of $649 on average.

Lower-income taxpayers are eligible to receive a credit of up to $1,400 per child, although they may receive less depending on their earned income. In contrast, higher-income taxpayers, with sufficient income tax liability, are eligible for up to a $2,000 credit per child. The highest-income taxpayers are ineligible for the credit due to the phaseout.

---

[14] IRS data on the average total child credit per taxpayer (the refundable and nonrefundable portion) are not available. The IRS provides data for the nonrefundable child credit and refundable portion (number of tax returns and total credit amount), but does not provide data on the total credit. Hence, because a taxpayer can receive both the nonrefundable and refundable portion, one cannot calculate the average credit amount.

Chapter 5

Who Can Claim a Child for the Child Tax Credit?*

Margot L. Crandall-Hollick

The child tax credit was expanded for one year—2021—by the American Rescue Plan Act of 2021 (ARPA; P.L. 117-2), and up to half of the 2021 credit was advanced to taxpayers in monthly payments issued between July and December of 2021. While ARPA expanded the credit and changed its delivery, the only change ARPA made to the qualifying child rules was to increase the maximum age limit of the child from 16 years to 17 years for 2021 only. This Insight provides a brief overview of who can claim a child for the child tax credit.

Qualifying Child Rules

In order for a taxpayer to be able to claim a child for the child tax credit on their tax return, the child must meet several requirements for that year as identified in Table 1. Failure to meet any of these requirements generally means the taxpayer cannot claim the child for purposes of the credit in that year.

Some of these requirements or tests are characteristics intrinsic to the child, like the child's age or whether the child supports themselves financially. Others—like the relationship and residency tests in Table 1—are

* This is an edited, reformatted and augmented version of Congressional Research Service Publication No. IN11853, dated February 10, 2022.

In: A Closer Look at the Child Tax Credit
Editor: Philip Palmer
ISBN: 979-8-89113-601-4

requirements specifically connecting the taxpayer and the child. These tests in particular can help identify which taxpayer can claim a child for the credit.

Table 1. Tests/requirements to claim a child as a qualifying child for the child tax credit

Test/Requirement	Description
Child vis à vis taxpayer	
Relationship[a]	The child must be the taxpayer's child,[b] grandchild (or great-grandchild),[b] sibling,[b] niece/nephew, or foster child placed with the taxpayer either by an authorized placement agency or court order.
Residency	The child must have lived with the taxpayer for more than half of the year.[c]
Child	
Age	In 2021, the child must be under 18 years old as of the last day of 2021. In all other years, the child must be under 17 years old as of the last day of the year.
Support	The child does not provide more than half of their own financial support.
Joint Return	The child has not filed a joint income tax return with their spouse.
Citizenship/Residency	The child must be a U.S. citizen, resident, or national.
Identification (ID) Number	The child's taxpayer ID must be provided (in addition to the child's name) in order for the credit to be issued to the taxpayer. The taxpayer ID must be issued on or before the due date of the return. From 2018 to 2025, the ID must be a social security number (SSN) associated with work authorization. After 2025, the ID can be any SSN, an individual taxpayer identification number (ITIN), or an adoption taxpayer identification number (ATIN).

Source: Internal Revenue Code (IRC) Sections 24 and 152.

Notes:

[a] A taxpayer's cousin generally does not meet the qualifying child's relationship test.

[b] This includes by adoption or remarriage (i.e., stepchildren) and "half" relatives (e.g., half siblings).

[c] There is an exception to this rule in certain cases of children of divorced or separated parents who meet requirements under IRC Section 152(e). In addition, exceptions to the residency test exist for certain temporary absences.

Relationship Test

Most types of relatives of a child meet the relationship test: parents, grandparents, aunts/uncles, and siblings all meet this test. Legal guardianship—where the child is placed with an adult by a court order—would meet this test (the child would be considered a "foster child" under this test), regardless of the actual biological relationship between the child and taxpayer.

Because of the relationship test, kinship care by some of the child's relatives (i.e., grandparents/great grandparents, aunts/uncles, siblings) would meet the relationship requirement. However, other types of kinship care—like informal caretaking of a child by a close family friend (i.e., no legal guardianship)— would not.

Residency Test

Under the residency test, children must live with the taxpayer for more than half the year. This is sometimes called the "six months and a day rule." The movement of children between different households from year to year may mean that a child meets the residency requirement with a particular taxpayer in one year but not in the next year. This may be of particular concern with the 2021 credit because the advance payments of the 2021 credit were based on older tax data, even though eligibility for the expanded credit depends on whether children meet these tests for 2021.

Specifically, the advance payments were based on an estimate of a taxpayer's 2021 child credit using 2020 income tax return information (or if unavailable, information from 2019 income tax returns). These older data were also used to estimate whether a child was the taxpayer's qualifying child for 2021.

Taxpayers with children who met these rules in 2020, but not in 2021, could be required to repay some of the advance payments. This may occur, for example, among certain divorced parents who trade off claiming the child for the credit from one year to the next.

If a child fails to meet the residency test of any taxpayer—for example, because the child spent three months each in four different family members' houses—the child would generally not be able to be claimed by any taxpayer as a qualifying child for the credit in that year.

Multigenerational Households and Tiebreaker Rules

The qualifying child rules of the child credit can lead to situations where more than one taxpayer may be able to claim a child for the credit. This can occur in multigenerational households, such as when a child lives for more than half the year with a parent and a grandparent. In cases where more than one taxpayer may be eligible to claim a child, there are specified tiebreaker rules to determine who can claim these children. These tiebreaker rules prioritize the claims of parents over those of nonparents. Among competing claims of nonparents, the rules prioritize the taxpayer with the highest adjusted gross income (AGI).

Chapter 6

The Child Tax Credit: What Lies Ahead?*

Margot L. Crandall-Hollick

The child tax credit has been temporarily modified several times in recent years. On January 16, Senate Finance Committee Chair Ron Wyden and House Ways and Means Chair Jason Smith announced that they had reached the deal on a "framework" that included further changes to the child credit.

Legislative text of this proposal (H.R. 7024) was released January 17, and a markup in the Ways and Means Committee occurred on January 19, during which time the bill, as amended, was voted out favorably by the committee by a vote of 40-3. This Insight provides background to those discussions by summarizing prior legislative changes to the credit and outlining the proposed changes to the child credit in H.R. 7024.

Recent Legislative Changes

Under permanent law—last in effect in 2017 and scheduled to go back in effect in 2026—the child tax credit allowed eligible households to reduce their income tax liability by up to $1,000 per child aged 16 or lower. Lower-income working taxpayers were eligible to receive part or all of this benefit as the refundable portion of the credit, sometimes called the additional child tax credit or ACTC. The ACTC phased in with earned income if households had at least $3,000 of earnings. For higher-income households, the child credit phased out.

---

* This is an edited, reformatted and augmented version of Congressional Research Service Publication No. IN12297, updated January 22, 2024.

In: A Closer Look at the Child Tax Credit
Editor: Philip Palmer
ISBN: 979-8-89113-601-4

The law commonly referred to as the Tax Cuts and Jobs Act (TCJA; P.L. 115-97) made several temporary changes to the permanent credit that are in effect through 2025. The TCJA increased the maximum credit amount to $2,000 per child, modified the ACTC formula to begin phasing in at $2,500 of earned income (compared to $3,000), capped the refundable portion of the credit at $1,400 per child (inflation-adjusted to $1,600 per child in 2023 and $1,700 per child in 2024), and increased the income levels at which the credit begins to phase out.

The American Rescue Plan Act of 2021 (ARPA; P.L. 117-2) layered additional temporary changes on top of the TCJA changes for 2021 only. ARPA increased the maximum credit to $3,000 per child ($3,600 per child for young children), eliminated the phase-in of the credit for low-income taxpayers so they were eligible to receive the full or maximum amount of the credit irrespective of how much earned income they had (this is sometimes referred to as "full refundability"), and expanded the eligibility age for children to include 17-year-olds. These changes expired as scheduled at the end of 2021.

Aside from the TCJA change to the maximum ACTC, none of the parameters of the credit are adjusted for inflation.

Details of these parameters can be found in the table at the end of this Insight. The impact of these changes on a hypothetical married couple with two children—one young (under 6 years old) and one older (6 to 16 years old)—is illustrated below.

Proposals in the 118th Congress

Many policymakers remain interested in expanding the credit, especially to benefit low- and moderate- income families, which research suggests benefited the most from the ARPA changes. Various proposals have been introduced to modify the child credit in the 118th Congress. Some of these proposals would reinstate a modified version of the ARPA changes (e.g., S. 1992, H.R. 3899, H.R. 5953).

Some policymakers, however, have expressed concerns that extending the ARPA changes would discourage some recipients from working. Under permanent law and the TCJA changes, the credit phases in with earned income for low-income households. This effectively requires a low-income single parent to work, or at least one parent among a low-income married couple to work. The ARPA credit, in contrast, had no work requirement, since the credit did not phase in with earned income.

Child Credit Amounts by Income Under Recent Laws

Married Couple with Two Children: One Young Child & One Older Child

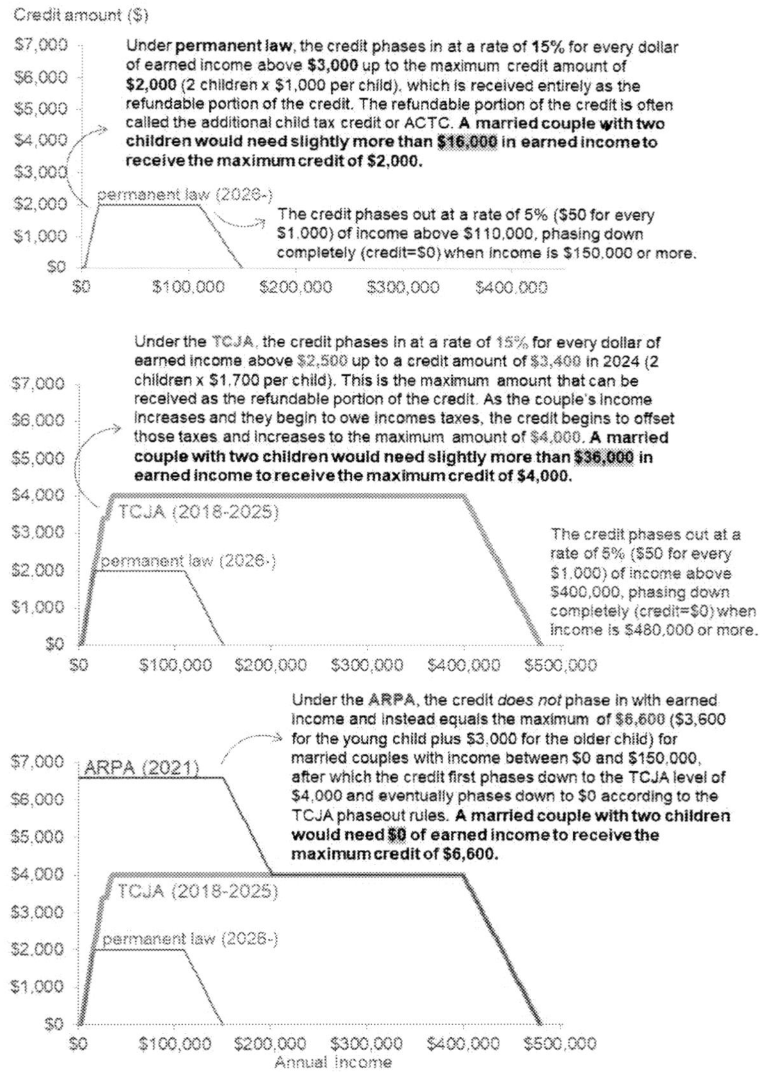

Source: CRS based on IRC Section 24.

Notes: For these figures, a young child is 0-5 years old. An older child is 6-16 years old. Under ARPA, older children include 17-year-olds.

Most research conducted during the pandemic did not find that the ARPA child credit discouraged people from working, although the findings may have been complicated by specific economic issues associated with the COVID-19 pandemic and the fact that the ARPA credit was in place for only one year. Most estimates of the impact of the ARPA credit on employment if the credit were to be extended for longer or made permanent predict a relatively modest impact on employment. (These estimates vary significantly with numerous required modeling assumptions.)

Concerns about the employment effects of an ARPA credit may have persuaded some policymakers to focus on expanding the existing credit for low-income families while retaining a phase-in, reflected in H.R. 7024.

H.R. 7024

H.R. 7024, released January 17, includes several provisions that would expand the child tax credit for low-income families, including

1. The ACTC would be calculated per child: After the ACTC amount is calculated under current law (15% of earned income above $2,500), it would then be multiplied by the number of children. This amount would still be subject to the ACTC limit (the ACTC maximum multiplied by the number of children). This provision would effectively phase in the credit faster for families with more children.
2. The maximum amount of the ACTC would increase: The ACTC maximum would rise from $1,600 to $1,800 per child in 2023 and from $1,700 to $1,900 per child in 2024 and equal $2,000 (adjusted for inflation) in 2025.
3. Taxpayers could use prior-year earned income to calculate the ACTC: Taxpayers could calculate the ACTC using their prior-year earned income if their current-year earned income was less than their prior-year earned income. (This is similar to a temporary provision enacted during the COVID-19 pandemic.) This would apply for 2024 and 2025.

The framework also proposes adjusting the child credit for inflation since 2022 in 2024 and 2025, meaning moderate- and higher-income taxpayers would likely receive a credit of more than $2,000 per child in 2024 and 2025.

Chair Smith's substitute amendment (agreed to during the January 19 markup) includes an additional provision that would direct the IRS, to the extent practicable, to recalculate the credit on 2023 returns based on the changes in the bill if a taxpayer had filed their return before these changes took effect (2023 returns can be filed beginning on January 29, 2024).

The Center on Budget and Policy Priorities (CBPP) estimates that of the 19 million children in low- income families that currently receive less than the maximum credit, 16 million of them would benefit from this proposal and 400,000 would be lifted out of poverty the first year it was in effect.

Child Credit Amount by Income

Married Couple with Two Children: One Young Child & One Older Child

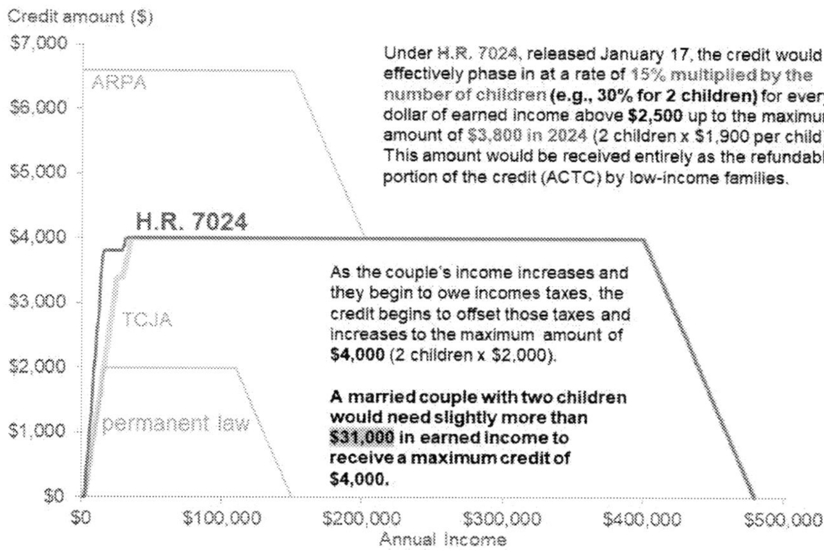

Source: CRS based on IRC Section 24 and the January 17 legislative text of H.R. 7024.
Notes: For this figure, a young child is 0-5 years old. An older child is 6-16 years old. Under ARPA, older children include 17-year-olds. In addition, under H.R. 7024, taxpayers could, for 2024 and 2025, calculate the ACTC using their prior-year earned income if their current-year earned income was less than their prior-year earned income, which is not illustrated in the chart.

Budgetary Impact

The average annual cost of the permanent law child credit is about $50 billion per year. The TCJA changes, if extended, are estimated by CBO to cost an additional $80 billion per year. For 2021, the ARPA changes increased the costs of the TCJA-modified credit by an additional $105 billion per year according to estimates from the Joint Committee on Taxation (JCT). The Joint Committee on Taxation estimates the cost of these changes (including those made by the substitute amendment) to be an average of $11 billion per year ($33 billion between FY2024 and FY2026)

Selected Child Credit Parameters

Under Selected Laws and H.R. 7024

Parameter	Permanent Law (2026)	TCJA	ARPA	H.R. 7024
Maximum credit	**$1,000** per child 0-16 years old	**$2,000** per child 0-16 years old	**$3,600** per child 0-5 years old **$3,000** per child 6-17 years old	**$2,000** per child 0-16 years old (adjusted for inflation for 2024 & 2025)
Maximum ACTC The additional child tax credit (ACTC) is the refundable portion of the credit for low-income taxpayers	**$1,000** per child 0-16 years old	**$1,600** per child 0-16 years old for 2023 **$1,700** per child 0-16 years old for 2024 *This amount is statutorily $1,400, adjusted for inflation*	**$3,600** per child 0-5 years old **$3,000** per child 6-17 years old	**$1,800** per child 0-16 years old for 2023 **$1,900** per child 0-16 years old for 2024 **$2,000** per child 0-16 years old for 2025 (this amount would be adjusted for inflation for 2025)
ACTC formula	15% of earned income above **$3,000 capped at $1,000** per child x number of children	15% of earned income above **$2,500 capped at $1,700** per child x number of children for 2024	**No phase-in.** Eligible low-income taxpayers receive the full or maximum ACTC amount, irrespective of earned income	15% of earned income above **$2,500 multiplied by the number of children** capped at the **maximum ACTC** per child x number of children

Source: CRS based on IRC Section 24 and the January 17 legislative text of H.R. 7024.
Notes: In addition, under H.R. 7024, taxpayers could calculate the ACTC for 2024 and 2025 using their prior-year earned income if their current-year earned income was less than their prior-year earned income.

Chapter 7

Factors Affecting the Cost of Extending the Expanded Child Tax Credit*

Margot L. Crandall-Hollick and Grant A. Driessen

As Congress has considered legislation extending the expanded child credit, questions have arisen aboutthe potential budgetary effects of such legislation and the factors that affect its projected cost.

The Congressional Budget Office (CBO) and the Joint Committee on Taxation (JCT) provide Congress with information about the projected budgetary effects of specific legislative proposals, typically in the form of cost estimates. These estimates are required to measure the budgetary effect of a legislative proposal in relation to projections of revenue and spending levels that are assumed to occur under currentlaw, typically referred to as the *current-law baseline*. Changes to refundable tax credits can affect both revenue and outlays. The portion of a refundable tax credit that reduces taxes owed (i.e., reduces positivetax liability) is scored as a decrease in revenue, while the portion of the credit that is greater than taxes owed (i.e., increases negative tax liability) is scored as an increase in outlays.

A variety of factors could affect the estimated budgetary effects of legislation that extends the expandedchild credit, including

- the details of the policy being extended,
- the duration of the extension,

---

* This is an edited, reformatted and augmented version of Congressional Research Service Publication No. IN11851, dated February 7, 2022.

In: A Closer Look at the Child Tax Credit
Editor: Philip Palmer
ISBN: 979-8-89113-601-4

- o other changes to the tax code that could affect child credit payments, and
- o economic and demographic projections. Each is briefly discussed below.

The Details of the Policy Being Extended

The estimated budgetary effects of a proposal depend in part on what is being extended. For example, is the legislation extending the 2021 child credit or is it extending a modified version of the 2021 credit? Some modifications—like those that expand eligibility—would increase the cost of the extension, all else being equal. Other modifications—like extending a smaller credit, limiting or eliminating full refundability, or reducing the income level at which the credit begins to phase out—would reduce the cost of an extension.

The Duration of the Extension

A shorter extension would generally be expected to have a lower budgetary cost than a longer extension. A longer extension's cost may also be affected by temporary tax provisions that, after they are scheduled to expire, would no longer be considered part of the current-law baseline.

This may be especially relevant to an expanded child credit extension, because the expanded credit is the result of temporary changes made by two laws which were both in effect in 2021—the Tax Cuts and Jobs Act (TCJA; P.L. 115-97) and the American Rescue Plan Act (ARPA; P.L. 117-2). (For more information on these changes, see Table 1 in R45124, The Child Tax Credit: Legislative History.) Each law temporarily expanded the credit, in terms of both the amount of the credit and eligibility, compared to the credit amounts under permanent law, as illustrated below.

Child Credit Amount by Income and Law

Married Joint Filer with One Young Child (0-5 years old)

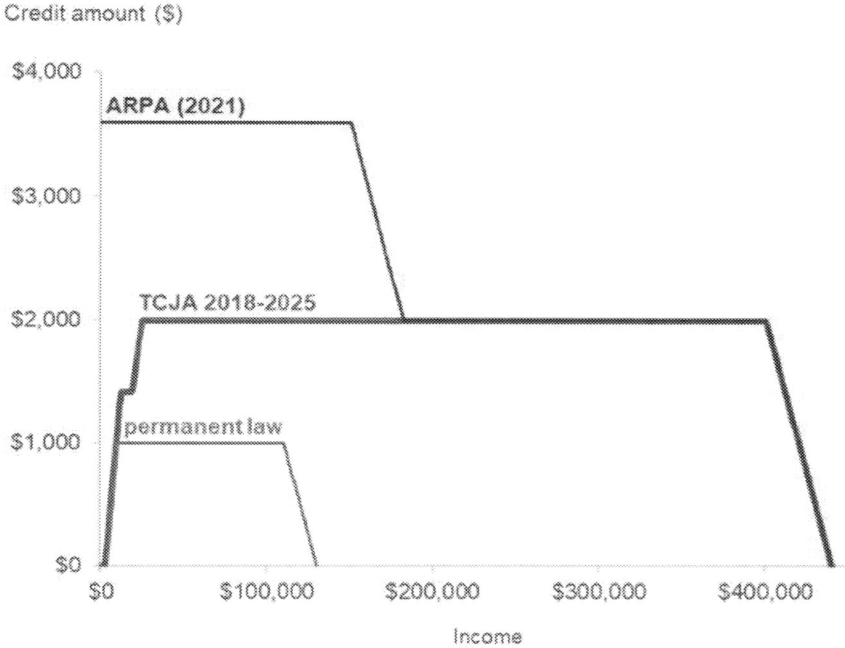

Source: CRS calculations based on Internal Revenue Code Section 24.
Notes: All household income is assumed to be from earned income (i.e., adjusted gross income=earned income) and taxpayers are assumed to only claim the standard deduction.

Upon the expiration of the ARPA expansion at the end of 2021, the credit has reverted back to levels under current law, as expanded by the TCJA, through the end of 2025. Beginning in 2026, the TCJA changes are scheduled to expire and the credit will revert to its permanent-law levels. In other words, if the expanded child credit in effect in 2021 were to be extended permanently, the annual budgetary cost in 2026 and beyond would appear higher than the annual cost through 2025, since the changes made by the TCJA were already assumed in the current-law baseline through 2025 (i.e., "current cost"), as illustrated in the figure below.

Estimated Cost of Child Credit with a Permanent Extension of the 2021 Expanded Credit

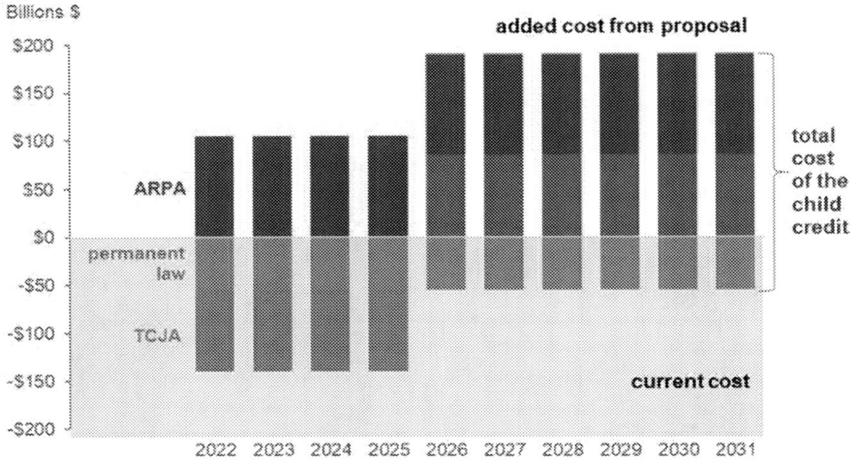

Source: CRS estimates based on IRS Statistics of Income data, Joint Committee on Taxation JCX 71-18 and JCX 14-21, and Congressional Budget Office letter to Senator Graham and Representative Smith dated December 10, 2021.

Notes: This is a stylized example to illustrate how expiring provisions can affect the cost of a proposed permanent extension of the expanded child credit. It does not reflect an actual budgetary score of the proposal. Notably, for this figure, fiscal years and calendar years are assumed to be the same. In reality, budgetary scores are usually calculated by fiscal year, while administrative IRS data on refundable tax credits usually reflect calendar years.

The total cost of the child credit (the pink, green, and grey bars in the figure above) ultimately reflects both the current-law baseline and any applicable changes to current law in that year.

CBO estimates making the 2021 credit permanent (including both the ARPA and TCJA changes) would cost $1.597 trillion over 10 years (FY2022-FY2031). Prior JCT estimates suggest the TCJA changes to the child credit would cost about $85 billion a year if permanently extended, while the ARPA changes could cost about $105 billion per year if permanently extended. Taken together, this means that, beginning in 2026, the cost of extending the 2021 policy would score at approximately $190 billion per year, versus $105 billion per year when TCJA is part of the current-law baseline. Hence, a shorter extension of one or two years would have a lower budgetary effect not only because it is in effect for fewer years, but because it will be in effect when the TCJA changes are part of the current-law baseline.

Other Changes to the Tax Code That Affect Child Credit Payments

If other changes to the tax code were included in a legislative package extending an expanded child credit—especially those that affect a taxpayer's income tax liability—they might directly affect child credit amounts and ultimately the projected cost of an extension. This could occur, for example, if the expanded credit extension was limited for lower-income taxpayers, which some have proposed.

Under current law, the child credit is structured so that the total amount is the sum of the credit that reduces income tax liability (the nonrefundable portion of the credit) plus the amount that is greater than income tax liability (the refundable portion of the credit). The refundable portion is limited to $1,400 per child. If a tax law change were to reduce income tax liabilities, and the refundable portion was limited in a proposed extension, the overall amount of the credit could fall for some low-income taxpayers. In other words, changes to the income tax could, in certain cases, directly affect credit amounts and hence the overall cost estimate of an extension. (The Build Back Better Act [BBBA; H.R. 5376]—which would extend the expanded credit for one additional year—does not limit the refundable portion of the credit.)

Policymakers could also consider other changes to tax and spending provisions, which may not directly affect the costs of the child credit extension, but could offset the cost of an overall legislative package that included an extension.

Economic and Demographic Projections

The cost estimate for any child tax credit modification will also depend on projections of future economic and demographic outcomes. Relevant economic factors to a child tax credit cost estimate include (1) the distribution of household income, as a tax filer's income determines both eligibility for the credit and amounts that may be claimed; (2) projections of future inflation, which will determine the rates at which households are pushed out of full and partial eligibility for the credit; and (3) the likelihood of future negative economic shocks, which generally tend to increase credit eligibility. Demographic projections of the number of households with qualifying children will also determine the projected cost of the credit, as the population of qualifying children will change over the course of the 10-year budget window (e.g., 9- to 17-year-olds eligible for the credit in the first year of the expansion would not be eligible by the last year of a 10-year budgetary window).

Chapter 8

Effects of the Expanded Child Tax Credit on Household Expenditures during the Interview Survey Reference Period: Preliminary Evidence from the Consumer Expenditure Survey*

Sophie M. Collyer
Thesia Garner
Neeraj Kaushai
Jiwan Lee
Jake Schild Waldfogel
and Christopher T. Wimer

Abstract

The Child Tax Credit (CTC) was substantially expanded through the American Rescue Plan Act of 2021, making the benefit more generous, fully refundable, and more periodic. Early studies documented the positive impact of the expanded CTC on reducing poverty and food hardship, but there is no research on its impact on household spending, and particularly spending on children. We apply a series of difference-in-difference estimates using newly available data from the Consumer Expenditure Survey (CE) collected through September 2021 to examine whether the expanded CTC increased expenditures, both overall and for

---

* This is an edited, reformatted and augmented version of BLS Working Papers of U.S. Department of Labor, U.S. Bureau of Labor Statistics Office of Prices and Living Conditions, Publication No. 549, dated April 2022.

In: A Closer Look at the Child Tax Credit
Editor: Philip Palmer
ISBN: 979-8-89113-601-4

targeted categories such as spending on children's education and development. We note that this paper provides only a first preliminary look at expenditures using partial and incomplete data from the first two months of the expanded payments. Future iterations will examine the full effects ofthe payments on more complete data. We find positive and statistically significant intent-to-treat effects for spending on food, children's clothing, and childcare, although results vary across specifications. This study, particularly once data for the full period are available, will add to a growing body of evidence on the effects of the expanded CTC on U.S. households' economic well-being, and provide information as toits potential role in improving child well-being.

Keywords: child tax credit, consumption

Introduction

The American Rescue Plan Act of 2021 (ARP), enacted in March 2021, significantly expanded the Child Tax Credit (CTC) in three major ways. First, it made the benefit more generous, increasing the maximum benefit size from $2,000 per child to $3,000 per child for children aged 6 to 17 years and $3,600 per child for children aged 0 to 5.[1] Included within this change was an increase in qualifying age from 16 and younger to 17 and younger. Second, it made the benefit "fully refundable," meaning tax filers were able to receive the full benefit of the credit regardless of their tax obligation.[2] Third, it converted the CTC's annual payment to payments delivered monthly from July to December of 2021.[3]

As a result of the expansions, from July through December 2021, most low- and middle-income households with children in the United States (U.S.)

---

[1] Before the ARP, eligible children included those under age 17 with a Social Security Number (SSN) who could be claimed as a dependent. Under the ARP, eligible children included those under age 18 with an SSN who could be claimed as a dependent.

[2] Previously, up to $1,400 of the $2,000 available through the CTC (per qualifying dependent) was refundable. Filers with income tax liability less than the refundable portion of the CTC would receive the difference as a refund. However, they woul d not benefit from the additional $600 available through the CTC that was non-refundable. Only filers with income tax liabilities larger than the refundable portion of the CTC were able to benefit. With the enacting of the ARP, there was no longer a minim um income at which a filer was able to receive the full benefit of the CTC.

[3] For most households, half of their annual payment was delivered in monthly installments between July and December of 2021, with the remaining half being delivered when they filed their taxes in 2022 for tax year 2021.

received monthly cash payments of $300 per child under age six and $250 per child between the ages of 6 and 17. Recipients had to have previously filed taxes, or alternatively enroll in the benefit using a government portal intended to allow non-filers (typically the lowest income households) to receive the benefit. The first monthly payment was distributed to the households of 59.3 million children in July 2021, while the last payment reached 61.2 million children in December 2021 (U.S. Department of Treasury, 2021).

Though now expired, the ARP-CTC is unprecedented in its reach and role in addressing the economic hardship of low-income households with children. Using new data from the Consumer Expenditure Survey (CE), this study examines the initial effects of the CTC expansion on consumer unit or household spending.[4] We stress that the results presented here are based on preliminary and incomplete CE data from just the first two months of payments. Our goal is not to interpret the results at present, but rather to lay out our approach and methodology for comment and revision. Nevertheless, for illustrative purposes, we present the preliminary results of our preferred methodology in the Results section.

Early studies established that the expanded CTC reduced material hardship (Parolin, Ananat, et al., 2021; Perez-Lopez, 2021), child poverty (Acs & Werner, 2021; Marr et al., 2021; Parolin, Collyer, et al., 2021), and childhood malnutrition (Waxman et al., 2021), while having no significant effect on parental employment (Ananat et al., 2022; Roll et al., 202a). Empirical research has not yet explored how household expenditures, and implicitly consumption, have changed due to the CTC expansion.

[4] The CE collects data on "Consumer Units," which in some cases differ from households. A consumer unit is defined as a group of people who "comprises either: (1) all members of a particular household who are related by blood, marriage, adoption, or other legal arrangements; (2) a person living alone or sharing a household with others or living as a roomer in a private home or lodging house or in permanent living quarters in a hotel or motel, but who is financially independent; or (3) two or more per sons living together who use their income to make joint expenditure decisions. Financial independence is determined by the three major expense categories: Housing, food, and other living expenses. To be considered financially independent, at least two of the three major expense categories have to be provided entirely, or in part, by the respondent." See https://www.bls.gov/cex/csxgloss.htm#:~:text=Consumer%20unit%20%2D%20A%20consumer%20unit,in%20permanent%20liv ing%20quarters%20in. The term consumer unit and household are often used interchangeably in the literature, although households are considered all people who live at an address and thus are not the same as consumer units. However, throughout the manuscript we refer to consumer units as households.

Our study adds to the literature on the impact of the CTC by examining overall expenditures on food, housing, and other key categories of spending. The consumption of goods and services is a primary indicator of living standards, and thus, a key component of measuring economic well-being (OECD, 2013). Moreover, parents' spending on children represents an important pathway to promote children's development and well-being (Jackson & Schneider, 2022; Kaushal et al., 2011; Kornrich & Furstenberg, 2013; Schneider et al., 2018). In particular, an increase in food consumption is known to improve children's nutrition and has long term positive impacts on economic well-being (Hamilton et al., 2022).

Additional income provided through cash transfers like the CTC may be characterized as improving child outcomes through two channels: family stress and family investments (Wimer and Wolf, 2020). The family stress model posits that economic hardship impairs family functioning, increasing parents' stress and undermining their mental health and ultimately children's development (Conger & Conger, 2002). Increased income can thus reduce family stress and improve child outcomes. The family investment model posits that increased income allows parents to purchase or invest in various things that enhance child development and well-being (e.g., books, toys, enriching activities, high-quality childcare, or nutritious food) (Yeung et al., 2002). This study focuses on the family investment model by investigating whether the expanded CTC affected households' expenditures on children as well as overall expenditures on categories such as food that contribute to child well-being.

Policymakers would like to know if households receiving the CTC are spending it in ways that benefit children, or if they are spending it on items that are not related to child well-being such as alcohol or tobacco. Thus, establishing how households spend the money is an important empirical question. A few studies have examined how households spend benefits similar to the CTC (Amorim, 2021; Jones et al., 2019; Gregg et al., 2005). Amorim (2021) examines the effects of income gains from cash transfers distributed from the Alaska Permanent Fund Dividend on child-related spending by exploiting exogenous variation in the values of the payment across time. The study uses CE data from the 1996–2015, and finds that immediately after receiving cash transfers, parents across the income distribution increase spending on clothing and durable goods that may improve children's material well-being. Using data from Canadian expenditure surveys, Jones et al., (2019) examined the effect of Canadian Child Benefits (CCB), very much like the ARP-CTC's payment design, on household expenditures and found that CCB increased the spending on basic needs such as transportation, childcare, and food at home, while decreased the expenditures on food in restaurants, alcohol and tobacco. Gregg et al., (2005) found that increased benefits for families with children in the UK led to increases in spending on children's clothing and footwear, books and toys, and fresh fruit and vegetables, and declines in spending on tobacco and alcohol; in addition, families receiving the increased benefits increased their ownership of cars and phones. However, we lack evidence on how families spent the CTC. While some studies have reported on how people receiving the CTC reported spending it (Karpman et al. 2021; Pilkauskas & Cooney 2021; Rachidi 2021; RAPID-EC 2021; Roll et al. 2021b; Zippel 2021), this study is the first to examine changes in spending patterns of households resulting from the CTC payments using a causal identification strategy.

This study applies a difference-in-difference approach, harnessing variation in the policy based on difference in time period, number of children in the household, and receipt/amount of the CTC. Newly available and comprehensive expenditure data from the CE allows us to examine household spending on (1) major categories, such as food, housing, alcohol and tobacco, leisure, etc., and (2) child-related spending including that for books, childcare, computers and tablets, and enrichment activities among households with children. This study seeks to contribute to a growing body of evidence on the effects of the expanded CTC on U.S. households' economic well-being and provide evidence as to its potential role in improving child health and education outcomes. In this paper, we use preliminary and incomplete data from the early months of the CTC expansion to put forward our preferred methodological approach to identifying causal effects of the policy, and then illustrate our approach using newly-available, though still preliminary and incomplete data.

The American Rescue Plan and Related Research

The ARP temporarily transformed the CTC into a nearly universal child allowance for 2021 through three fundamental changes:[5] (1) expanded

[5] The changes to the CTC in the ARP follow those outlined in the American Family Act (a bill first introduced in both the Senat e and House of Representatives in 2017 and reintroduced in 2019) with one exception: in the AFA, the credit would begin to phase out for heads of household with earnings above $120,000 or and joint filers with Adjusted Gross Incomes (AGI) over $180,000. In the ARP, the credit began to

eligibility, (2) higher credit amounts, and (3) delivery of credit in monthly installments for the second half of 2021. Prior to this temporary expansion to the CTC, tax filers could receive a maximum CTC of $2,000 per child per year at tax time.[6] However, the credit was not fully-refundable. Instead, it phased in with earnings, and tax filers claiming dependent children needed to earn a certain amount in order to qualify for the maximum credit.[7] Overall, one in three children did not receive the full benefit value because their parents did not earn enough to qualify.

Children with single parents, those in rural areas, Black and Latino children, and those in larger households were disproportionately ineligible for the full credit (Curran and Collyer, 2020; Collyer, Harris, and Wimer, 2019).

The ARP expanded CTC eligibility to almost all children, including those in households with the lowest incomes who were previously excluded, by removing the earnings requirement and making the credit fully refundable. Second, it raised the maximum annual credit amounts to $3,000 for children ages 6-17 and $3,600 for children under age 6.[8] Third, beginning mid-July 2021, it delivered the credit in monthly installments of up to $250 per older child or up to $300 per younger child, for a period of six months.[9] Note that while the ARP expanded eligibility for the CTC, monthly payments did not reach all eligible households.[10] We take several steps to account for the imperfect coverage of the monthly CTC payment when evaluating the policy's effects spending, as discussed in our Data and Methods section.

---

phase out for families with AGIs above $112,500 or $150,000 per year, depending on filing status, but it only phased out until matching the credit values that a family would receive under prior law. This alteration was made because the Biden administration committed to not raising taxes for those with incomes below $400,000 per year.

[6] See additional information on the history of the Child Tax Credit, see Crandall-Hollick (2021), Crandall-Hollick (2018), and arfinkel et al., (2016).

[7] See Curran and Collyer, 2020 for details on how much a filer needed to earn to qualify for the full credit.

[8] Included within this change is an increase in the maximum qualifying after from 16 to 17.

[9] Because the payments began halfway through the year, families will receive half of the full amount of their credit in 2021 an dthe remainder when they file taxes in 2022. Note that children born in 2021 were not eligible for monthly payments. Their families can instead claim the entirety of the credit at tax time.

[10] Families who did not file taxes in the prior year, presumably due to having an income below the tax -filing threshold, generally needed to register with the Internal Revenue Service (IRS) in order to receive their monthly credit. Several estimates sugges t that the total number of children in eligible tax units is around 64 to 67 million children (Parolin et al., 2021) , more than the 60.9 million to whom the IRS distributed CTC payments to in August 2021 and to 61.2 million children in December 2.

Early research suggests the expanded CTC has generated large reductions in child poverty (Acs & Werner, 2021; Marr et al., 2021; Parolin, Collyer, et al., 2021) and reduced food insufficiency among households with children (Parolin, Ananat, et al., 2021; Perez-Lopez, 2021). A few studies have reported that households with children increased spending on childcare and school-related expenses (Roll, Hamilton, & Chun, 2021; Perez-Lopez & Mayol-Garcia, 2021). Other studies have asked parents directly how they spent their payments, finding that the most commonly reported expenses are on food, bills, and other necessities (Pilkauskas & Cooney, 2021). To date, no study has estimated the effect that the monthly CTC payments had on spending across the host of categories available in the CE data or used data on spending collected both before and after the delivery of the monthly CTC payments.

Data and Methods

Data

This study uses micro-level data from the CE, a nationally representative survey sponsored by the U.S. Bureau of Labor Statistics that collects spending, demographics, and other financial information for households living in the U.S. The survey is divided into two methods of data collection, the Interview Survey and the Diary Survey. This research utilizes the data collected as part of the Interview portion of the CE since it covers a larger proportion of all spending by households. In addition, the Interview reference period is the three months prior to the interview as opposed to the Diary Survey, which is used to collect expenditures during a week. The CE sample is a rotating panel recruited every survey month, with households[11] to be interviewed once in each of four consecutive quarters.[12] Given this survey structure, we observe expenditures at overlapping three-month intervals. For example, data collected in August 2021 refer to expenditures from May to

[11] Recall that when we are referring to households, the CE actually collects data for a unit dubbed the "consumer unit." Consumer unit is defined as "all members of a housing unit related by blood, marriage, adoption or some other legal arrangement; or tw o or more persons living together who are identified as making joint expenditure decisions; or a single person who is livi ng with others but is financially independent" (BLS 2005).

[12] Due to survey non-response, CUs may participate int the CE for fewer than 4 times. Population weights are created to be applied to quarterly expenditures to produce estimates that are representative of the U.S. population.

July 2021; data collected in September 2021 refer to expenditures from June to August 2021.

In response to the passage of the ARP, the BLS included a module of questions in the CE survey asking about the CTC starting with the October 2021 interviews. Although advanced CTC payments have not been previously issued, the BLS has included questions about the COVID-19 Economic Impact Payments, as well as previous recovery rebate programs. The CTC questions were developed based on the questions used in the recovery rebate modules. However, October data have not been released yet. So, we are unable to report on the responses to these questions.[13] Furthermore, without data on actual receipt of the CTC monthly payments, we are unable to estimate the treatment-on-treated effect. However, we have data through September, which means two interview months (August and September) have reference periods that (partially) overlap with the distribution of the monthly payments.[14]

Using TAXSIM estimates included in with CE microdata, we are able to calculate the additional CTC received as a result of the expansion.[15] First, we calculate the monthly value of the CTC that a tax unit would have been eligible for under the pre-ARP tax law. Then we calculate the monthly value of the CTC under the APR expansion (as described in detail earlier in the ARP and Related Research section)[16] and take the difference between this

[13] Once the full 2021 dataset is released by the BLS, we will update our analysis to cover the entire period the advanced CTC payments were distributed (i.e. through December 2021).

[14] The reference period for August is May, June, and July. The reference period for September is June, July , and August. The advanced CTC payments began being distributed in July and continued through December. This period of disbursement overlapswith one month in the August interview reference period and two months in the September interview reference period.

[15] Using data collected during the Interview, the BLS creates tax units and then employs the NBER TAXSIM model to provide imputations of adjusted gross income, and the number and age (i.e, 0-6, 6-17, 18+) of dependents at the tax unit level.

[16] To calculate the pre-ARP CTC in the CE data, we first calculate the federal income tax liability of tax units in the data (according to the 2021 tax brackets and marginal tax rates, see Tax Foundation, 2022), and then calculate the value of the CT C they would have received under prior law. For those with AGIs below pre-ARP CTC phaseout thresholds, this was calculated as the lesser of: (1) $2,000 per qualifying dependent, and (2) the sum of 15% of their earned income and their tax liability. Fo r those with AGIs above the phaseout thresholds, we calculate the maximum credit for their family size and then reduced in at a rate 5% for each dollar over the phaseout threshold. We also used data on tax units to calculate the credit the received under the ARP expansion. This expansion granted all families with adjusted gross incomes below $112,500 (joint filers) or $75,000 (heads of household) a credit of $3,000 per child ages 6 -17 and $3,600 per child under age 6, half of which was paid out in monthly

and value of the pre-ARP CTC. This monthly difference is then multiplied by the number of months within the reference period that monthly payments could have been received, which yields a 3-month reference period value of the additional CTC received for each tax unit. We then aggregate the 3-month reference period additional payments for all tax units within a household to get a household-level measure of the additional CTC received.[17] Table 1 shows the average dollar value of the expected additional CTC received for August and September Interviews. With this measure, we are able to estimate the intent-to-treat effect (ITT). The models and the identification strategy we use are described in the Methods section.

Expenditure Categories

The CE provides comprehensive and detailed information on household spending. To examine the ARP-CTC's effects on household expenditures, both overall and child-related, we construct variables for 17 outcome categories.

First, we use data on ten major expenditure categories: housing and utility; food; alcohol and tobacco; clothing; transportation; health; leisure; personal care; education and reading; miscellaneous; and total expenditures. Second, using CE data on detailed item expenditures, we construct the following seven categories of child-related expenditures: children's clothes; books and toys; childcare; school items; computers and tablets; enrichment activities; and sports items. Details on the measures of each expenditure category are presented in Appendix Tables 1 (major categories) and 2 (child-related categories). Table 2 shows the average 3-month reference period total expenditures for households with and without children, pre- and post-distribution of the monthly CTC payments.

installments between July and December 2021. Above these thresholds, the credit phased out at a rate of 5% for each dollar in AGI, until reaching the credit that families received under prior law. The policy parameters then followed those of previous law, beginning the final phaseout of the credit for joint filers with AGIs over $400,000 and heads of household with AGIs over $200,000.

[17] Ideally, we would be able to conduct our analysis at the tax unit level, but CE expenditure data are reported at the household level, which can contain multiple tax units. Therefore, our measure of the additional CTC payment received needs to be aggregated to the household level.

Table 1. Average addition expected 3-month reference period value of the CTC to be received per household

Additional Expected 3-Month Reference Period CTC Received		
	All Households	With children < 17 y/o
Total	$104.85	$365.88
	(5.81)	(16.51)
Income Category		
Under $25,000	$113.97	$752.24
	(15.16)	(72.25)
$25,000 to $50,000	$107.74	$385.92
	(11.99)	(29.69)
$50,000 to $100,000	$110.69	$342.94
	(8.37)	(17.37)
$100,000+	$87.84	$214.72
	(6.48)	(12.82)
Race		
White, non-Hispanic	$74.79	$312.65
	(4.80)	(15.19)
Black, non-Hispanic	$165.75	$515.94
	(29.96)	(79.27)
Hispanic	$174.17	$414.54
	(16.49)	(30.74)
Asian, non-Hispanic	$103.30	$276.38
	(15.53)	(31.91)
Other, non-Hispanic	$184.16	$447.99
	(46.33)	(88.05)

Notes: Averages are calculate using data from August and September Interviews only. The additional CTC received is reported at the household-level. All averages are weighted using FINLWT21 and the 44 replicate weights.

Table 2. Average 3-month reference period total expenditure

3-Month Reference Period Total Expenditures				
	With children < 17 y/o		Without children < 17 y/o	
	Pre	Post	Pre	Post
Total	$20,019.34	$21,208.95	$13,549.96	$14,636.23
	(628.86)	(617.48)	(160.97)	(293.21)
Income Category				
Under $25,000	$10,259.68	$10,675.38	$8,507.72	$8,742.39
	(321.96)	(663.97)	(148.88)	(255.09)
$25,000 to $50,000	$12,217.95	$12,463.79	$10,323.07	$10,604.53
	(286.25)	(968.75)	(215.94)	(376.81)
$50,000 to $100,000	$18,392.40	$17,394.71	$14,660.62	$14,317.27
	(1906.27)	(723.01)	(367.68)	(403.10)
$100,000+	$28,473.31	$31,599.51	$23,737.87	$27,166.02
	(767.83)	(1151.33)	(449.51)	(869.97)

	3-Month Reference Period Total Expenditures			
	With children < 17 y/o		Without children < 17 y/o	
	Pre	Post	Pre	Post
Race				
White, non-Hispanic	$22,435.58	$24,908.68	$14,129.97	$15,091.11
	(587.26)	(901.49)	(207.66)	(359.77)
Black, non-Hispanic	$17,589.95	$15,796.76	$11,043.90	$10,449.23
	(3661.53)	(1339.28)	(352.19)	(472.90)
Hispanic	$15,181.90	$15,258.64	$12,037.12	$13,807.25
	(376.12)	(987.92)	(304.58)	(707.24)
Asian, non-Hispanic	$21,188.21	$24,907.17	$15,948.02	$20,619.31
	(883.58)	(2545.84)	(821.06)	(2076.11)
Other, non-Hispanic	$17,867.94	$14,565.66	$12,199.82	$17,623.68
	(1408.42)	(1428.53)	(752.87)	(3116.16)

Notes: "Total Expenditures" is based on the CE definition of total spending. "Pre" includes data collected during interviews from January 2021 through July 2021. "Post" includes data collected during interviews from August 2021 through September 2021. All averages are weighted using FINLWT21 and the 44 replicate weights.

Methods

Our empirical models all rely on a difference-in-difference framework. We are interested in understanding how the expansion of the CTC affected expenditures. Analyzing the difference in pre-CTC expansion and post-CTC expansion spending for treated units would yield a first difference estimate of the treatment effect. However, a first difference specification will not control for variation in spending due to month-to-month differences ("monthly" variation) and changes in supply and demand of goods and services due to COVID-19 restrictions, which may be correlated with when the monthly payments began being distributed. Variation due to the pandemic can be separated into two subcategories. The first type of variation we will refer to as "pre-pandemic" variation, and is the variation in spending that occurs between pre- and post-start of the pandemic. The second type of variation is "within pandemic" variation and is the variation in spending that occurs between months due to changes in COVID-19 restrictions.

To control for these various sources of variation, we first estimate the difference between the pre- and post-CTC expansion spending for households with and without children. Households without children do not benefit from the expansion of the CTC, and therefore, act as our control units. Equation

(1) shows the model that will be estimated.

$$Eit = \beta 0 + \beta 1 * Childit + \beta 2 * Childit * 1[CTCt > 0] + \nabla Xit \quad \alpha t + eit \tag{1}$$

We first evaluate the CTC expansion using a binary treatment indicator (i.e., the post-CTC expansion period), which is represented as the indicator function $1[CTC(t) > 0]$. As described in the data section, our dependent variable is three-month expenditures for various spending categories. We only use data from 2021 in order to control for "pre-pandemic" variation in spending.[18] Expenditures are reported by household i and collected in interview month t.[19] $Child\_it$ is a binary variable equal to 1 if the household has at least one child under age 18 and 0 otherwise. Vector Xit represents a set of household characteristics, namely age of the reference person, this person's gender, race/ethnicity, and education, and for the household the total income, state of residence, and the number of people in the household. αt represents a full set of controls for the interview month, which account for seasonal variation.

With a binary treatment, we are using only the variation in spending between possible recipients and non-recipients to identify the treatment effect. Possible recipients are represented by households interviewed in August or September that have at least one child aged 17 or less. We have two types of non-recipients, households who have at least one child, but were not interviewed in August or September and households without a child aged 17 or less. Variation in spending for pre- and post-treatment is controlled for with interview month fixed effects (αt). We control for "monthly" variation and "within pandemic" variation by including a dummy variable for the presence of a child. The coefficient ($\beta 2$) on the interaction term provides the difference-in-difference estimate of the association between the expanded CTC and expenditures by households with children. Recall, we do not have data on receipt of the monthly payments. Instead, we assume all households with children receive a monthly payment, so $\beta 2$ represents the Intent-to-Treat (ITT) effect.[20]

---

[18] All households are reporting expenditures from after the start of the pandemic, so there is no difference in spending due to spending pre- or post-start of the pandemic.

[19] Recall, the reference period for expenditures is the three months prior to the interview.

[20] When the remaining quarters of 2021 CE data are made available, we will apply a two-stage least squares methodology to estimate the treatment-effect on the treated. For this

Expanded CTC payments were first sent out on July 15, 2021, and the last payments (as of this writing) were sent out in mid-December of 2021. Ideally, we would measure the effect of expanded CTC payments on monthly expenditures, but CE data are collected at the 3-month reference period level.[21] A respondent who is interviewed in August will report expenditures for May, June, and July. Since part of the reference period occurs after the CTC expansion, this respondent is considered "treated" under the binary specification even though only one month of expenditures occur post-expansion. A similar "partial treatment" also occurs for interviews occurring in September 2021, where only two months of expenditures (July and August) occur post-expansion. A potential shortcoming of using equation (1) to estimate the treatment effect is that it treats households interviewed in August and September as if they received the same treatment intensity, but they did not. As noted earlier a respondent who is interviewed in August 2021 will report expenditures for May, June, and July. Only during one month of this reference period could a household have received a monthly payment. In contrast, a respondent interviewed in September 2021 will have a reference period of June, July, and August, which means this respondent would have been treated for two months. By treating CUs interviewed in August and September as having the same treatment intensity we are diluting our treatment effect. We attempt to correct for this potential bias, as well as improve the statistical power of our model, by exploiting the variation in the amount of the monthly CTC payment.[22]

Equation (2), shown below, is identical to equation (1) with the only difference being the indicator function, $1[CTC(t) > 0]$, has been replaced with $CTC(t)$, which represents the dollar value of the additional CTC that is expected to be received after the expansion. By using the variation in the expected amount to be received we are implicitly controlling for the

approach, we use the expected benefit (based on the calculation described above) as an instrumental variable and the observed receipt (as reported by families in the CEX surveys) as the endogenous variable.

[21] Some of the expenditures for the CE interview are collected at the monthly level, but a majority are only reported for the en tire three-month reference period, which is why we use the data at the (overlapping) three-month frequency.

[22] Since the variation in treatment intensity can be described as a discrete measure, we could separate in binary treatment variable into three categories of treatment intensity (e.g., CTC=0.33 in August 2021 and March 2022; CTC=0.67 in September 2021 and February 2022; CTC=1 in other months after August 2021) and estimate equation (1) using this alternative specification. This option will be explored while revising this work.

variation in treatment intensity that occurs between August and September interviews. Ceteris paribus, $CTC(Aug) < CTC(Sept)$ simply because August interviewees will only receive one month of the payment whereas September interviews will be assigned two months. Moreover, this specification allows us to use not only variation between recipients and non-recipients, but also variation in spending by households who are expected to receive different size payments. Again, β_2 represents our estimate of the ITT effect.

$$E_{it} = \beta_0 + \beta_1 * Child_{it} + \beta_2 * Child_{it} * CTC_t + \nabla X_{it} + \alpha_t + e_{it} \tag{2}$$

Both equations (1) and (2) use families without children to control for any "monthly" variation in spending, as well as to control for "within pandemic" variation due to changes in supply and demand of goods and services resulting from changes in COVID-19 restrictions. For these models to lead to an unbiased estimator, households with and without children need to have similar "monthly" and "within- pandemic" variation in spending. However, it could be the case that households with children have different month-to-month trends in spending and are impacted differently when COVID-19 restrictions change. For example, households with children will have expenditures for school and childcare that are different from month to month and not incurred by households without children and unrelated to the receipt of monthly payments. Additionally, changes in policies about school openings and closing will impact households with children but not households without children. As a result, the estimate of the ITT effect in equation (1) and (2) could be biased. We account for this difference in seasonal spending by restricting our sample to only those households with children.

If we simply restrict our sample to only households with children, we reduce our model to a firstdifference. Therefore, when we restrict our sample to only households with children, we also pull in datafrom January 2019 to September 2019 interviews. Equation (3a) shows the new specification with a binary treatment variable. Equation (3b) shows the continuous treatment specification.

$$E_{it} = \beta_0 + \beta_1 * 1[CTC_t > 0] + \gamma_t + \lambda_t + \nabla X_{it} + e_{it} \tag{3a}$$

$$E_{it} = \beta_0 + \beta_1 * CTC_t + \gamma_t + \lambda_t + \nabla X_{it} + e_{it} \quad (3b)$$

Unlike in equations (1) and (2), our treatment and control groups are dictated by the year in whichthe interview took place rather than the presence of children. γ_t represents this year fixed effect, taking a value of one if the household was interviewed in 2021. This fixed effect controls for "pre-pandemic" variation, variation in spending between 2021 (treatment) and 2019 (control). It also controls for the month-to-month ("monthly") variation in spending that occurs for households with children that is the same between 2021 and 2019. To control for the pre- and post- treatment variation, we include a full set of fixed effects for the interview month (λ_t). The ITT effect with an indicator for when a household is expected to receive a monthly payment during their reference period (i.e., August and September 2021).

In equation (3b) the treatment variable is the dollar value of the expected monthly payment received during the reference period. All other variables are the same as in equation (3a). The ITT effect is represented by β_1. Our identification strategy is similar to the identification strategy used to estimate theITT effect in equation (1) and (2).

Unlike with equations (1) and (2), we are not concerned about differences in "monthly" variationdue to the presence of children. However, one might still be concerned about the potential for changes in COVID-19 restrictions to affect spending ("within pandemic" variation). Most of the impact on spending from these restrictions were felt during 2020. By 2021 many of the restrictions that were constraining consumption during 2020 had already been relaxed and there was not much variation between the pre- and post-treatment periods. Therefore, we do not believe the pandemic era will cause much of a bias in equations (3a) and (3b), but we can use a triple-difference framework to help account for the any impact changes in restrictions had on spending.[23] We will provide a detailed description of this model in future iterations of this paper. A more detailed description of the technical details underlying the identification strategy is provided in the Technical Appendix.

[23] See Berck and Villas-Boas 2016 for an explanation of triple difference modeling.

Results

This section presents the ITT estimates for the models detailed above in the Methods section.

Note all the models were estimated using the survey weight (FINLWT21). Additionally, the dollar value of the additional CTC received is scaled by $100. So, a 1 unit increase in the continuous model is equivalent to a $100 increase in the CTC monthly payment. As noted earlier, these results are meant only to provide an illustration of our approach, and should not be used yet to interpret the causal effects of the expanded CTC. In future iterations, when full data across the treatment period become available, we will be able to present and interpret results more definitively.

Table 3 shows the estimates of the ITT effect ($\beta 2$) from equation (1) and (2). The ten different expenditure categories correspond to the ten major expenditure categories described in the Data section. Panel I in the table presents the treatment effect for the binary specification. Panel II presents the results for the continuous specification. In general, the results are insignificant, which is not surprising given the data only contained two interview months of treated observations and those treated observations received a relatively small "dose" of the treatment.

That being said, we do see positive and weakly significant treatment effects under the binary specification for food and clothing. The positive coefficient on food is in line with other research that has found the CTC expansion has helped reduce food insecurity (Parolin, Ananat, et al., 2021). We also find a statistically significant negative treatment effect for transportation when using the continuous treatment. This result contradicts our hypothesis that the CTC would have a positive effect on spending. However, this could be a result of differences in seasonal spending between consumer units with and without children. Specifically, the treatment period reflected July and August spending which corresponds to when schools are closed for the summer. Thus, consumer units with children may be spending less on transportation because it is the summer, which is not a decrease that is likely to be experienced by consumer units without children.

We can test this theory by looking at Table 4. This table presents the estimates when using equations (3a) and (3b), which restricts the sample to only consumer units with children and pulls in expenditures from 2019. When using the binary treatment, the treatment effect on food and clothing are still positive and weakly significant. We also see the treatment effect on personal care becoming statistically significant. Turning to the continuous treatment (panel II), the treatment effect on transportation is still negative, but the magnitude of the effect has reduced, and it is not statistically significant. Both changes suggest there was some difference in the seasonal spending patterns of consumer units with and without children. However, the coefficient is still negative, but this could be a result of differences in pandemic era spending. The triple-difference specification will help us disentangle what is going on with this treatment effect.

Finally, Table 5 presents the estimates of the ITT effects on child related expenditures using equations (3a) and (3b). Looking at the binary treatment in panel I, the treatment effect for children's clothes is positive and statistically significant. When we compare the magnitude of this treatment effect to the treatment effect we saw for clothing generally, it appears a majority of the additional spending on clothing generally is attributable to spending on children's clothes. The binary treatment effects for the rest of the spending categories are insignificant.

Turning to the continuous treatment effects in panel II, we see a positive and statistically significant coefficient on children's clothing. Consumer units who we expect to receive the advanced CTC payment spend $0.09 out of every $1 on children's clothing. Based on the average predicted gain in CTC payment ($365.88) recipients will increase spending on children's clothing by $31.54, which is within the margin of error for the binary treatment effect. In addition to children's clothing, spending on childcare has a positive and statistically significant coefficient.

While these results are promising, for the same reasons mentioned above about why large standard errors are not a big concern for us at this point, we do not want to read too much into the statistical significance we find. The results we present in here will likely change when we incorporate data from the rest of 2021.

Table 3. Difference-in-differences estimate of effect of expanded CTC on spending on major expenditure categories among households with children compared to households without children, binary and continuous treatment

I: Binary Treatment										
	Total	Food	Housing	Transport	Health	Clothing	Alcohol & Tobacco	Leisure	Personal Care	Misc.
Estimation method	*ITT*	*ITT*	*ITT*	*ITT*	*ITT*	*ITT*	*ITT*	*ITT*	*ITT*	*ITT*
	439.92	159.17	134.07	8.08	23.83	57.11	0.76	163.24	-2.32	14.55
	(836.20)	(75.79)	(220.60)	(183.90)	(72.86)	(29.92)	(19.26)	(141.30)	(8.32)	(46.96)
II: Continuous Treatment										
	Total	Food	Housing	Transport	Health	Clothing	Alcohol & Tobacco	Leisure	Personal Care	Misc.
Estimation method	*ITT*	*ITT*	*ITT*	*ITT*	*ITT*	*ITT*	*ITT*	*ITT*	*ITT*	*ITT*
	-238.52	-2.30	-34.75	-57.30	-16.15	4.70	0.05	17.96	-2.10	5.99
	(124.11)	(12.06)	(27.79)	(17.63)	(9.95)	(4.90)	(3.57)	(18.99)	(1.22)	(4.40)
N observations	*15,432*	*15,432*	*15,431*	*15,432*	*15,432*	*15,432*	*15,432*	*15,431*	*15,432*	*15,432*

Notes: Standard errors clustered at the household level are reported in parenthesis. All estimates are calculated with FINLWT 21 survey weights. The coefficients in Panel I can be interpreted as the dollar increase in spending over the three months during which the household is expected to have received the CTC. The coefficients in Panel II can be interpreted as the increase in spending per $100 of additional CTC received over the 3 -month reference period.

Table 4. Difference-in-differences estimate of effect of expanded CTC on spending on major expenditure categories among households with children in 2021 compared to those in 2019, binary and continuous treatment

I: Binary Treatment										
	Total	Food	Housing	Transport	Health	Clothing	Alcohol & Tobacco	Leisure	Personal Care	Misc.
Estimation method	*ITT*	*ITT*	*ITT*	*ITT*	*ITT*	*ITT*	*ITT*	*ITT*	*ITT*	*ITT*
	1022.30	286.17	417.52	245.46	28.31	60.31	2.46	119.04	27.04	84.09
	(873.01)	(85.29)	(267.04)	(183.86)	(78.63)	(37.52)	(20.24)	(129.12)	(9.47)	(56.87)
II: Continuous Treatment										
	Total	Food	Housing	Transport	Health	Clothing	Alcohol & Tobacco	Leisure	Personal Care	Misc.
Estimation method	*ITT*	*ITT*	*ITT*	*ITT*	*ITT*	*ITT*	*ITT*	*ITT*	*ITT*	*ITT*
	-166.45	6.08	-19.00	-21.16	-9.07	6.44	-1.32	7.30	0.06	8.15
	(106.12)	(13.07)	(29.46)	(16.30)	(10.06)	(5.25)	(3.52)	(15.96)	(1.16)	(4.45)
N observations	*8,955*	*8,955*	*8,954*	*8,955*	*8,955*	*8,955*	*8,955*	*8,955*	*8,955*	*8,955*

Notes: Standard errors clustered at the household level are reported in parenthesis. All estimates are calculated with FINLWT 21 survey weights. The coefficients in Panel I can be interpreted as the dollar increase in spending over the three months during which the household is expected to have received the CTC. The coefficients in Panel II can be interpreted as the increase in spending per $100 of additional CTC received over the 3-month reference period.

Table 5. Difference-in-differences estimate of effect of expanded CTC on spending on child-related items and childcare among households with children in 2021 to those in 2019, binary and continuous treatment

I: Binary Treatment							
	Children's clothes	Books and toys	Computers, tablets and tech	School related items	Sports items	Childcare	Enrichment activities
Estimation method	*ITT*	*ITT*	*ITT*	*ITT*	*ITT*	*ITT*	*ITT*
	48.07	6.24	14.67	96.77	12.88	40.66	3.19
	(17.82)	(14.69)	(16.88)	(75.88)	(22.93)	(45.86)	(54.57)
II: Continuous Treatment							
Estimation method	*ITT*	*ITT*	*ITT*	*ITT*	*ITT*	*ITT*	*ITT*
	8.62	0.63	2.18	-14.15	-0.10	8.10	-5.83
	(3.10)	(1.91)	(2.13)	(10.10)	(3.16)	(4.82)	(4.34)
N observations	*8,955*	*8,955*	*8,955*	*8,955*	*8,955*	*8,955*	*8,955*

Notes: Standard errors clustered at the household level are reported in parenthesis. All estimates are calculated with FINLWT 21 survey weights. The coefficients in Panel I can be interpreted as the dollar increase in spending over the three months during which the household is expected to have received the CTC. The coefficients in Panel II can be interpreted as the increase in spendi ng per $100 of additional CTC received over the 3 - month reference period.

Conclusion

Households with children faced significant economic challenges during the pandemic as a result of lost jobs, school closures, and a lack of childcare. The expansion of the CTC provided more generous benefits, modified the rules to allow more households to receive the credit, and implemented monthly payments in hopes of alleviating some of this burden. Early studies have established the expanded CTC has reduced material hardship, improved food security, and reduced child poverty. However, none of these studies have looked at the direct impact of the CTC expansion on spending. This paper helps fill this gap by beginning to explore how household expenditures have changed due to the CTC expansion using data from the Consumer Expenditure Survey. Future iterations of the paper will revisit these preliminary and incomplete results as fuller data across the treatment period become available.

We implement a difference-in-difference approach and use variation between recipients and non- recipients as well as variation due to differences in the CTC amount a household receives to identify the treatment effect. Because the full year of 2021 data is not yet available and the CE only started to ask about receipt of the CTC in October 2021, our analysis is limited to estimating the intent-to-treat effects. Estimates of these effects suggest receipt of the CTC is most likely to impact spending related to children. Our results show an increase in spending on children's clothing and childcare in response to the CTC. Spending on food also was shown to increase. Spending on categories unrelated to children, such as alcohol and tobacco, did not appear to be impacted by the CTC. However, our dataset includes only two Interview Survey reference months that can be considered treated, and even so, the treatment is relatively small for these observations. Results vary across specifications, and our estimates are intent-to-treat only. Therefore, we want to caveat the results presented in this paper. When we update our analysis to use the full 2021 year of data, we will have many more treated observations with larger treatments and we will be able to estimate the treatment-on-treated effect, so we fully expect our results to change.

Appendix Table 1. Major expenditure categories

Category	Description
Housing and utility	Shelter cost; utility cost; household operations; house furnishings and equipment
Food	Food at home and away from home (including meals as, and not as, pay)
Alcohol and tobacco	Alcoholic beverages and tobacco and smoking supplies
Clothing	Clothing and footwear for men, women, boys, and girls, and other apparel products and services
Transportation	Cars and trucks, other vehicles, gasoline and motor oil, maintenance and repairs, vehicle insurance, rental, leases, licenses, and public transportations
Health	Health insurance, medical services, prescription drugs, and medical supplies
Leisure	Fees and admissions to entertainment activities, televisions, radios, and sound equipment, pets, toys, and playground equipment, and other entertainment
Personal care	Wigs, hairpieces, or toupees, electric personal care appliances, and personal care services for males and females, including haircuts
Education and reading	Tuition, schoolbooks, supplies, and equipment for college, elementary and high school, day care center, and other schools, and other school-related expenses; newspapers and magazines and books
Miscellaneous	Miscellaneous expenditures including funeral, cash contributions, insurance and pension
Total	Total of above

Appendix Table 2. Child-related expenditure categories

Category	Description
Children's clothes	Infant and children clothing and footwear
Books and toys	Books and toys including infant furniture and equipment
Childcare	Babysitting and childcare and day care
School items	School related items including tuition, schoolbooks, supplies, and school lunch
Computers and tablets	Computers, tablets, digital book readers, and other related software and accessories including CD
Enrichment activities	Enrichment activities and outings including trips club membership tickets to events fees for lessons musical instruments
Sports items	Sports item including athletic gear, bicycles, and camping items

Technical Appendix

The purpose of this section is to provide a detailed technical explanation for the estimation strategy described in the Data & Methods section of the paper. It should be noted, the model described in this section does not exactly match the model presented in the main paper. The model presented in this section is a simplified version of model in the main paper. We use a simplified version of the model in order to make the explanation of the identification strategy and potential biases easier to understand. However, everything discussed in this section can be extended to the model we estimate,

$$Expict = \alpha c + \alpha i + \beta i\ t + \gamma i\ CTCict + \delta iyict + \eta i\ hsizeict$$

- i = pre- or post-pandemic (i.e., 2019 or 2020)
- c = presence of qualifying dependent
- t = time period (pre- or post-July, when the CTC advanced paymentsbegan)
- Exp_{ict} expenditure for an observation in time period t, with children c, and in year i
- α_C an indicator for whether or not the observation has a qualify dependent
- α_i an indicator for whether or not the observation occurs during the pandemic era
- CTC_{ict} the Child Tax Credit
- y_{ict} income
- $hsize_{ict}$ the number of people living within the observation

First difference (time): compare pre-ARP (t = 0) to post-ARP (t = 1)
All observations occur during the pandemic era (i = 1) *

$$Expi,c,t = 1 - Expi,c,t = 0 = ac + \alpha i + \beta i\ (t = 1) + \gamma i\ CTCi,c,t = 1 + \delta iyi,c,t = 1 + \eta i\ hsizei,c,t = 1 - [ac + \alpha i + \beta i\ (t = 0) + \gamma i\ CTCi,c,t = 0 + \delta i\ yi,c,t = 0 + \eta i\ hsizei,c,t = 0\ ]$$

$$\Delta tExpict = \beta i\ t + \gamma i\ (CTCi,c,t = 1 - CTCi,c,t = 0\ ) + \delta i\ (y_{i,c,t=1} - y_{i,c,t=0}) + \eta_i(hsize_{i,ct,=1} - hsize_{i,c,t=0})$$

- $\Delta tExpict$ the change in expendituresbetween pre- and post-July
- ac drops because (on average) the presence of qualifying dependent does not change
- αi drops because all observations occur during the pandemic era (i = 1)
- $\beta i\ t$ effect on expenditures from being post July
- $(CTCi{,}c{,}t = 1 - CTCi{,}c{,}t = 0\ )$ the additional child tax credit receivedpre-July and post-July
- $(yi{,}c{,}t = 1 - yi{,}c{,}t = 0\ )$ the change income pre-July and post-July
- $(hsizei{,}ct{,} = 1 - hsizei{,}c{,}t = 0\ )$ the change in household size pre-July and post-July

Second difference (children): compare observations with (c = 1) and without (c = 0) children

$$\Delta t\ Expi{,}c = 1{,}t - \Delta t\ Expi{,}c = 0{,}t$$

$$= \beta i\ t + \gamma i\ (CTCi{,}c = 1{,}t = 1 - CTCi{,}c = 1{,}t = 0\ ) + \delta i\ (yi{,}c = 1{,}t = 1 - yi{,}c = 1{,}t = 0\ )$$

$$+ \eta i\ (hsizei{,}c = 1{,}t = 1 - hsizei{,}c = 1{,}t = 0\ )$$

$$[\beta i\ t + \gamma i\ (CTCi{,}c = 0{,}t = 1 - CTCi{,}c = 0{,}t = 0\ ) + \delta i(yi{,}c = 0{,}t = 1 - yi{,}c = 0{,}t = 0\ )$$

$$+ \eta i\ (hsizei{,}c = 0{,}t = 1 - hsizei{,}c = 0{,}t = 0\ )]$$

$$\Delta tc\ Expict = \gamma i\ [(CTCi{,}c = 1{,}t = 1\ - CTCi{,}c = 1{,}t = 0\ ) - (CTCi{,}c = 0{,}t = 1\ - CTCi{,}c = 0{,}t = 0\ )]$$

$$+ \delta i[(yi{,}c = 1{,}t = 1 - yi{,}c = 1{,}t = 0\ ) - (yi{,}c = 0{,}t = 1 - yi{,}c = 0{,}t = 0\ )]$$

$$+ \eta i\ [(hsizei{,}c = 1{,}t = 1 - hsiz\ ei{,}c = 1{,}t = 0\ ) - (hsiz\ ei{,}c = 0{,}t = 1 - hsizei{,}c = 0{,}t = 0\ )]$$

$$\Delta tc\ Expict = \gamma i\ (CTCi{,}c = 1{,}t = 1 - CTCi{,}c = 1{,}t = 0\ )$$

$$+ \delta i[(yi{,}c = 1{,}t = 1 - yi{,}c = 1{,}t = 0\ ) - (yi{,}c = 0{,}t = 1 - yi{,}c = 0{,}t = 0)]$$

$$+ \eta i\ [(hsizei{,}c = 1{,}t = 1 - hsiz\ ei{,}c = 1{,}t = 0\ ) - (hsiz\ ei{,}c = 0{,}t = 1 - hsizei{,}c = 0{,}t = 0)]$$

- $\Delta tc\ Expict$ the difference in expenditures between pre- and post-July for an observation with children compared to the difference in expenditures between pre-and post-July for an observation without children

- The level difference between observationswith children and withoutchildrenof the level different between pre- and post-July
- Did expenditures between pre- and post-July for observations with children change at a different rate than observations withoutchildren

- $(CTCi{,}c = 1{,}t = 1 - CTCi{,}c = 1{,}t = 0\ )$ the additional child tax credit receivedpre-July and post-July
  - $(CTCi{,}c = 0{,}t = 1 - CTCi{,}c = 0{,}t = 0\ )$ drops out of the equation because $Ci{,}c = 0{,}t = 1\ = CTCi{,}c = 0{,}t = 0\ =\ 0$
- $[(yi{,}c = 1{,}t = 1 - yi{,}c = 1{,}t = 0\ ) - (yi{,}c = 0{,}t = 1 - yi{,}c = 0{,}t = 0\ )]$ is the change in pre- and post-July income for observations with children comparedto the change in pre- and post-July income for observations without children
  - If you believe there is zero change pre- and post-July income for both observations with children and observations without children then this effect will drop out of the diff-in-diff equation
  - If you believe the change pre- and post-July income for observations with childrenis the same as the change for observations without childrenthen this effect will drop out of the diff-in-diff equation
  - If you believe the change pre- and post-July income for observations with childrenis different from the change for observations without children then this effect will not drop out of the diff-in-diff equation and the treatmenteffect estimate will be biased
- $[(hsize_{i,c = 1,t = 1} - hsize_{i,c = 1,t = 0}) - (hsize_{i,c = 0,t = 1} - hsize_{i,c = 0,t = 0}\ )]$ is the change in pre- and post-July household size for observations with children compared to the change in pre- andpost-July household size for observations without children
  - If you believe there is zero change pre- and post-July household size for both observations with children and observations withoutchildrenthen this effect will drop out of the diff-in-diff equation
  - If you believe the change pre- and post-July household size for observations with children is the same as the change for observations without children then this effect will drop out of the diff-in-diff equation

- o If you believe the change pre- and post-July household size for observations with children is different from the change for observations without children thenthis effect will not drop out of the diff-in-diff equation and the treatment effect estimate will be biased
- If you believe δi and/or ηi do not drop out of the diff-in-diff equation then the treatment effect will be biased
  - o The bias is a result of observations with children being fundamentally different than observations without children
  - o To address this, we can alter the diff-in-diff to compare only observations with children

First difference (time): compare pre-ARP (t = 0) to post-ARP (t = 1)

This is the same as before except all observations have a qualifying dependent (c = 1) *

$Expi,c,t = 1 - Expi,c,t = 0 = ac + \alpha i + \beta i\ (t = 1) + \gamma i\ CTCi,c,t = 1 + \delta iyi,c,t = 1 + \eta i\ hsizei,c,t = 1 - [ac + \alpha i + \beta i\ (t = 0) + \gamma i\ CTCi,c,t = 0 + \delta i\ yi,c,t = 0 + \eta i\ hsizei,c,t = 0\ ]$

$\Delta tExpict = \beta i\ t + \gamma i\ (CTCi,c,t = 1 - CTCi,c,t = 0\ ) + \delta i\ (yi,c,t = 1 - yi,c,t = 0\ ) + \eta i\ (hsizei,ct, = 1 - hsizei,c,t = 0\ )$

- $\Delta_t Exp_{ict}$ the change in expendituresbetween pre- and post-July
- a_c drops because all observations have a qualifying dependent(c = 1)
- α_i drops because (on average) the observations in pandemic era do not change
- $\beta_i t$ effect on expenditures from being post July
- $(CTC_{i,c,t} = 1 - CTC_{i,c,t} = 0)$ the additional child tax credit receivedpre-July and post-July
- $(y_{i,c,t=1} - y_{i,c,t=0})$ the change income pre-July and post-July
- $(hsize_{i,ct,=1} - hsize_{i,c,t=0})$ the change in household size pre-July and post-July

Second difference (pandemic era): compare observations in the pandemic era (i = 1) to observations in the pre-pandemic era (i = 0)

$\Delta_t Exp_{i=1,c,t} - \Delta_t Exp_{i=0,c,t}$
$= \beta_i t + \gamma_i (CTC_{i=1,c,t=1} - CTC_{i=1,c,t=0}) + \delta_i (y_{i=1,c,t=1}$
$- y_{i=1,c,t=0})$
$+ \eta_i (hsize_{i=1,c,t=1} - hsize_{i=1,c,t=0})$
$- [\beta_i t + \gamma_i (CTC_{i=0,c,t=1} - CTC_{i=0,c,t=0}) + \delta_i (y_{i=0,c,t=1}$
$- y_{i=0,c,t=0})$
$+ \eta_i (hsize_{i=0,c,t=1} - hsize_{i=0,c,t=0})]$

$\Delta_{tc} Exp_{ict} = \gamma_i [(CTC_{i=1,c,t=1} - CTC_{i=1,c,t=0}) - (CTC_{i=}$
$_{0,c,t=1} - CTC_{i=0,c,t=0})]$
$+ \delta_i [(y_{i=1,c,t=1} - y_{i=1,c,t=0}) - (y_{i=0,c,t=1} - y_{i=0,c,t=}$
$_{0})]$
$+ \eta_i [(hsize_{i=1,c,t=1} - hsiz\,e_{i=1,c,t=0}) - (hsiz\,e_{i=0,c,t=1} -$
$hsize_{i=0,c,t=0})]$

$\Delta_{tc} Exp_{ict} = \gamma_i (CTC_{i=1,c,t=1} - CTC_{i=1,c,t=0})$
$+ \delta_i [(y_{i=1,c,t=1} - y_{i=1,c,t=0}) - (y_{i=0,c,t=1} - y_{i=0,c,t=}$
$_{0})]$
$+ \eta_i [(hsize_{i=1,c,t=1} - hsiz\,e_{i=1,c,t=0}) - (hsiz\,e_{i=0,c,t=1} -$
$hsize_{i=0,c,t=0})]$

- $\Delta_{tc}\ Exp_{ict}$ the difference in expenditures between pre- and post-July for an observation in the pandemic era compared to the difference in expenditures between pre-and post-July for an observation in the pre-pandemic era
    - The level difference between observationsin the pandemic era and pre-pandemic era of the level different betweenpre- and post-July
    - Did expenditures between pre- and post-July for observations in the pandemic era change at a different rate than observations in the pre-pandemic era
- $(CTCi = 1,c,t = 1 - CTCi = 1,c,t = 0)$ the additional child tax credit receivedpre-July and post-July
    - $(CTCi = 0,c,t = 1 - CTCi = 0,c,t = 0)$drops out of the equation because $Ci = 0,c,t = 1 = CTCi = 0,c,t = 0 = 0$

- $[(yi,c = 1,t = 1 - yi,c = 1,t = 0) - (yi,c = 0,t = 1 - yi,c = 0,t = 0)]$ is the change in pre- and post-July income for observations in the pandemic era compared to the change in pre- and post-July income for observations in the pre-pandemic era
  - If you believe there is zero change pre- and post-July income for both observations in the pandemic era and observations in the pre-pandemic era then this effect will drop out of the diff-in-diff equation
  - If you believe the change pre- and post-July income for observations in the pandemic is the same as the change for observations in the pre-pandemic era then this effect will drop out of the diff-in-diff equation
  - If you believe the change pre- and post-July income for observations in the pandemic era is different from the change for observations in the pre-pandemic erathen this effect will not drop out of the diff-in-diff equation and the treatmenteffect estimate will be biased
- $[(hsize_{i = 1,c,t = 1} - hsize_{i = 1,c,t = 0}) - (hsize_{i = 0,c,t = 1} - hsize_{i = 0,c,t = 0})]$ is the change in pre- and post-July household size for observations in the pandemic era compared to the change in pre- and post-July household size for observations in the pre-pandemic era
  - If you believe there is zero change pre- and post-July household size for both observations in the pandemic era and observations in the pre-pandemic era then this effect will drop out of the diff-in-diff equation
  - If you believe the change pre- and post-July household size for observations in the pandemic is the same as the change for observations in the pre-pandemic era then this effect will drop out of the diff-in-diff equation
  - If you believe the change pre- and post-July household size for observations in the pandemic era is different from the change for observations in the pre-pandemic erathen this effect will not drop out of the diff-in-diff equation and the treatmenteffect estimate will be biased
- If you believe δ_i and/or η_i do not drop out of the diff-in-diff equation then the treatmenteffect will be biased

- The bias is a result of observations in the pandemic era being fundamentally different than observations in the pre-pandemic era
- We could try to correct this by using only data from the pandemic era, but this is what we did in first diff-in-diff model.
- There does not appear to be another way we can use on pandemic era data and create a treatment and control group without using the presence of a qualifying dependent
- Therefore, we can turn to the triple difference

$$(\Delta_t Exp_{i=1,c=1,t} - \Delta_t Exp_{i=1,c=0,t}) - (\Delta_t Exp_{i=0,c=1,t} - \Delta_t Exp_{i=0,c=0,t})$$

$$= \{\beta_{i=1} t + \gamma_{i=1}(CTC_{i=1,c=1,t=1} - CTC_{i=1,c=1,t=0}) + \delta_{i=1}(y_{i=1,c=1,t=1} - y_{i=1,c=1,t=0})$$

$$+ \eta_{i=1}(hsize_{i=1,c=1,t=1} - hsize_{i=1,c=1,t=0})$$

$$- [\beta_{i=1} t + \gamma_{i=1}(CTC_{i=1,c=0,t=1} - CTC_{i=1,c=0,t=0}) + \delta_{i=1}(y_{i=1,c=0,t=1} - y_{i=1,c=0,t=0})$$

$$+ \eta_{i=1}(hsize_{i=1,c=0,t=1} - hsize_{i=1,c=0,t=0})]\}$$

$$- \{\beta_{i=0} t + \gamma_{i=0}(CTC_{i=0,c=1,t=1} - CTC_{i=0,c=1,t=0}) + \delta_{i=0}(y_{i=0,c=1,t=1} - y_{i=0,c=1,t=0})$$

$$+ \eta_{i=0}(hsize_{i=0,c=1,t=1} - hsize_{i=0,c=1,t=0})$$

$$- [\beta_{i=0} t + \gamma_{i=0}(CTC_{i=0,c=0,t=1} - CTC_{i=0,c=0,t=0}) + \delta_{i=0}(y_{i=0,c=0,t=1} - y_{i=0,c=0,t=0})$$

$$+ \eta_{i=0}(hsize_{i=0,c=0,t=1} - hsize_{i=0,c=0,t=0})]\}$$

$$\Delta_{tc} Exp_{i=1,c,t} - \Delta_{tc} Exp_{i=0,c,t}$$

$$= \gamma_{i=1}[(CTC_{i=1,c=1,t=1} - CTC_{i=1,c=1,t=0}) - (CTC_{i=1,c=0,t=1} - CTC_{i=1,c=0,t=0})]$$

$$+ \delta_{i=1}[(y_{i=1,c=1,t=1} - y_{i=1,c=1,t=0}) - (y_{i=1,c=0,t=1} - y_{i=1,c=0,t=0})]$$

$$+ \eta_{i=1}[(hsize_{i=1,c=1,t=1} - hsize_{i=1,c=1,t=0}) - (hsize_{i=1,c=0,t=1} - hsize_{i=1,c=0,t=0})]$$

$$- \{\gamma_{i=0}\,[(CTC_{i=0,c=1,t=1} - CTC_{i=0,c=1,t=0}) - (CTC_{i=0,c=0,t=1} - CTC_{i=0,c=0,t=0})]$$
$$+ \delta_{i=0}\,[(y_{i=0,c=1,t=1} - y_{i=0,c=1,t=0}) - (y_{i=0,c=0,t=1} - y_{i=0,c=0,t=0})]$$
$$+ \eta_{i=0}\,[(hsize_{i=0,c=1,t=1} - hsize_{i=0,c=1,t=0}) - (hsize_{i=0,c=0,t=1} - hsize_{i=0,c=0,t=0})]\}$$

$\beta i = 1\ t$ and $\beta i = 0\ t$ are both added and subtracted, so they drop out

$$\Delta_{tci}\, Exp_{i,c,t} = \gamma_{i=1}(CTC_{i=1,c=1,t=1} - CTC_{i=1,c=1,t=0})$$
$$+ (\delta_{i=1} - \delta_{i=0})[(y_{i,c=1,t=1} - y_{i,c=1,t=0}) - (y_{i,c=0,t=1} - y_{i,c=0,t=0})]$$
$$+ (\eta_{i=1} - \eta_{i=0})[(hsize_{i,c=1,t=1} - hsize_{i,c=1,t=0})$$
$$- (hsize_{i,c=0,t=1} - hsize_{i,c=0,t=0})]$$

- $\Delta tci\ Expi,c,t$ is the difference in expenditures pre- and post-July controlling for the difference in expenditures pre- and post-July for observations with and without qualifyingdependents and controlling for expenditure pre- and post-July for observations in the pandemic and pre-pandemic era
  - $(CTCi = 1,c = 1,t = 1 - CTCi = 1,c = 1,t = 0\ )$ the additional child tax credit receivedpre-July and post-July
  - $CTC_{i=1,c=0,t=1} = CTC_{i=1,c=0,t=0} = CTC_{i=0,c=1,t=1} = CTC_{i=0,c=1,t=0} =$
  - $CTCi = 0,c = 0,t = 1 = CTCi = 0,c = 0,t = 0 = 0$
- $(\delta i = 1 - \delta i = 0\ )$ represents the difference betweenthe pandemic era change in pre- and post- July income for observations with children compared to the pandemic era change in pre- and post-July income for observations without children and the pre-pandemic era change in pre- and post-July income for observations with children comparedto the pre-pandemic era change in pre- and post-July income for observations without children
  - If you believe the difference for the pandemic era is the same as the difference in the pre-pandemic era then this term will drop out of the triple difference equation

  - This means you believe the difference in income across the year between observations with and without qualifying dependents during the pandemic era is the same as the difference in income across the year between observations withand without qualifying dependents during the pre-pandemic era
- $(\eta_{i=1} - \eta_{i=0})$ represents the difference betweenthe pandemic era change in pre- and post- July household size for observations with children compared to the pandemic era change inpre- and post-July household size for observations without children and the pre-pandemic era change in pre- and post-July household size for observations with children compared to the pre-pandemic era change in pre- and post-July household size for observations without children
  - If you believe the difference for the pandemic era is the same as the difference in the pre-pandemic era then this term will drop out of the triple difference equation
  - This means you believe the difference in household size across the year between observations with and without qualifying dependents during the pandemic era is the same as the difference in household size across the year between observations with and without qualifying dependents during the pre-pandemic era.

References

Acs, G., & Werner, K. (2021). *Expanding the Child Tax Credit Could Lift Millions of Children out of Poverty*. Urban Institute. https://www.urban.org/research/publication/expanding-child-tax-credit-could-lift-millions-children-out-poverty.

Amorim, M. (2021). Socioeconomic Disparities in Parental Spending after Universal Cash Transfers: The Case of the Alaska Dividend. *Social Forces*, soab119. https://doi.org/ 10.1093/sf/soab119.

Ananat, E., Glasner, B., Hamilton, C., & Parolin, Z. (2022). *Effects of the Expanded Child Tax Credit on Employment Outcomes: Evidence from Real-World Data from April to December 2021* (WorkingPaper No. 29823; Working Paper Series). National Bureau of Economic Research. https://doi.org/10.3386/w29823.

Berck, P. & Villas-Boas, S.B. (2016) A note on the triple difference in economic models, *AppliedEconomics Letters*, 23:4, 239-242, DOI: 10.1080/13504851.2015.1068912.

Coleman-Jensen, A. Rabbitt, M.P., Gregory, C.A., & Singh, A (2021). "Household Food Security in the United States in 2020." 298. Economic Research Report. U.S. Department of Agriculture.

Conger, R. D., & Conger, K. J. (2002). Resilience in Midwestern Families: Selected Findings from the First Decade of a Prospective, Longitudinal Study. *Journal of Marriage and Family*, *64*(2), 361– 373. https://doi.org/10.1111/j.1741-3737.2002.00361.x.

Gregg, P., Waldfogel, J., & Washbrook, E. (2005). *Expenditure Patterns Post-Welfare Reform in the UK:Are Low-Income Families Starting to Catch Up?* (SSRN Scholarly Paper ID 1159330). Social Science Research Network. https://papers.ssrn.com/abstract = 1159330.

Hamilton, L., Roll, S., Despard, M., Maag, E., Chun, Y., Brugger, L., & Grinstein-Weiss, M. (2022). Theimpacts of the 2021 expanded child tax credit on family employment, nutrition, and financial well-being: Findings from the Social Policy Institute's Child Tax Credit Panel (Wave 2) (No.

173). Global Economy and Development Program at Brookings. https://www.brookings.edu/research/the-impacts-of-the-2021-expanded-child-tax-credit-on-family-employment-nutrition-and-financial-well-being/.

Jackson, M. I., & Schneider, D. (2022). Public Investments and Class Gaps in Parents' Developmental Expenditures. *American Sociological Review*, *87*(1), 105–142. https://doi.org/10.1177/00031224211069975.

Jones, L. E., Milligan, K., & Stabile, M. (2019). Child cash benefits and family expenditures: Evidence from the National Child Benefit. *Canadian Journal of Economics/Revue Canadienne d'économique*, *52*(4), 1433–1463. https://doi.org/10.1111/caje.12409.

Karpman, M., Maag, E., Kenney, G. M., & Wissoker, D. A. (2021). Who Has Received Advance Child Tax Credit Payments, and How Were the Payments Used?. *Washington, DC: Urban Institute.*

Kaushal, N., Magnuson, K., & Waldfogel, J. (2011). *How is family income related to investments in children's learning?* (G. J. Duncan & R. Murnane, Eds.; pp. 187–206). Russell Sage Foundation.https://www.russellsage.org/.

Kornrich, S., & Furstenberg, F. (2013). Investing in Children: Changes in Parental Spending on Children,1972–2007. *Demography*, *50*(1), 1–23. https://doi.org/10.1007/s13524-012-0146-4.

Marr, C., Cox, K., & Sherman, A. (2021). *Build Back Better's Child Tax Credit Changes Would ProtectMillions From Poverty—Permanently.* 19.

Meyer, B., Murphy, C., & Sullivan, J.S. (2022). Changes in the Distribution of Economic Well-Being During the COVID-19 Pandemic: Evidence form Nationally Representative Consumption Data. https://www.nber.org/system/files/working_papers/w29878/w29878.pdf.

OECD. (2013). *OECD Framework for Statistics on the Distribution of Household Income, Consumption and Wealth.* OECD. https://doi.org/10.1787/9789264194830-en.

Parker, J., Schild, J., Erhard, L., & Johnson, D. (2022). *Household Spending Responses to the Economic Impact Payments of 2020: Evidence from the Consumer Expenditure*

Survey (No. w29648; p. w29648). National Bureau of Economic Research. https://doi.org/10.3386/w29648. Also available as BLS Working Paper 544 https://www.bls.gov/osmr/research- papers/2021/pdf/ec210100.pdf.

Parolin, Z., Ananat, E., Collyer, S., Curran, M., & Wimer, C. (2021). *The Initial Effects of the Expanded Child Tax Credit on Material Hardship* (No. w29285; p. w29285). National Bureau of EconomicResearch. https://doi.org/10.3386/w29285.

Parolin, Z., Collyer, S., Curran, M. A., & Wimer, C. (2021). *Monthly Poverty Rates among Children afterthe Expansion of the Child Tax Credit*. 14.

Perez-Lopez, D. J. (2021). *Household Pulse Survey Collected Responses Just Before and Just After the Arrival of the First CTC Checks*. Census.Gov. https://www.census.gov/library/stories/2021/08/economic-hardship-declined-in-households-with-children-as-child-tax-credit-payments-arrived.html.

Pilkauskas, N., & Cooney, P. (2021). Receipt and usage of child tax credit payments among low-income families: what we know. University of Michigan: Poverty Solutions.

Rachidi, A. (2021) New survey data raises questions about the expanded Child Tax Credit. Washington DC: American Enterprise Institute.

RAPID-EC (2021c) Parents' Expectations About the Child Tax Credit (December). The Child Tax Credit is Buffering Families from Financial Hardship. University of Oregon.

Roll, S., Hamilton, L., & Chun, Y. (2021a). *Expanded Child Tax Credit Payments Have Not ReducedEmployment*. 4.

Roll, S., Chun, Y., Brugger, L., & Hamilton, L. (2021b). How are families in the US using their Child Tax Creditpayments? Evidence from Census Data. Social Policy Institute, Washington University in St. Louis & Appalachian State University.

Schneider, D., Hastings, O. P., & LaBriola, J. (2018). *Income Inequality and Class Divides in ParentalInvestments*. https://doi.org/10.1177/0003122418772034.

Waxman, S., Sherman, A., &Cox, K. (2021) Income Support Associated With Improved Outcomes forChildren, Many Studies Show. Washington DC: Center on Budget and Policy Priorities.

Yeung, W. J., Linver, M. R., & Brooks–Gunn, J. (2002). How Money Matters for Young Children's Development: Parental Investment and Family Processes. *Child Development*, *73*(6), 1861–1879.https://doi.org/10.1111/1467-8624.t01-1-00511.

Zippel, C. (2021) 9 in 10 Families with Low Incomes Are Using Child Tax Credits to Pay for Necessities,Education. Washington DC: Center on Budget and Policy Priorities.

Index

A

B

C

D

E

R

S

T

U